D0906166

2-23-77

WALPOLE AND THE WITS

WALPOLE AND THE WITS

The Relation of Politics to Literature, 1722–1742

Bertrand A. Goldgar

UNIVERSITY OF NEBRASKA PRESS
LINCOLN & LONDON

Publishers on the Plains
UNP

Library of Congress Cataloging in Publication Data

Goldgar, Bertrand A   1927–
    Walpole and the wits.

    Includes bibliographical references and index.
    1. English literature—18th century—History and
criticism.   2. Politics and literature.   3. Walpole,
Robert, Earl of Orford, 1676–1745.   4. Politics in
literature.   I.   Title.
PR448.P6G6   820'.9'005   76–6809
ISBN 0–8032–0893–6

To Ben and Anne

CONTENTS

ACKNOWLEDGMENTS

I AM GRATEFUL to the Clarendon Press for permission to reprint most of my essay on *Gulliver's Travels* and the opposition, which first appeared in *The Augustan Milieu: Essays Presented to Louis A. Landa* (1970); and to the Department of Publications, University of Iowa, for allowing me to reprint a substantial portion of an essay on Fielding's *Coffee-House Politician,* which was first published in *Philological Quarterly* in July, 1970. I wish to acknowledge also that the Cholmondeley (Houghton) manuscripts at Cambridge University Library were consulted with the kind permission of the late 5th Marquess of Cholmondeley. Quotations from Swift's *Poems,* Pope's *Correspondence,* Swift's *Correspondence,* and Gay's *Poetical Works* are used by permission of the Oxford University Press. Quotations from *The Twickenham Edition of the Poems of Alexander Pope* are used by permission of Methuen and Company Ltd.; the individual volumes are incorporated in *The Poems of Alexander Pope: A One-Volume Edition of the Twickenham Text,* ed. John Butt.

I am indebted to the American Philosophical Society for a grant which enabled me to begin research on this project and to the Lawrence University Research Council for summer grants which enabled me to continue it. I am grateful also to my colleague Leonard Thompson for his suggestions on various sections; to Michael Harris, Institute of Historical Research, University of London, for his help with the journalistic background; and to my former teacher Louis Landa for his continuing encouragement and advice. Finally, I wish to extend my special thanks to Martin Battestin, who offered invaluable counsel on the entire manuscript.

WALPOLE AND THE WITS

INTRODUCTION

IN 1742 DAVID HUME estimated that Sir Robert Walpole "is the subject of above half the paper that has been blotted in the nation within these twenty years." He might have gone on to remark on an even more interesting phenomenon, that almost every literary figure in England in those two decades contributed to the mass of writing about Sir Robert and that almost all of their contributions were hostile to the Walpole administration. Swift, Pope, Gay, Fielding, Thomson, and a host of lesser figures exercised their talents to attack the person and the policies of the prime minister. Some acted independently, some under the direct influence of the political opposition; but, whatever the individual motives may have been, the leader of the opposition, William Pulteney, was exaggerating only slightly when he asserted that "the *gay,* the *polite,* and *witty Part of the World"* was united in ridicule of the government and its supporters.[1]

The literary-political alignment described by Pulteney is familiar enough to students of the eighteenth century, and biographers or critics of most of the individual writers involved have paid due attention to this facet of their subjects' careers. Maynard Mack's *The Garden and the City* (1969), for example, has given us a remarkable insight into Pope's political poetry. Yet little effort has been made to gain an overview of the problem or to consider it as a single phenomenon—and such apparent unanimity of political attitudes among a whole generation of writers can hardly be regarded as less than phenomenal. No literary history has been published which traces with any precision of detail the actual relations of politicians and men of letters in the period. Nor has any attempt been made to answer the central questions which arise from such interrelations. Was there an organized "literary opposition"? Were the writers who opposed Walpole bound together by a common ideology, or was their opposition a more complex and multifaceted phenomenon, woven of rather different individual strands of private interest and personal associations? To what extent did works like *Gulliver's Travels* or *The Beggar's Opera* actually make a mark in the world of the politicians themselves? What effect did the political atmosphere have on the reception of individual works of the imagination or on the attitude toward a whole genre like satire? And underlying these questions is a problem—all too recognizable at the time—of somewhat deeper significance, a problem about the status of literary art itself, about the widening rift between what Auden called the poet and the city and what the eighteenth century knew simply as "men of letters" and "men of business."

The present study intends to provide answers to such questions through a detailed account of the points of intersection between the literary and political worlds during Walpole's administration. As such, its primary concern is with individual careers and concrete events rather than with the political ideology which, according to some recent studies, underlay both the political and literary opposition to Walpole. In *Bolingbroke and His Circle* (1968), for example, Isaac Kramnick has described the "style of thought" shared by Bolingbroke and his literary friends Swift, Pope, and Gay; their bias was traditional, idealizing an aristocratic society which they saw threatened by the corruptions of the Walpole regime, with its "moneyed men," its new financial institutions, and its projecting spirit. Their satire, their gloom, says Kramnick, was a reaction to changes in the traditional political and social order, changes welcomed by a "new man" like Defoe. H. T. Dickinson, in his biography of Bolingbroke (1970), has reiterated the influence of Bolingbroke's ideas on the political attitudes of his literary allies; and, similarly, Jeffrey Hart, in *Viscount Bolingbroke: Tory Humanist* (1965), has placed the literary figures of the opposition in the tradition of Renaissance humanism, a tradition which emphasized the ethical qualities needed in a ruler and assumed that men of letters are by definition public figures dedicated to the establishment of a just social order.

On the other hand, some historians, like Archibald Foord and J. B. Owen, have analyzed the parliamentary politics of the period in a way which minimizes the ideological divisions. They have tended to accept the claim of opposition writers that "Court and Country" must replace "Whig and Tory" as significant political distinctions, and they have found merit in the claim made by Walpole's press that his opponents were interested more in places than in principles. If the various groups composing the opposition agreed on anything, it was only hostility to Walpole; and, as Foord puts it, "unity upon a principle of negation does not guarantee uniformity in positive aims and methods. Satan's adversaries do not all worship at the same shrine."[2]

There is no need to enter here into this historiographical quarrel between Namierians and anti-Namierians. It may or may not be accurate to say, with Kramnick, that the political opposition was unified by a particular set of ideas; but my concern is with literary rather than political history, and it appears to me only partly useful to speak of all the men of letters of the period as sharing a common political philosophy. Of course, as every literary scholar knows, Swift, Pope, and Gay did indeed bring to bear upon political issues the kind of bias which Kramnick describes, a bias traditional, Tory, humanistic, and aristocratic. And it has long been obvious that the principles of Bolingbroke's *Idea of a Patriot King* played a significant role in the background of both "Patriot" poetry and Pope's later political satire. But the figures in the opposition's literary fringe were not politicians, nor, except for Swift, even political thinkers; they were writers pursuing literary careers, and a broad sketch of their social or political values, while important in its own right, simply does not tell us all we need to know about their role in practical politics or the effect of particular political episodes upon their work and their careers. Nor does it enable us to assess the impact of their literature upon the political climate. However similar their biases, their responses and their contributions to the immediate political scene were diverse. Fielding's curious dallying with the administration (and the students of Bolingbroke's ideas have little to say about Fielding) forms something like a paradigm of the typical relations between Walpole and the wits; but his political behavior was not quite the same as Pope's or Thomson's or Glover's. Only by examining in detail the relations of such writers with the government and the opposition can we get an accurate picture of the real interconnections of politics and literature in the period.

The purpose of this book, then, is to examine with some precision the behavior of literary figures under the immediate pressure of partisan politics in order to illuminate the changing relations between the world of literary values and the world of political power. In Walpole's day, for perhaps the first time in England, the most talented writers of a generation faced a government which made no bones about its hostility to men of letters and its contempt for their role in society. My prime focus of concern is upon their reaction to this new, pragmatic stance assumed by those in power, a stance which so clearly impugned the traditional value accorded to literary expression and the traditional social and political role accorded to men of letters. A second area of concern is the impact of specific poems, plays, or satires upon practical politics, and a third is the shift in mood and literary mode of the best writers in response to changes in the political sphere. Although such areas are best explored, I think, through the details of a narrative history, the first chapter considers two general themes which tend to recur throughout the period; the chapters which follow, ordered chronologically, then offer a guide through the wilderness. Since in charting that wilderness I concentrate upon figures who were self-consciously poets or men of letters and who felt themselves threatened by the antiliterary bias of the administration, I have excluded Defoe from consideration. And since the plays of the period have been treated systematically by John Loftis (*The Politics of Drama in Augustan England,* 1963), I have dealt with the drama only in special cases, like that of Fielding, where my point of view differs from his. I am indebted in a general way to the one previous attempt to synthesize this material, Mabel Hessler's doctoral dissertation "The Literary Opposition to Sir Robert Walpole" (University of Chicago, 1934); her focus, however, is on explicating the political satire and political ideas of individual authors, considered separately, rather than on the questions about literary-political interactions with which my work is concerned.

Given its emphasis upon literary history rather than political thought, it will be obvious that the methodology of this book is resolutely biographical. My research has concentrated upon the genesis of literary works and their immediate political impact, and my analyses of literary works have been restricted to their political implications, with no effort made to elucidate them fully as poems or plays or satires. Indeed, I have assumed in my readers some familiarity with the political satire of the better-known works, like *Gulliver's Travels* or *The Beggar's Opera,* and have thus limited my treatment to an account of their role in the context of partisan politics. I have also assumed throughout that the climate of reception of a literary work is the best gauge of its political implications and that the best evidence for establishing that climate is to be found in the political press of both sides. Such a method has been all the more necessary because of the indirect and oblique manner in which major literary figures in the 1730s addressed themselves to the question of partisan politics. During the last four years of Queen Anne's reign, writers like Swift, Addison, Steele, and Defoe were all actively engaged in writing directly about political issues themselves. During the Walpole period, on the other hand, literary figures (except for Fielding) were not major contributors to political journalism or pamphleteering. Instead, the relationship between politics and literature much of the time was a matter of the political utility of works that on the surface were not political at all and the political commitment of writers who on the surface—in their public reputations—were neutral or apolitical. The brouhaha over Addison's *Cato* in 1713 is an instance of the kind of thing which became commonplace between 1726 and 1742. The biographical and critical problems posed by such indirection make the task of the literary historian both more exacting and more rewarding.

1 LITERATURE AS A POLITICAL ISSUE

THOUGH THE BODY of this study will present a detailed history of the interaction between wits and politicians, one fundamental point needs to be established at the outset about the relations between literature and politics in the Walpole period; quite simply, it is that they *were* related. So obvious a point needs to be highlighted if only because we tend now to take for granted their separation rather than their connection. "The poetic imagination," writes Auden, "is not at all a desirable quality in a statesman."[1] Literary figures, we assume, have no special role in political life, and literature itself is concerned with the private, not the public self. Thus a critic writing about politics and the novel must be at some pains to defend his subject against the prevalent view that political ideas contaminate a work of art.[2] Needless to say, Swift, Pope, and Gay, influenced by the humanist tradition, might have been bewildered by such attitudes;[3] political discourses did not seem to them inevitably separated from literary modes of expression, and political events were clearly a fit topic for treatment in a literature that looked outward to society rather than inward to the self.

At the same time, however, it is essential to recognize that the alienation of literary figures from the world of public action was well under way in the 1730s and, above all, that such alienation was encouraged and hastened by the character of the Walpole regime. Moreover, the widening rift between belles-lettres and practical affairs became clearly evident and was openly discussed in the course of the most significant political-literary controversies of the period. With this theme in mind, I will examine in the present chapter two such controversies, one arising from the government's attitude toward men of letters and the other from the government's attitude toward one particular genre, satire. Both were of immediate political significance, with the first becoming an important motif of opposition propaganda, but both also entailed the raising of larger questions about the status of literary expression in the world of practical politics.

Politics and the Decay of Letters

Late in the history of the opposition, Chesterfield, writing in the antigovernment paper *Common Sense,* pointed with mock astonishment to the remarkable alignment of literary figures against the administration:

. . . I challenge the Ministerial Advocates to produce one Line of *Sense,* or *English,* written on their Side of the Question for these last Seven Years. . . . Has there been an Essay, in Verse or Prose, has there been even a Distich, or an Advertisement, fit to be read, on the Side of the Administration? —But on the other Side, what Numbers of Dissertations, Essays, Treatises, Compositions of all Kinds, in Verse and Prose, have been written, with all that Strength of Reasoning, Quickness of Wit, and Elegance of Expression, which no former Period of Time can equal? Has not every body got by heart, Satires, Lampoons, Ballads, and Sarcasms against the Administration? And can any body recollect, or repeat one Line for it? —What can be the Cause of this? . . . Even the infamous and pernicious Measures of King *Charles* the II's Reign . . . were palliated, varnish'd, or justified by the ablest Pens. By what uncommon Fatality then, is this Administration destitute of all Literary Support?[4]

By what uncommon fatality, indeed? I have suggested already that an ideological answer may not, by itself, be entirely adequate. It needs, at the least, to be supplemented by another answer to Chesterfield's question, one familiar but significant. The fact is that Walpole, in contrast to such ministers of the recent past as Godolphin, Halifax, Somers, and Oxford, refused to encourage or even to show much interest in men of letters, whose works he considered irrelevant to the serious affairs of government. Many of the writers who attacked him were moved to do so perhaps by principle, but certainly by their resentment at the preferment of the unworthy and the neglect of artistic merit on the part of the ministry, the very institution which they had formerly regarded as the source of patronage and guardian of excellence. And the ensuing controversy over the role of men of letters in the body politic became easily transformed into a controversy over the nature and value of literary art.

Even Coxe, Walpole's nineteenth-century biographer, is forced to admit that Sir Robert's record as a patron of letters was remarkably poor, especially when compared with that of some of his predecessors. Though hardly agreeing with contemporary comments that Walpole was a man of "little or no Learning," Coxe concedes that Walpole paid little attention to the muses and spent great sums on inferior writers to defend his policies. "The truth is," he says, "Sir Robert Walpole neither delighted in letters, nor considered poets as men of business. He was accustomed to say, that they were fitter for speculation than for action, that they trusted to theory, rather than to experience, and were guided by principles inadmissible in practical life."[5] An account by Kenneth Greene of the system of patronage under Walpole bears out Coxe's impression. There were gifts to Young, Savage, and a few others who flattered the minister, and even Pope received £200; but, by and large, writers who sought patronage for purely literary efforts were less successful than those who could contribute to Walpole's political success by their writing. Though patronage did not come completely to an end under Walpole, Greene concludes, and though dozens of hopeful poets lavished praise upon him in their verses or dedications, he was generally indifferent to their pleas. One may argue, of course, that other sources of patronage were available and that literary art obviously continued to flourish in the first half of the century; but the fact remains that a significant number of Walpole's contemporaries believed that his administration had veered away from an earlier tradition of government support of men of letters.[6] Such was the situation which caused Aaron Hill to write bitterly in the Epistle Dedicatory to his *Advice to Poets* (1731) of the effect of the patronage system on contemporary letters, and Richard Savage to ridicule the system in his poem, "A Poet's Dependance on the Statesman" (1736).

With Swift it is a constant theme, both in his private utterances and his published attacks on the court. When writing to Gay he spoke of the poet's "triumphial comfort of never having received a penny from a tasteless ungratefull court, from which you deserved so much, and which deserves no better Genius's than those by whom it is celebrated," and to Lady Elizabeth Germain he complained that "however insignificant wit, learning, and virtue may be thought in the world, it would perhaps do government no hurt to have a little of them on it's side."[7] The failure of persons of talent and genius to receive pensions, places, or other marks of patronage is also a crucial motif in his *Letter to the Writer of the Occasional Paper* (1727), in *Gulliver's Travels,* and in many of his poems critical of the Walpole administration. It is evidently an issue about which Swift felt deeply, and we may assume that it did much to alienate from the government not only Swift but many literary figures less politically oriented than the Dean.

It is hardly remarkable to find Walpole refusing to consider poets worthy of his attention nor to find poets responding to neglect with hostility. What is remarkable, though, is the extent to which the minister's treatment of men of letters became itself a major motif in the propaganda of the opposition. The chief literary periodical of the opposition, the *Craftsman,* in one of its early numbers (13 February 1726/7) speaks of the universal complaint of a decay of learning in Great Britain and presents a heavily ironic defense of Walpole as patron of the arts:

> Let him [the malcontent] afterwards turn his Eye to the *Commonwealth of Letters,* and I will challenge him, with the same Confidence, to instance any Period of Time, when *wit* and *polite Literature* were more openly and amply encourag'd than at present; not excepting even the two famous Reigns of *Augustus* and *Louis le Grand.* How many *Men of Wit* could I mention, who have been lately advanc'd to Posts of great Profit and Honour? What a multitude of generous Presents, Pensions, and Stipends could I enumerate, if I thought it agreeable to the modesty of the Donors? Methinks I behold a *Maecenas,* a *Pollio,* a *Somers,* or an *Hallifax* in almost every great Family. But how am I struck with Raptures, when I cast my Eyes on HIM, who sits at the Helm, and does not disdain to Patronize the *Muses,* at the same Time that He supports and adorns the *State.*

And the same paper, two years later (8 February 1728/9), lists as a symptom of a declining minister his willingness to give encouragement to any writer who will openly support him, "contrary to his natural Antipathy to all Men, who have the least Pretence to *Wit* and *Literature.*"

These comments in the *Craftsman* are typical of the hundreds of similar passages in the opposition press indicting Walpole for his neglect of letters. Apparently, in the 1720s and 1730s the status of men of letters and the relationship between literature and society were still considered crucial enough to make the government's attitude toward the arts a major theme of political propaganda.

Opposition journalists were not content to decry the neglect of good writers by the government; they also ridiculed the "inferior" writers who seemed to be favored by the court. As we shall see, the granting of the laureateship to Colley Cibber and the patronage bestowed on Stephen Duck, though seemingly outside the realm of politics, became political issues in the hands of antigovernment pamphleteers. Moreover, every ridiculous farce or wretched poetaster became grist for their mill, since such works and such writers could be viewed as indicative of a general decay of letters symptomatic of a more generalized decay of the national image. Thus the *Craftsman* (15 June 1728) mockingly criticizes "Verses on the Recovery of the Lord Townshend," dedicated to Walpole and written by one Leonard Howard, a gentleman employed in the post office who "by the Spirit of his Writing, discovers the Effects of that generous Encouragement, which his Noble Patron is so remarkable for extending to the *Muses.*" The absurd farce *Hurlothrumbo* (1729), by Samuel Johnson of Cheshire, was patronized by Walpole's son and was also seized upon as good evidence of the corrupt state of national taste. *Fog's Weekly Journal* (5 July 1729), after first ironically defending the piece from a charge of "disaffection," says such reports may "hinder our present generous Patrons of Arts and Sciences from continuing their Encouragement to other Men of Genius like this Author," and concludes: "It is certain, we may judge not only of the Religion and Morals of the Age, but also of the Politeness, the Wit, the Good Sense, and even the Politicks of the upper People, by the writings which are best receiv'd, and most encourag'd by them."

The kind of irony to which opposition papers often rose (or descended) is illustrated in another *Craftsman* piece (22 August 1730) on the same theme, this time in the form of a letter from "Courtly Grub" defending Walpole as a patron of the arts; even if Walpole never distinguished himself by conferring places upon the *best* writers, "Grub" argues, "certainly no Minister ever made himself more remarkable by his Profusion of *Pensions* among the *Worst;* which I think a much more generous and munificent Part; because *good Writers* may be able to support themselves by their *own Works;* whereas *bad Ones* must depend upon his *Protection.* If he never shower'd down his Favours upon such Men as *Prior, Addison, Congreve* or *Swift;* even your Brother *Fog* allows that he gave no small Encouragement to these sublime Productions, *Hurlothrumbo* and *Tom Thumb.*" And in exactly the same way a writer in the *Grub-street Journal* (27 January 1731/2) gravely remarked, "I may take upon me to affirm, that learning is, in this age, so far from being discouraged, that even the meanest pretenders to it meet with constant protection and assistance."

Opposition journalists never tired of contrasting the rewards given to writers of merit by other ministers, such as Somers, Halifax, or Oxford, with the neglect of such writers by Walpole, who had, it was claimed, hired all the victims of *The Dunciad* to represent him in pamphlets and in newspapers.[8] This topic was made the subject of an amusing exchange of epigrams in 1734. The first poem appeared in the *Grub-street Journal* on 19 September and sounded a note typical of that paper, which was only nominally neutral in its politics:

> Tho' Wit by vulgar souls be set at nought,
> And some great men think little of a *thought:*
> Yet through all ages every prop of state
> Has likewise lent a helping hand to *that:*
> And, in proportion to his own great parts,
> Has prov'd a friend to wit and liberal arts.
> Thus HALLIFAX, who touch'd himself the lyre,
> Rewarded CONGREVE, ADDISON, and PRIOR.
> SOMMERS, GODOLPHIN, cherish'd doctor SWIFT;
> Nor did wise HARLEY turn the Dean adrift:
> And so the Primier, who had next the staff,
> Smil'd on CONCANEN, CIBBER, MITCHELL, RALPH.

This sally does not seem totally apt in retrospect; though Matthew Concanen was made attorney general of Jamaica and Cibber was amply rewarded, Joseph Mitchell received little in return for his many effusions praising the minister, and Ralph later changed sides. At any rate, the poem provoked an angry response in the *Daily Courant* of 24 September, consisting mainly of an attack on Swift and Harley but also pointing out that Young, Thomson, and Dodington had all praised Walpole in verse. More effective and more interesting, however, was another response printed on 26 September by the *Grub-street Journal* itself:

> Silence, rude scribler; nor, with envious spite,
> Bark, like a dog, at bards thou canst not bite.
> What tho' CONCANNEN, CIBBER, MITCHELL, RALPH,
> Are smil'd on, by the Primier with the staff?
> So POPE, YOUNG, WELSTED, THOMPSON, FIELDING, FROWDE,
> Have, each by turns, to his indulgence owed.
> So thousands more (were thousands such) wou'd share
> Th' unbounded blessings of his friendly care!
> But, upon thee, what patron in our isle,
> Is blockhead, knave, or fool enough to smile?

The reference to Pope is interesting, since it is a rare public allusion to Walpole's gift of £200 for work on the *Odyssey,* and the reference to Fielding supports the suspicion that he received some sort of financial help from Walpole in the early thirties. But beyond these details, the entire exchange is illustrative both of the ease with which purely literary judgments could become the pivot on which political satire could turn and of the significance with which the ministry's attitude toward the literary world was endowed by political journalists for both sides.[9]

But the argument was sometimes put on a more serious plane. Walpole's policy of ignoring the claims of the literati was occasionally yoked, not without violence, to what the opposition regarded as his political sins. The *Craftsman* argued that tyrants and wicked politicians have always been enemies to men of letters, whose calling it is to dispel ignorance and represent things in a true light; the government's failure to encourage writers was thus linked to that favorite opposition cry, that

Walpole posed a threat to liberty of the press. Antigovernment propagandists even maintained that the tragic themes chosen by dramatists reflected the policies of the administration, either filled with public spirit and panegyric or with selfishness and corruption, depending on the quality of the government at the time the play was written. But the most common method of elevating the tone of such criticism was to speak glowingly of the reign of Augustus and the encouragement by Maecenas of Virgil, Horace, and Livy—a tactic almost invited by the habit of some government writers of depicting in all seriousness George II as a new Augustus and Robert Walpole as the "new Maecenas [who] ornaments our State," despite the fact that the reputation of Augustus was beginning to decline.[10]

In its leader for 1 August 1730, *Fog's Journal* agrees that the Augustan Age was worthy of emulation but does not find it duplicated in the 1730s: "Poets and Philosophers are the fit Ornaments . . . of a polite and sensible Court, such as was that of *Augustus,* but Fidlers, Singers, Buffoons, and Stock-jobbers, would best suit the Court of a *Tiberius* or a *Nero,* where Stupidity, Lewdness, and Rapine sat in Council, and exerted all their Strength, in Opposition to every Thing that was sensible and ingenious." Like the *Craftsman, Fog's* connects hostility to the arts with a tyrannical hostility to all who see and understand too much. Such unjust rulers surround themselves with the tools of their corruption, whereas a Maecenas dedicates his private hours to the conversation of a Virgil or a Horace. After this rather fanciful picture *Fog's* points to the superiority of arts and letters over military prowess and to the debt posterity owes to great men like Maecenas and Richelieu who encouraged them. The elevated tone of this theme is abruptly altered, though, when *Fog's* finally makes the expected political application with the usual mock defense of Walpole; it is true, the writer says, that everyone asks what man of wit or genius ever tasted of his beneficence, but such critics have forgotten his support of *Hurlothrumbo* and his presence at *Tom Thumb.* Thus the irony of George II as a new Augustus and Walpole as his Maecenas was obvious to many besides Pope.[11]

Such attacks on Walpole's neglect of literary merit continued to the very end of his administration. The propagandists in the opposition press were not, of course, necessarily interested in literature at all; they merely seized upon the theme as a handy weapon against the minister, and their contexts often betrayed their real interests. Thus when a writer in the *Champion* (6 September 1740) pointed out, rather less than accurately, that Walpole's "Glories never warmed a *Pope*, a *Swift*, a *Young*, a *Gay*, or a *Thompson*, to celebrate his Name," he was merely setting the stage for a detailed catalogue of the hacks employed by Walpole as newspaper writers. But however sincere such writers may have been, they apparently could assume sufficient interplay between the literary and political interests of their audience to make this reiterated indictment worth their while. Even after Walpole's fall in 1742 the *Craftsman* continued harping on this theme, and James Ralph's summary in 1743 of the state of letters for the past two decades epitomizes the whole trend of this particular motif of opposition propagandizing:

> Can anyone mention a Period of Years . . . when ingenious Arts, Improvements in mathematical, natural, or any other Branch of useful Knowledge, were cultivated under greater Discouragements, were less countenanced and rewarded at C——t, than under the late Admin——n? Did even the Muses ever sing to so little Purpose, or were they ever so little inspired with the Praises of the Great? . . . The Spirit of Satire went forth amongst all who could write better, and the Names of *Dunce* and *Blockhead* were every where dealt about and applied. . . . All these Things happened in the Days, and under the Reign of W——e.[12]

How did the writers supporting Walpole attempt to answer this recurrent charge? Sometimes they quarreled merely with the details of the indictment, arguing that Richelieu and Oxford and Augustus were not worthy models for a patriotic British minister to emulate, or pointing out that some writers had indeed received patronage. The progovernment *Free Briton* in its issue for 13 August 1730 cited the example of Thomson, who, it was claimed, received a gift of £50 for dedicating to Walpole his poem on the death of Newton; then he "published his Gratitude the following *Winter*, libell'd the Ministry in formidable Poetry [and] applied to them again in the *Spring*." After such a notable instance of ingratitude, the *Free Briton* goes on, it is little wonder that Walpole's attitude towards poets should be marked with caution and distrust. Men of letters, the essay concludes, "do little consult the Interests of Learning, when they bring its Artillery into the Cause of Party."

More often, however, the defenders of Walpole made a frontal assault on the very notion of "wits" being given important places in government. Their assumption was that literary or scholarly accomplishments are frivolous entertainments that are useless in the real world of men and affairs. The *Free Briton* (6 August 1730) ridicules the notion that poets and philosophers are fit ornaments of a court: "The *General*, I presume, ought to give the Word of Command in *Rhime*." And the *Senator*, a progovernment paper written in the wake of Gay's success with *The Beggar's Opera*, paints a sarcastic picture of the progress of the wit to the patriot:

The Clown in *Aesop*, who wanted to be either Secretary of State or Butler, was not more absurd than our modern male-content Pretenders; of which there are Multitudes who upon the meer Credit of translating an Epigram, or saying a few lively Things at Midnight, do really believe themselves most consummately qualify'd for the very next Employment that shall fall in his Majesty's Service. If they are disappointed of this; if the Prime Minister thro' meer humane Frailty should chance to prefer his near Relation, or perhaps a try'd and constant Friend before our ingenious Gentleman, who makes Jests, and writes Epigrams; Then, all goes wrong, the World is near its End, and the poor Kingdom, for meer want of Wit, is on the very Precipice of Destruction![13]

Wit is no qualification for high office, nor is appreciation of poetry essential to the function of a minister. The only "learning" necessary for a minister, say Walpole's defenders, is a knowledge of human nature: "And I should rather chuse a Minister from among those who well understood Human Nature, and the Art of Governing Wisely, than from those who could distinguish the true Sublime in Poetry, or penetrate the Depths of Philosophy." Richelieu and other ministers may boast of plays and poetry, but Walpole has been expert in the more demanding art of defending the State from her enemies.[14] The point is made rather nicely in an epigram in another ministerial organ, the *Daily Gazetteer*, for 9 April 1740:

> The Cause you ask, and fain would know it,
> Why W—— ne'er retain'd a *Poet.*
> He wants not *Fancy*'s feeble Aid,
> Nor is of *Satire*'s Shaft afraid.
> On *History* he grounds his *Hope;*
> Let *St. John* trust for fame to *Pope.*

But they did not rest their case on epigrams. A more serious indictment of poetic interest as an actual hindrance to the accomplishment of great affairs is typified by this onslaught in the *Daily Courant* (23 March 1731):

Tho' Poetry is a fine Amusement, and a Taste in it a great Accomplishment in Youth . . . ; yet common Observation shews, that in Private Life 'tis so bewitching that wherever it gets firm Possession, it excludes from the Mind even a necessary Attention to Matters of more Moment: And shall a man be thought fittest to be trusted with the Concerns of the Publick for Talents, which, Experience shews us, render him incapable of managing his own?

Referring to the claim that Walpole had hired all the hacks of *The Dunciad* to appear in print on his behalf, the *Daily Courant* points out that it is absurd to call a man a dunce merely because he lacks skill "in making words clink." Similarly, the *Free Briton* ridicules the man in government who can give his attention to pretty turns and easy expressions when he ought to be engaged in great and national affairs. But if men of wit are unfit to hold office, then surely the dull and stupid are perfect managers of affairs of state—or so went *Fog's* mocking answer to such arguments.[15]

If this entire dispute has an air of unreality for the modern reader, it is only because the chasm between the active and the contemplative life, between the pragmatist and the artist, the poet and the statesman, is now simply axiomatic. But in the two decades of Walpole's ministry, the distinction was not so readily accepted. It had not, after all, been very long since Prior was a plenipotentiary at the conference of the Treaty of Utrecht and Addison a secretary of state. In his dedication to Halifax of the fourth volume of the *Tatler* (1711), Steele could write:

Your patronage has produced those arts, which before shunned the commerce of the world, into the service of life; and it is to you we owe, that the man of wit has turned himself to be a man of business. The false delicacy of men of genius, and the objections which others were apt to insinuate against their abilities for entering into affairs, have equally vanished. And experience has shown, that men of letters are not only qualified with a greater capacity, but also a greater integrity in the despatch of business.[16]

Whatever Halifax thought of this view, it was certainly not shared by Walpole. But as we have seen, "men of letters" were still held in such respect that opposition propagandists could make political capital out of the government's failure to notice them, and the gloating reminder in opposition journals that the witty world was united against the administration was at least important enough to sting Walpole's writers into some rejoinders. Moreover, the situation which this common motif in political journalism reflects, however distorted and exaggerated its depiction may be, must surely have had its effect on the political behavior of literary figures. Walpole was not likely to reward writers whose social or political biases and whose personal associations marked them as likely enemies to his administration; yet his failure to provide patronage, his contempt for men of letters, itself exacerbated and reinforced the hostility of the wits, whose humanist background led them to expect not only favor but a measure of power, regardless of their political leanings or their partisan friendships. As a result of this circle of events, Walpole became "Bob, the Poet's Foe," and the rift widened between the poet and the city.

Satire, Panegyric, and Politics

Not only were the government's patronage of literary figures and the alleged "decay of letters" under Walpole political issues of some significance, even the *kind* of literature that should be written was a question subject sometimes to political debate. James Ralph's comment that the spirit of satire went forth among all the better writers—that is, among those who opposed Walpole—was accurate enough, and the "literary" issue of the morality of satire and its proper limits became in essence a political dispute as well. By the end of the period of Walpole's

administration, it was a commonplace that "satire" was somehow
to be associated with the opposition to the ministry and the
court, and "panegyric" with the "courtiers" who defended the
administration.

This is not to say that Pulteney and others were truthful when
they claimed that all the wit was on their side. Progovernment
newspapers, pamphlets, and poems did not hesitate to employ
all the techniques of ridicule and personal satire against Bolingbroke, Pulteney, and the opposition press; and much of their
work was more clever and effective than has sometimes been
admitted. But, perhaps recognizing that the preponderance of
literary talent supported the opposition, political writers defending the ministry adopted a lofty moral tone about the evils of
satire and discoursed like literary critics on the value of wit.
Much of their criticism derived from the fact that the *Craftsman*
and other opposition papers necessarily depended rather heavily on allegory, myth, innuendo, puns, mock advertisements,
and other forms of devious "wit" to attack the prime minister
and his policies. And, of course, the very methods which satirists
may use to escape punishment are those which are also likely to
sharpen the edge of their satire and enrage their victims. The
criticism of the government writers went deeper, though, than
an attack on devious methods; their objections implied that
satire itself is out of place in a healthy society. Thus, after
complaining that the antigovernment papers depend wholly on
wit and ridicule, one pamphlet affirms that the state of affairs in
England has never been better; we are urged to recognize that
"in the year 1721 we were rescued from the jaws of destruction;
that *publick Credit* hath since flourished; . . . that Peace hath
poured all her blessings on us; that Universal Plenty hath
quieted all our Discontents."[17] Similarly, in an antigovernment
poem called "The World Unmask'd" (1738) the poet is sarcastically advised by a friend to forego satire in favor of panegyric on
the court:

> To Great *Augustus* Praises tune your Lyre,
> The Subject will heroic Thoughts inspire,
> And as his Image dignifies the Coin,
> His Name will consecrate each worthless Line,
> And, without Genius, make a Poem shine:

> Else cou'd the Court approve of *Cibber's* Verse,
> Did not the Lyre Great *Caesar's* Praise rehearse;
> Why then's your blotted Page with Satire stain'd
> As if a *Nero* or *Domitian* reign'd?[18]

Clearly, satire is here ironically viewed as a genre that one could reasonably expect to flourish only in corrupt society or under a wicked prince.

It is not surprising, then, to find the government papers attacking satire as a genre as well as particular satires against Walpole. The *London Journal* (14 September 1728), for instance, argues that "Satyr and Libelling have been practised from the Beginning of Letters in every Nation, yet I'd be glad to know what Vices do they really prevent." Such writing, it goes on to say, is more likely to encourage vice by "depriving Virtue of its just Reward." Lord Hervey, himself fairly adept at malicious wit, nonetheless complained of the "Propensity to Satyr" and expressed the hope that there were still some readers who "may be more shock'd at the Morals of a Satyrist, than pleased with his Wit and will not suffer the Depravity of their Natures to be flattered at the Expence of their Principles." Other progovernment writers echoed Hervey's suggestion that satire appeals to the depravity of human nature; either the satirist or his appreciative audience was said to be moved by jealousy, lack of benevolence, and spleen. One poem depicts all the opposition writers as a powerful band who combine wit with envy and Bolingbroke as a gifted man who "Hopes by his Satyr to redeem his Post,/ And gain by Wit, what Treachery has lost."[19]

Not only is satire attacked as ill-natured and inefficacious, but the closely associated terms of "humour" and "raillery" and even laughter itself are belittled, especially when they are applied to political affairs. Politics is serious business, the government writers seem to say; it has no place for literary frivolity. Any book or pamphlet written in a ludicrous manner, we are warned, is from an unworthy mind and is written with a seditious design; jesting, says another writer, is the business of the other party; our business is to defend the integrity of Walpole, not his wit and humor. If Britain, argues yet another, is as sick as the malcontents suggest, then it is surely our duty not to laugh at her, but to relieve her—doctors are valued not for their wit and polite taste but for their skill and experience.[20] The *Senator* (12 March 1727/8), with *The Beggar's Opera* and possibly *Gulliver's Travels* in mind, launches a full-scale attack on "our common Laughers," who are helpless in conversation with "Men of Sense, Business, or True Wit":

He that first defin'd Man to be a Risible Animal, certainly meant to tell us at the same Time that he was a very ridiculous one: The Follies, Vices, or Misfortunes of any other Creature, being by no means a proper Subject of Mirth or Diversion, whether our own are so or no.

But there is little to be feared from all the masters of wit and ridicule, counsels another writer, with considerable shrewdness: "No Man can be so weak as to think that a People of Good Sense, such as the *English* are, will ever be laughed into an Opposition to the Government." Witty sayings, he points out, may arouse our admiration without gaining our votes, and he adds this passage, which puts the writings of the opposition wits in perhaps a more accurate perspective since it recognizes their distance from the centers of power where political decisions are actually made:

Believe me, Sir, these Writings and Sayings have not the Effect that we may imagine. They do indeed open a great many Mouths against the Government; they are little to be regarded. The Men of Interest and Wealth in the Nation are they who make least Noise; as they have a great deal to lose they are more cautious, and don't care to disoblige any Party by speaking too freely, and for this Reason all the Talkers and Laughers are on the Side of the Opposition.[21]

The extent of the reaction to the use of wit, humor, and satire, however, belies such confidence. Many of those associated with the administration's cause obviously were fearful of the political effects of the satire and wit turned against them. The *Daily Courant* was more typical of the progovernment attitude when it warned on 7 June 1735 that in the last years of Queen Anne the strain of raillery was used for the worst purposes, and "how can we avoid believing, that it is to no good End we find it now revived?"

What most frustrated the writers for the government was that the literary qualities of satire or raillery, its distortions, subtleties, and witty hyperbole, made it the more appealing as it wandered farther from plain statement and direct argument on political affairs. Thus the *Senator* (24 August 1728) complains that common sense, plainly stated, fails to excite the attention of the public, so that artful writers now forego the simple methods of instruction and attempt to make the manner recommend the subject, *"How* a thing is said, being now the chief Inducement to listen to it, as well as generally the true Reason of saying it." Another writer attacking the *Craftsman* argues that, despite Shaftesbury, ridicule is no substitute for reason and no test of truth; it lays down no propositions and cannot satisfy the mind of an impartial inquirer. Similarly, Lord Hervey views sneering and invective as appealing to our passions rather than our understanding, and a letter in the *Daily Courant* claims that presenting arguments fairly and plainly is more pleasing to the readers "than the most smart Pieces of Satyric Wit could be; for with us 'tis the Reason, not the Language, that gains Credit to the Writer."[22] This case is argued fully, and a bit plaintively, in a pamphlet called *A Series of Wisdom and Policy,* which sets out to answer a pamphlet by Pulteney. The following paragraph is worth noting:

Why the Enemies of the Government have made so much Noise in the World, its Friends so little by their Writings, is because the one have had the labouring Oar, the *defensive* and *argumentative* Part, which few understand and fewer attend to; the other the declamatory, satirical and defamatory Part, which all have a Taste for. The entertaining Part has been carry'd on by a *well compact* and *united* Body . . . the other by a disjointed straggling Body. . . . This hath given further Scope to Wit and Drollery, and by playing off one Court-Advocate against another, in trivial and immaterial Points, have gain'd Devotees and Admirers; while their antagonists more *deep* are unread, as being unrelish'd by the *Shallows* of the age.[23]

What these writers are all expressing is, of course, partly the frustrated recognition that satire can be answered only in kind; defenders of the government did attempt to respond to ridicule with ridicule, and with some success despite their opponents' disparaging comments. But more than that, I think, the emphasis on "reason" and "common sense" in their complaints calls into question the value of satire as a vehicle of instruction and tends to disparage literary qualities as obstacles on the avenue to truth. Such, at least, is indicated by the tone of a defense of satire in the *Craftsman* for 9 February 1739/40. The essayist cites Horace as his authority for the use of ridicule on serious subjects and claims that more people may be laughed out of their vices and follies than argued out of them. But if, he goes on, the government apologists have somehow missed reading Horace despite the excellent translations and imitations of him available (a sly puff for Pope's anti-Walpole Horatian poems), then they need only turn to the writings of Addison and Steele. If it is further objected that Addison and Steele ridiculed private vices instead of public, then Addison's *Freeholder* would serve as an instance of wit applied to political affairs. Moreover, he concludes, there are many examples from the pulpit of eminent divines combating sin with wit. Thus, once again, we find that the paper warfare in the political press reaches out to include questions ordinarily thought of as purely literary.

Another literary question paramount in the minds of political commentators is the distinction between general and personal satire, or simply between satire and libel. The legal implications of such questions and their connections with controversy over freedom of the press need not be described here, but it should be recognized that to a considerable extent literary theorizing played a part in such disputes. The *London Journal*, for instance, argued that "just" satire is leveled at vice or folly, but that when particular persons are pointed out as guilty of that vice or folly, then the satirist is guilty of libel. All personal satire, in other words, is libel. The *Gazetteer* on several occasions insisted that the proper subjects of satire are general vices such as avarice or lust or affectation, not the particular vices of particular persons. Indeed, personal satire is not considered "true satire" by these writers, but mere "abuse," since "no Satire can be *Moral* that has not a good natured Tendency: nor can it ever tend to the Good of Mankind, to *suppose* Men wicked, and then use 'em ill."[24] Addison and Steele were constantly advanced as examples of great writers who tempered satire with benevolence or eschewed it altogether, and the authority of both Horace and Boileau was invoked to the same end. Thus the long-standing critical contrast between smiling with Horace and railing with Juvenal, as well as that between personal and general satire, entered the political arena as a result of the ridicule of Walpole by the *Craftsman* and by the circle of Swift and Pope.[25] Perhaps it is in this semipolitical light that we should view Pope's defense of personal satire in his famous letter to Arbuthnot, especially since he takes pains to proclaim sarcastically that his panegyrics are not "Incense worthy of a Court" and that "much freer Satyrists than I have enjoy'd the encouragement and protection of the Princes under whom they lived." When Cibber, in his *Apology* (1740), contrasts satire and panegyric and condemns the malicious wit of "our weekly Retailers of Politicks" who make bold with a government "that had unfortunately neglected to find their Genius a better Employment," he might well have been writing an essay in Walpole's *Daily Gazetteer*.[26]

Against all this criticism of personal satire, the *Craftsman* and other opposition papers offered several arguments, none very convincing. For one thing they claimed that their satires *were* general, that no particular persons were intended, and that, as the *Craftsman* (9 March 1727/8) put it, "as long as I confine myself to *general Expression* or wrap up my Invectives against Vice in *Dreams, Fables, Parallels,* and *Allegories,* I must insist on it that I keep within the proper Bounds of a *Satirist,* as prescribed by Criticks, Moralists, and Divines in all Ages." Of course, if the guilty recognize their portraits or if the government engages in absurd overreading, then no writing against vice can escape the charge of libel, not even Tillotson's sermons or *The Whole Duty of Man.* It is doubtful that anyone took very seriously this disingenuous defense, which made such a virtue out of legal necessity. As the *Senator* pointed out, the *Craftsman* could hardly print the words "bad Minister" in italics without being well understood in every alehouse in town.

The sincerity of the second argument offered in opposition papers was hardly more credible, though it seemed to concede that personal satire was freely engaged in. This defense was simply to view the function of satire as supplementing or even supplanting the role of the laws and the magistrate, on the ground that, if fame and infamy were in the power of the magistrate, then the magistrate himself would never be infamous. To this the *Gazetteer,* in a paper bitterly attacking Pope, responded contemptuously; such personal satire as can be found in Pope is actually against the law, but this will hardly

matter to a great poet since *of course* "a Paper of Verses is of
infinitely more value than any Law whatever."[27] The fact is that
no convincing defense of personal satire could be offered by the
opposition writers. The political situation demanded an attack
on particular people in the administration; satire and ridicule
were the weapons most effective with their audience, most
suitable to their talents, and—if handled subtly—least likely to
bring legal punishment. And to write satire was necessarily to
forego nice distinctions or judicious argument. There is some
truth in the closing remarks of the *Gazetteer* essay which attacked
Pope; both satire and panegyric, the writer says, are necessarily
larger than life—a true picture would show that the only
difference between the "Patriot" and the "Courtier" is that "the
former wants to get what the latter has."

It is important to note, however, that even the most general
satires could have political implications. As we shall see when
examining the relation of *Gulliver's Travels* to the opposition,
even satire broadly indicting the degeneracy of the times was by
implication specifically indicting the court and the ministry. If
the state is corrupt, then the source of that corruption must by
tradition be the head of the state, or at least his ministers. Thus,
by a simple reversal of that logic, depiction of the corrupt state
of society, even if free of personal reflections, is a form of
criticism of the king and his government. Such, at least, seems to
have been the attitude taken by the papers and journals supporting Walpole.

The *London Journal* for 31 July 1731, for instance, accused the
Craftsman of depicting all things as corrupt merely to slander
Walpole: " . . . because he is in Power, all things are out of order;
Nature and *Providence* are but *just safe,* and scarce left unar-
raigned; For *his sake,* the *whole Nation* hath been abused, Corruption and Degeneracy universally charged." The *Craftsman* had,
indeed, been requested by one of its readers to show how
"generally depraved" the present age has grown, how corruption has spread through all orders and professions, so that it is
not surprising to find the *London Journal,* in other issues,
ridiculing those who write "Satyrs upon the Age," who proceed
from the mistaken assumption that "Men are by Nature bad"
merely to prove that "Men in Power are ill Men." Another of
Walpole's propaganda organs, the *Free Briton,* also complains

that "Nature in general has been painted all Black, and Government in particular decry'd like a Pestilence." Sometimes, too, these diatribes against "false Philosophy" were accompanied by panegyrics on the honesty, sobriety, and wisdom of the English people. But however "philosophical" the air of these discourses, they all end by attacking opposition leaders or defending the administration.[28]

Whatever the form of the satire, then, whether general or personal, *Gulliver's Travels* or *Epilogue to the Satires,* it might be linked with the political opposition to Walpole. As with the first theme discussed, the attitude of the ministry to men of letters, we need not be surprised to find literary problems of such interest to the political world. The chapters which follow will trace in some detail the intersection of the political and literary worlds in the two decades of Walpole's administration. They will concern themselves, in other words, with the political aspects of particular literary works and particular literary careers. But throughout this sometimes confusing history of the maneuverings of politicians and the shifting loyalties of poets, the questions I have just surveyed will tend to recur. And they are questions not only about the value of specific genres like satire but also about the status of literary expression itself in the narrow arena of political struggle.

2 THE SCRIBLERIANS AND THE NEW OPPOSITION, 1723–1728

THOUGH WALPOLE assumed power in 1721, it was not until the summer and fall of 1726 that a parliamentary opposition with any semblance of effectiveness was formed; indeed, nearly every political event in the early years of his ministry seemed to work against the interests of those opposed to his politics.[1] It is hardly surprising, then, that no identifiable literary opposition emerged until after the efforts of the various malcontent factions began to coalesce and intensify. When Bolingbroke and William Pulteney made a working agreement to oppose Walpole in 1726, their political schemes coincided with the reunion and revival of the "Tory Wits," Pope, Swift, Gay, Arbuthnot—a revival marked by the publication of *Gulliver's Travels* only a few weeks before the beginning of the chief opposition organ, the *Craftsman*. Even before that important summer, however, these writers were reacting to the new political world with resentment and hostility but also with some evident desire to reach an accommodation.

The Atterbury Affair and After

One important event early in Walpole's term of office must especially have aroused the fear and antagonism of some of the old circle of wits who had constituted the Scriblerus Club in the last years of Queen Anne. This was the arrest on 24 August 1722 of Francis Atterbury, bishop of Rochester and close friend of both Pope and Swift, on a charge of treasonable correspondence

with the Pretender. Though Atterbury's complicity in a Jacobite
plot of large proportions is now known for certain, the evidence
available to the government was flimsy, and his "trial" before the
House of Lords was notable for impassioned speeches by the
bishop and his friends, for the testimony of Walpole himself,
and for the prosecution's extraordinary reliance on the "conjec-
tures of decypherers" who attempted to break the code in
Atterbury's correspondence. Though there was insufficient evidence to bring him to a court of law, the Lords passed a bill of
pains and penalties, and he was banished in the summer of
1723. It was the Lords and Atterbury's fellow bishops who
passed the bill overwhelmingly, but throughout all his difficulties it was Robert Walpole whom the bishop considered as "The
Author of all I suffer."[2]

Some members of the Scriblerus Circle were involved in the
affair directly. Bathurst, the close friend of Swift, Pope, and
Gay, gave an impassioned speech during the trial, attacking the
lack of legal evidence and the "sinister Arts" used by the government in prosecuting the bishop; and both Erasmus Lewis, Swift's
friend, and Pope himself testified before the House in Atterbury's behalf. While Atterbury was confined in the Tower, he
and Pope exchanged moving and affectionate letters; it was in
the course of this correspondence, at least in part conducted
secretly, that Atterbury asked Pope to testify "to say some what
about my way of Spending my Time at the Deanery, which did
not seem calculated towards managing Plots and Conspiracys."[3]
Pope faced his task with trepidation and apparently performed
poorly, but both Atterbury's counsel William Wynne and the
duke of Wharton made use of his testimony in their speeches of
defense. Yet Atterbury's purpose in seeking Pope's testimony is
obscure; he had more impressive friends to attest to his character, and the fact that he did not mention the plot while
discussing poetry with Pope signifies very little. As Thomas
Reeve, pressing the government's case, pointed out when belittling Pope's evidence, "No doubt my Lord Bishop hath con-
versed with Persons on different Subjects to whom he would
communicate nothing of an Affair of this Nature."[4]

There is a slight question, too, about the veracity of Pope's
testimony, since, as Sherburn indicates, the possibility of his
having Jacobite sympathies and even of his perjuring himself

cannot be completely ruled out.[5] At any rate, Pope found himself figuring unpleasantly in the paper warfare that broke out over the bishop's arrest and trial. He had been denounced as a Jacobite long ago by old enemies like Dennis, he had only recently been embarrassed by the government's suppression of his edition of the *Works* of the Jacobite duke of Buckingham, and now once again he found himself accused of Jacobitism in progovernment journals like *Pasquin*. Moreover, as has recently come to light, he received a bad fright at just this time (May and June 1723) when his sister's husband, a reputed Jacobite named Charles Rackett, and his nephew, Michael Rackett, were arrested as suspected members of the Windsor Blacks, a gang whose prowling in Windsor forest has been explained as a form of social protest. Pope may well have sympathized with their motives, but he obviously would have wanted to use whatever influence he possessed to secure their release. It is small wonder that he made an effort in letters to members of the administration to vindicate himself "from the notion of being a Party man."[6]

Swift, too, as an old friend of the bishop, was much aroused by the Atterbury affair. Though maintaining the pose that he was no longer "in the world" and had forsworn politics, he followed the event with interest. "It is a wonderful thing," he wrote sarcastically to a friend, "to see the Tories provoking his present majesty, whose clemency, mercy, and forgiving temper, have been so signal, so extraordinary, so more than humane, during the whole course of his reign, which plainly appears . . . from a most ingenious pamphlet just come over, relating to the wicked Bishop of *Rochester*." He ridiculed the prosecution of the bishop in the famous passage on plots and conspiracies in Part III of *Gulliver's Travels* and also in two poems written but not published during the bishop's imprisonment.[7] The government had broken the code in Atterbury's correspondence by studying references to a lame dog sent to the bishop from France, and Swift made the most of this piece of cryptography in his poem "Upon the horrid *Plot* discovered by *Harlequin* the B—— of R——'s *French* Dog," full of obvious puns on "dog" and invective against both Walpole and Atterbury's fellow bishops. Similarly, in a poem sent to Charles Ford on his birthday in January 1723 Swift warned his friend to stay away from London, where his foes (like

"Bloody Townshend," secretary of state and Walpole's brother-in-law) triumph over laws, condemn without evidence, and invent plots whenever it seems politically expedient. Such poems may seem a curious way for the Dean to forswear politics, but of course they were meant only as expressions of private resentment.

Atterbury's eminence as a man of letters made his exile an obvious target for those who already were depicting England under Walpole and George I as an environment hostile to the fine arts. Pope, writing to Swift about the bishop's departure and Bolingbroke's return, expressed his concern for the intellectual rather than the political significance of such an "exchange": "'Tis sure my particular ill fate, that all those I have most lov'd & with whom I have most liv'd, must be banish'd. ... Sure this is a Nation that is cursedly afraid of being overrun with too much politeness, & cannot regain one Great Genius but at the expense of another."[8] Ten years later, when this motif of opposition propaganda was well entrenched, Whitehead in *The State Dunces* made it his major comment on the Atterbury affair:

> And well it was that *Prelate* was sent hence,
> Who was *fast-leagu'd* with *Wits* and *Men of Sense*,
> *Sworn Foes* to *Appius* and his *blundring Tools*,
> Under whose *Auspices* this Isle he rules.[9]

Even in 1723 such comments were apparently widespread, for the *London Journal* (5 October 1723) took the trouble to ridicule those who deplored the lack of wit among the bishops now that this *"Miracle of Wit* and *Oratory* and *Poetry"* has gone: "Let the *Charms of Wit*, and *Song*, and *Epigram*, perish, when Justice makes its Demands." Though one may doubt whether Atterbury's exile represented a great loss to English letters, his literary pretensions enabled the opposition to harp once more on "Bob, the Poet's Foe" and also contributed, no doubt, to the resentment of his literary friends at his treatment by the government.

Not all the wits, however, reacted like Pope and Swift to the Atterbury episode. On 15 February 1723, a tragedy called *Humphrey, Duke of Gloucester*, written by Ambrose Philips, one of the "Whig wits" whom Swift had broken with in the last years of

Queen Anne, was performed. Philips's play, which in its printed
form was dedicated to William Pulteney, chairman of the
Committee of Inquiry into the conspiracy, immediately became
the center of controversy in the political press. It was clear to all
that the evil Cardinal Beaufort was meant to represent the
bishop of Rochester, especially since Philips included lines
justifying the use of bills of attainder against traitors whose
dignity, wealth, or cleverness placed them beyond the reach of
written laws. His play was mightily puffed in such ministerial
papers as *Pasquin* (6 March), the *British Journal* (9 March), and
the *St. James Journal* (February), all of which took pains to apply
the play to present circumstances in case anyone had missed the
point. The *London Journal* (2 March 1722/3) printed a poem by
Leonard Welsted praising Philips for turning from pastoral
poems to patriotic drama, and the *British Journal* (9 March)
found room for a poem with the remarkable title, "To Mr.
Philips, on his *Humphry Duke of Gloucester,* by a Gentleman of the
House of Commons, present when the Grenadier wept who
stood on the Stage whilst it was acted." As might be expected,
Mist's crypto-Jacobite *Weekly Journal* in several papers (23 February, 9 March 1722/3) attacked Philips bitterly, presumably on
artistic grounds but making no secret that the attack on Atterbury was really what offended most. In one issue (25 May)
Philips is contrasted with good poets like Pope and Fenton (a
nonjuror) and condemned by Apollo "not to go any where but
upon all Four, this being thought the most suitable Punishment
from his known Talent at Creeping"—a clear allusion to Philips's play as an effort to gain preferment.

Mist's judgment was fairly accurate, for Philips followed his
play first with an ode praising Pulteney, and then, in June of
1724, with a eulogy of Walpole in the style which justly earned
him the name "Namby Pamby":

> Steerer of a mighty realm,
> Pilot, waking o'er the helm,
> Blessing of thy native soil,
> Weary of a thankless toil,
> Cast repining thought behind,
> Give thy trouble to the wind.[10]

As M. G. Segar points out, it was impolitic of Philips to follow compliments to Pulteney with praise of Walpole, since the two politicians were already becoming estranged, but from this point on he devoted himself completely to seeking favor from the Pulteney and the Carteret families. Yet, after he arrived in Ireland in November 1724 as secretary to Primate Boulter, all his "creeping" seemed to do him little good, as Swift wrote to Pope. Pope, in turn, voiced his regret at Philips's failure to gain promotion, since it spoiled these lines he planned to use in *The Dunciad:*

> But what avails to lay down rules for Sense?
> In [George]'s Reign these fruitless lines were writ,
> When Ambrose Philips was preferr'd for wit![11]

Philips's attempt to capitalize on Atterbury's troubles would not have endeared him to Pope, and Swift's sarcastic comment on Philips's lack of success in Ireland speaks for itself: "Yet we think it a Severe Judgment that a fine Gentleman, and so much a finer for hating Eclesiasticks should be a domestic humble Retainer to an Irish Prelate."[12]

Reaction among literary figures to the trial of Atterbury, then, varied according to the personal associations and personal expectations as well as the politics of the individual writers. But in the absence of an effective political opposition to the government, the hostile emotions evoked in the Pope-Swift circle were not transformed into public attack on the ministry. Resentment at the imprisonment of a witty friend is not the same as political involvement, and none of the Scriblerians were yet engaged in anything remotely like a "literary campaign" against Walpole. As Swift put it during the bishop's imprisonment in explaining his abandonment of politics, "I am sometimes concerned for persons, because they are my friends, but for things never, because they are desperate."[13]

As a matter of fact, several of Swift's friends, however desperate they found "things," were themselves seeking or receiving favors from the court or the ministry in the period between Atterbury's trial and the beginning of the Bolingbroke-Pulteney opposition in 1726. Gay, for instance, who was made a commissioner of state lotteries in 1723, sought constantly in the years following to gain favor and preferment at court through Fortescue and others, and was constantly disappointed. Even in 1723 he could write cynically to Mrs. Howard, "I cannot indeed wonder that the Talents requisite for a great Statesman are so scarce in the world since so many of those who possess them are every month cut off in the prime of their Age at the Old-Baily," and by the fall of 1725 he was expressing himself bitterly about his failure to win a more lucrative post.[14] Swift and Pope saw nothing wrong with Gay's efforts to obtain favors from Walpole and the court of George I but only with the failure of those in power to support a needy poet. Literary genius, they felt, ought to be regarded as beyond partisan politics, and wits should be encouraged whatever their politics and whoever their friends. There was no hypocrisy in this view, at least not on Swift's part, for he had constantly sought to gain posts for the "Whig wits" in his days of influence with the Oxford-Bolingbroke ministry. But they were quick to see a political reason for Gay's lack of success; Swift suggested in 1723 that Gay might be under "original sin" for having dedicated the "Shepherd's Week" to Bolingbroke, and Pope wrote Swift in 1725, "Our friend Gay is used, as the friends of Tories are by Whigs, (and generally by Tories too) Because he had Humour, he was suppos'd to have dealt with Dr Swift; in like manner as when any one had Learning formerly, he was thought to have dealt with the Devil." They were probably right that Gay's association with such figures as Swift, Bolingbroke, and the Jacobite Shippen cost him favor, though Irving points more precisely to Gay's reliance on Mrs. Howard as not likely to recommend him either to Princess Caroline or to Walpole.[15] At any rate by the end of 1725 Gay was writing fables for the infant Prince William in what was to be his last literary attempt to gain favor at a Hanoverian court.

Pope's effort in these years to gain patronage from the ministry was both more successful and more quiet—so quiet, indeed, that it has received less attention than it deserves. The known fact is that on 29 April 1725 Pope received £200 as His Majesty's "Encouragement to the Work . . . of Translating the Odysses of Homer into English Verse."[16] Since Pope never referred directly to this grant from the Treasury, one must piece the story together from his letters. As early as February of 1723, when Atterbury was in the Tower and Pope was under a political cloud because of Buckingham's *Works,* Carteret, then secretary of state, was attempting to "promote" Pope's plan for translating the *Odyssey;* at that time Pope professed his distaste at being obliged to a government he had displeased: "I take my self to be the only Scribler of my Time . . . who never receiv'd any Places from the Establishment, any Pension from a Court, or any Presents from a Ministry. I desire to preserve this Honour untainted to my Grave." He followed this "Eclairaissment," as he called it, with a similar declaration to Harcourt. Sherburn suggests that the letter to Carteret alludes to the possibility of the grant Pope received two years later and, further, that Pope was discharging his obligations for the grant by crediting ten sets of the *Odyssey* to Walpole and Townshend in the preliminary subscriptions of 1724—"I would not deny my obligations," said Pope, "& tis all I owe Them." At any rate it is clear that, despite his fine words to Carteret, Pope, like other scribblers of his time, did receive a present from a ministry. Moreover, he maintained friendly relations with the minister himself, dining frequently at Walpole's table and instructing Fortescue to represent to Sir Robert that "I am much more his Servant, than those who would flatter him in their Verses."[17] At the same time he continued to associate freely with Bolingbroke, Swift, Burlington, Bathurst, Pulteney, and others opposed to the minister.

In this early period, at least, Pope seems once again to have tried to place himself on some lofty literary plane far above political animosities. His motive, as E. P. Thompson has hypothesized, may have been concern for the welfare of Charles and Michael Rackett, whose cases Walpole may have held in abeyance to insure the poet's good behavior—a form of blackmail that would cease to have meaning only in 1728, when his brother-in-law died.[18] But whatever the reason, Pope tried with some success to maintain good relations with both sides. He called himself only half a Tory when writing to Swift, and, expressing to Fortescue his concern about an indiscretion that might reach Walpole's ears, he complained, "We live in unlucky times, when half one's friends are enemies to the other."[19] The times were unlucky, indeed, for literary men who wished to escape the influence of politics on their lives and careers; Pope's attempt now to chart such a course was to prove no more successful than a similar effort on his part had been in 1712.

Pope's tacking, which enabled him to win a substantial favor from the government despite maintaining his ties with the "Tory wits" and being accused of Jacobite sympathies, was in contrast not only to Gay's naive politicking for a place but also to Swift's defiance of the government in these years. There is no need to repeat here the story of *The Drapier's Letters* and the trouble they caused the English ministers, but it should be noted that, in the view of one scholar, the real antagonists were Swift and Walpole. Wapole's handling of the events in Ireland in 1724 was unusually obtuse, largely, according to J. H. Plumb, because he lacked a proper understanding of the effectiveness of public opinion—a mistake not likely to be made by Swift.[20] However, for Swift this was an Irish affair, unrelated except indirectly to any opposition movement in the English parliament. As a matter of fact, the uproar in Ireland enabled Walpole to rid himself of a chief rival within the government, Carteret, who by a deft irony was made lord lieutenant and forced to support Walpole's Irish policy against his friends Swift and the Brodericks. Nonetheless, the victory in Ireland made Swift a formidable foe, and when he came over to England in the spring of 1726, Primate Boulter warned the English ministers to keep an eye on the Dean and discover "What he shall be attempting on your side of the water."[21] The warning was issued with better reason than Boulter knew, for Swift was bringing with him the manuscript of *Gulliver's Travels,* and an opposition group which could use that satire to good advantage was just then being formed.

The Wits and the Forming of the Opposition

The two major events which led to the new opposition had both occurred in 1725. In May of that year an act was passed which restored to Bolingbroke his estates; it did not, however, restore to him his seat in the House of Lords, lest "his bad leavan should sower that sweet untainted mass," as he put it to Swift.[22] In 1725, too, William Pulteney, the friend of Pope and Gay, broke with Walpole and was dismissed from his place at court.

With his cousin Daniel he attempted unsuccessfully to lead an opposition in the parliament of 1726; but the spark of Bolingbroke was needed to weld discontent into an effective opposition. Though Bolingbroke had been accused of caballing with Pulteney even while his case was being heard, it was only in the summer of 1726 that an alliance between these two brilliant and ambitious men was effected. Bolingbroke's country retreat, Dawley Farm, became the gathering place not only of such politicians as Bathurst and the Pulteneys but also of the Scriblerian wits Arbuthnot, Pope, Swift, and Gay.

Not every important figure in the literary world, however, was so careless in the choice of political associations in that summer of 1726. Edward Young, at least, was actively courting the ministry. He was friendly with Bubb Dodington (the "Bufo" of Pope's *Epistle to Dr. Arbuthnot*), who was now one of the lords of the Treasury and to whom Young dedicated the third satire of his "Universal Passion" (1725). That piece of flattery was followed in 1726 by the dedication of "Satire the Last" to Walpole, the "pilot of the realm" and the model for all courtiers. But the *coup de maître* of Young's campaign was *The Instalment,* written to celebrate the installation of Walpole as Knight of the Garter in May of 1726. A year earlier Walpole had been instrumental in the revival of the Order of Bath so that more honors would be available to the deserving—a motive ridiculed by Swift in these lines:

> Thus my Subjects with pleasure will obey my Commands
> Tho as empty as Younge and as saucy as Sandes
> And he who will leap over a Stick for the King
> Is qualified best for a Dog in a String.[23]

Now the minister himself was honored by appointment to the Order of the Garter, an event which was accompanied by such a display of wealth and splendor that it aroused popular resentment and which produced such a spate of complimentary verses that Mist advised his readers to place them under their pillows as a sure cure for insomnia.[24] The praise of Walpole in Young's poem is remarkably fulsome, even for an age inured to the conventions of eulogy. He needs no muse, for a Walpole is his theme. Walpole's azure ribbon (he was known as "Sir Blue-String" from now on) and radiant star will guide the vessel of Britain through war or peace. He is "The *fruit* of Service, and the *bloom* of Fame,/ *Matur'd* and gilded by the royal Beam." Nor is Young too bashful to include himself in these verses:

> My breast, O WALPOLE, glows with grateful fire
> The streams of Royal bounty, turn'd by Thee
> Refresh the dry domains of Poesy.

The reference to the streams of royal bounty alludes to the pension of £200 a year which Young had just been granted and which lends an unintentional irony to his line, "False praises are the Whoredoms of the Pen." There is, perhaps, more truth than sincerity in his comment on his good fortune:

> My fortune shews, when Arts are WALPOLE's care,
> What slender worth forbids us to despair:
> Be this thy partial smile from censure free;
> 'Twas meant for *Merit,* tho' it fell on *Me.*[25]

Dodington had himself addressed a poetic epistle to Walpole that year, advising him, when dispensing his favors, to reward truth and probity rather than genius and "parts"; half of his advice, at least, seems to have been heeded.

As might be expected in the rapidly intensifying political atmosphere of 1726, such a poem from a man of Young's reputation could not go unnoticed in the circles opposed to Walpole. His fellow poet James Thomson confined his remarks to the literary quality of the poem: "The Dr's very Buckram has run short on this Occasion: his affected Sublimity even fails Him, and down He comes, with no small Velocity."[26] But one pamphlet appearing shortly after the poem cleverly mingled literary with political criticism. We have a right, says this anonymous author, to expect good English and common sense from one of Young's learning, yet we find neither these qualities nor any share of prudence or discretion. Indeed, after a close examination and considerable distortion of Young's text, this pamphlet concludes that the reader is faced with a curious dilemma: "either that our Author had a malicious Design of *traducing* this *eminent Patriot*, under a pretence of *extolling* him; or else, that he . . . has the worst knack at *Flattery* of any Man living." With this gambit established, Young's critic quickly assumes the former, that the poem is a mock panegyric, and he proceeds then with an ironic defense of Walpole against the "designing Sycophant" who is secretly insulting him in verse. How does Young dare to say Walpole has "thrown the proud Enclosure down"? This great minister has attempted to keep up the national enclosures (Young had meant merely the aristocratic tradition of the Order of the Garter). "When was there a more free and uncorrupted *Parliament;* or a Bench of more eminent, learned, and pious *Bishops?* . . . We are publickly assured, that the *national Debt sinks* gradually under his Hands, and is in a fair way of being speedily discharged; even *though it were to be increased* to a much larger Sum."[27] Such political barbs are superimposed upon ridicule of Young's poetic abilities, which throughout are contrasted with Pope's. It may well be, as the *Dictionary of National Biography* suggests, that Young was a writer for the government or performed other specifically political tasks, but neither this pamphlet nor other opposition sources make any such accusation. The *Craftsman* merely refers to him as Walpole's "*own immortal Poet,* who is himself a witness and partaker of his *munificence*," and for Swift seven years later he is still merely the symbol of a poet corrupted by a court:

> Whence *Gay* was banish'd in Disgrace,
> Where *Pope* will never show his Face;
> Where *Y[oung]* must torture his Invention,
> To flatter *Knaves*, or lose his *Pension*.[28]

There were many, however, who said that Swift himself was not above seeking patronage from Walpole in the summer of 1726, despite his appearances at Dawley Farm and his friendship with Bolingbroke. He had come over to England in March; then in April he had two meetings with Walpole, the first at the minister's invitation and the second at Swift's request. Little is known about the first meeting, except that Swift and some of his friends, possibly Harcourt and Peterborough, dined at Chelsea with Walpole and that Swift attempted to put in a good word for John Gay. Williams suggests, quite plausibly, that Walpole's invitation was his way of keeping an eye on the "wild Dean." At any rate, it was the second, private interview arranged by Peterborough at Swift's request that caused rumors to spread that Swift offered his pen in exchange for a living in England, rumors which still find their way into current biographies. And about this interview we know a great deal, since the following day Swift wrote Peterborough an account which he asked his friend to show to Walpole. His purpose in the meeting was to lay before the minister the grievances of Ireland, "not only without any view to myself, but to any party whatsoever"; it was, as Swift admits, a fruitless effort, "for, I saw, he had conceived opinions from the examples and practices of the present and some former governors, which I could not reconcile to the notions I had of liberty." As Oliver Ferguson has demonstrated, the arguments used by Swift in this interview were the same as those used by Archbishop King in a similar effort that summer to plead Ireland's case with the government, so that it appears he and King were acting in a concerted fashion on behalf of Ireland.[29] Certainly, there is no reason to doubt the truth of Swift's account of this interview and not a scrap of evidence to impugn the statements he made a few months later in a letter to James Stopford:

I was latterly twice with the chief Minister; the first time by invitation, and the second at my desire for an hour, wherein we differed in every point. But all this made a great noise, and soon got to Ireland, from whence upon the late death of the Bishop of Cloyne, it was said I was offered to succeed, and I received many letters upon it, but there was nothing of truth, for I was neither offered, nor would have received, except upon conditions which would never be granted. For I absolutely broke with the first Minister, and have never seen him since.[30]

No doubt Swift would have been pleased with a bishopric, but it was in Leicester House, Mrs. Howard, Princess Caroline, and a new government at the death of George I that he placed his hopes, not in Robert Walpole.

Nor should too much significance be attached to the gathering of Swift and his friends with Bolingbroke and the Pulteneys at

Dawley during this summer of 1726. The tendency has been to assume that the "leading spirits of the opposition" held meetings there with the Scriblerian wits and that, as one commentator puts it, "a consistent effort was made to develop a friendship with those literary men whose services might be found of value."[31] Yet such statements, again, need qualification. Certainly Swift, Pope, Gay, and Arbuthnot were there in the company of Bathurst and other politicians. But whatever was agreed to between Bolingbroke and Pulteney, there is no evidence of any literary "club" being formed to attack the government; as far as we can tell, there was no agreement made among the wits to enter into the political schemes of their friends and no parceling out of satiric chores. Pope was still deliberately keeping himself aloof from politics, and Gay was writing fables and hoping still for preferment at court. Indeed, it was only after Swift had returned to Ireland at the end of the summer that Pulteney made overtures to him about a matter "that I do not think so discreet to trust to a letter," overtures which Swift rejected when he described himself to Pope as unwilling to engage in a "Useless Correspondence" with Pulteney. Pope, in turn, praised Swift for declining the gambit:

Another thing with which you have pleased me, was what you say to Mr. P. by which it seems to me that you value no man's civility above your own dignity, or your own reason. Surely, without flattery, you are now above all parties of men, and it is high time to be so, after twenty or thirty years observation of the great world. . . . I question not, many men would be of your intimacy, that you might be of their Interest: But God forbid an honest or witty man should be of any, but that of his country. They have scoundrels enough to write for their passions and their designs; let us write for truth, for honour, and for posterity. If you must needs write about Politicks at all, (but perhaps 'tis full as wise to play the fool any other way) surely it ought to be so as to preserve the dignity and integrity of your character with those times to come, which will most impartially judge of them.[32]

Swift modestly replied that he was too old to act otherwise and thus necessity appeared a virtue, but it is clear that whatever his reasons he had no taste for political journalism at the moment. Certainly none of this sounds much like an "organized" literary opposition.

The fact is that the Scriblerian wits were never involved in an organized opposition to Walpole in the sense of a planned and coordinated literary-political campaign of the kind which would be mounted by the circle around Prince Frederick in the late 1730s. Though their sympathies were with their close friends in the parliamentary opposition, they did not consider themselves "party-writers," and their satiric attacks on Walpole were written not in accord with any political scheme but as independent expressions of their own hostility to the administration. As I have indicated, not the least element in that hostility was the attitude of the Walpole government toward the literary world itself. Obviously, their wit was useful to the opposition even if not "written to order." Swift was at work on *Gulliver's Travels* before he met Pulteney, before Bolingbroke returned to England, and before there was an effective opposition to the government, but, as will be demonstrated, his satire was nonetheless both commonly regarded as opposition propaganda and highly serviceable to the cause of his friends in Parliament.

For that matter, the coalition between Bolingbroke Tories and Pulteney Whigs which was now to constitute the "country interest" was not an "organized" opposition party in any modern sense. Archibald Foord characterizes the new opposition in this way:

Our evidence concerning its formation and early operation suggests that in its original character it was a personal working agreement between the two constituent factions for relentless assault upon Walpole, to which purpose they sought, by direct negotiation and the exploitation of popular issues, to gather support from all other malcontents both within and without the Ministry. No specific contract bound its members, and within its counsels lurked no "shadow Cabinet." Its oracles alleged the customary reason for opposition, the need to purify a corrupt Government, and everything pointed to a desire for preferment, regardless of others, as the true motivation in the hearts of most.[33]

Though from this unstable base the opposition expanded and became more institutionalized, it did not become more homogeneous; as Foord puts it, "the Opposition remained a loose confederacy, for ever on the verge of dissolution" (p. 135). If those actually engaged in the struggle for power were without a formal structure or organization, it is not surprising that their literary friends pursued an independent course in their own attacks on the "great man."

The beginning of a new and vigorous opposition was marked in the popular mind not by any secret agreements at Dawley nor by any new moves in Parliament, but by the appearance on 5 December 1726 of the *Craftsman* by "Caleb D'Anvers," which from then till the fall of Walpole was to be the chief organ of the opposition. This new journal was at first written chiefly by Bolingbroke, Pulteney, and a minor wit named Nicholas Amhurst. In its early years the Scriblerian wits were accused of writing for it; "I have been set forth to the World," said Caleb on 25 November 1727, "as a *noble Lord,* a *discontented Courtier,* an *Ecclesiastical Dignitary,* a *learned Physician,* a *celebrated Poet,* an *expell'd Academick,* and a *Grubstreet Garreteer*"—i.e., as Bolingbroke, Pulteney, Swift, Arbuthnot, Pope, and Amhurst. Yet there is no evidence that Swift, Pope, or Gay contributed papers, though presumably it was to seek Swift's aid with the *Craftsman* that Pulteney had made his approach to the Dean a few months earlier. It is interesting to find Arbuthnot's name included in a list of noblemen who are to receive packets of the journal (the list was among papers seized by government agents in one of the many raids on the *Craftsman*); but, again, an avid reader is not necessarily a contributing author, and without more evidence the good doctor cannot be connected with the paper further.[34] As a matter of fact, there are not a large number of essays in the *Craftsman* worth attributing to the Swift-Pope circle even on dubious internal evidence. Though occasionally amusing and sometimes brilliantly satiric, the constant allegorizing of Walpole as the Norfolk Steward or Dr. King with a "golden Specifick" or even as "a certain Great Man" grows tedious after a time, as do Bolingbroke's interminable historical parallels of Walpole to all bad ministers of the past. If a typical issue of the *Craftsman* is on a level superior to that of a typical government paper, this does not mean it approaches the level of Swift's *Examiner. Fog's Journal* (the successor to Mist's!) is, in my estimation, much

wittier and certainly more concerned with matters of literary
interest.

But there can be no question that the *Craftsman* made a
powerful impact; after its appearance the political atmosphere
intensified and a full scale paper war ensued. In the winter and
spring of 1727 Bolingbroke's series of pamphlets called *The
Occasional Writer* excited angry attacks, and significantly in the
very first of those pamphlets Bolingbroke called attention to the
ministry's disregard of literary merit. Pretending that he is a
venal writer offering his services to Walpole, he asserts as a
general principle that "M—— of S—— pay no regard to the
brightest talents, when they are misapplied, and esteem all
talents to be so, which are not wholly employed about the
present time, and principally dedicated to the service of their
A——n."[35] From the very beginning, then, this appears to have
been a major motif in opposition propaganda and one to which
the government writers were sensitive, as the angry answers to
this point in *The Occasional Writer* attest. It is amusing to find
Leonard Welsted, no friend of the Scriblerus group, echoing
this theme in a discourse to Walpole (July 1727) intended to gain
the minister's support for a projected translation of Horace;
after first flattering Walpole as a patron of the arts, Welsted
suddenly tacks about, bemoans the decay of letters, cites as his
authority no less a person than Mist, and attempts to recoup any
possible losses from this bold maneuver by the following passage:

> I know very well, that this quotation will make no great figure in the
> way of learning . . . ; however, since it was to the purpose, I have set it
> down, and the rather, Sir, as it gives me an occasion to hint to You, that
> this is a subject the disaffected are particularly fond of, and that they
> play off most of their Engines of wit from this quarter, not altogether
> so much, perhaps, from their affection for the *Belles Lettres,* as for more
> important reasons; an Esteem for learning and liberal Arts is, they
> know, one of the most specious covers, that can be made use of for
> discontent.[36]

This unusual ploy did not succeed; Welsted was ignored, and
the plans for translating Horace died.

In this exacerbated climate of political journalism in the early months of 1727, it was more likely than ever that literary works would be looked at closely for political implications. Indeed, even Italian opera became a subject of political controversy, with the *British Journal* (4 March 1726/7) defending it and the *Craftsman* (13 March) attacking it as sybaritic and inappropriate for the British national character. It was at this "boisterous" time, as Bolingbroke called it, that the first series of Gay's *Fables* appeared, dedicated to Prince William. Compared to the lampoons on Walpole daily appearing in the press, the political satire in these fables is negligible.[37] Their themes are typically generalized attacks on sycophantic courtiers, tyrants, and informers, or indictments of general moral faults like avarice, envy, and pride. Only No. VII, "The Lyon, the Fox, and the Geese," could be really suspect; here, a fox, chosen viceroy by the lion, is extravagantly praised, whereupon a goose reflects:

> What praise! what mighty commendation!
> But 'twas a fox who spoke th'oration.
> Foxes this government may prize
> As gentle, plentiful and wise;
> If they enjoy these sweets, 'tis plain,
> We geese must feel a tyrant reign.
> What havock now shall thin our race!
> When ev'ry petty clerk in place,
> To prove his taste, and seem polite,
> Will feed on geese both noon and night.[38]

This might have appeared a clear jibe at Walpole, his eulogizers, and his accumulation of private wealth at the expense of the nation, especially since unlike most of the fables it uses words like "government" and "administration" and thus gives its general theme more specific application.

Yet despite this mild satirical poem and despite the fact that the Walpole circles were sensitive about even general satire on courtiers, it is difficult to understand how these fables could have harmed Gay's chances, given their appearance at a time of truly virulent political pamphleteering. On the other hand, we have Swift's testimony in the *Intelligencer* No. III that Gay *was* thought too bold in his account of court life: "And although it be highly probable, he meant only the *Courtiers* of former Times,

yet he acted unwarily, by not considering that the Malignity of
some People might misinterpret what he said, to the Disadvan-
tage of present *Persons* and Affairs."³⁹ Moreover, *Intelligencer*
No. X gives an instance of how Gay's poems might have been
misapplied. In Swift's poem called *"Tim* and the *Fables,"* a violent
Whig ("Timothy the Scourge of the Tories") believes that Gay's
innocent fable of the monkey who had seen the world is a
political satire leveled at him:

> He now began to storm and rave;
> *The cursed Villain! now I see*
> *This was a Libel meant at me;*
> *These Scriblers grow so bold of late,*
> *Against us Ministers of State!*
> *Such Jacobites as he deserve,—*
> *Dammee, I say, they ought to starve.*⁴⁰

The *Intelligencer* appeared, of course, after Gay had written *The
Beggar's Opera* and thus become clearly hostile to the administration; if there were Timothys in 1727 who overread the fables,
they did not voice their feelings in print very often, for the
political journals ignored the fables when they first appeared. In
1728, though, a poem called "The Oak and the Dunghill,"
attributed to Edward Roome, mocked the "Patriot Dunghill" so
jealous of the mighty oak (Walpole), and it doubtless amused the
town to find the opposition satirized in a form clearly imitating
fables by the author of *The Beggar's Opera.*⁴¹

Shortly after the publication of the *Fables*, another aspiring
poet chose a somewhat safer way to gain favor from the
government circles. In May appeared James Thomson's *Poem
Sacred to the Memory of Sir Isaac Newton*, dedicated to Sir Robert
Walpole. Thomson, a year earlier, had ridiculed Young's *Instal-
ment* and the absurd poems of the "Planet-blasted Fool" Joseph
Mitchell, who, said Thomson, "has had a Fling at Walpole too."⁴²
Now, apparently, Thomson decided to have his own fling at
Walpole. His dedication is a typical panegyric; Walpole is our
most illustrious patriot, "engag'd in the highest and most active
Scenes of Life, balancing the Power of *Europe,* watching over our
common Welfare, informing the whole Body of Society and

Commerce, and even like Heaven dispensing Happiness to the Discontented and Ungrateful."[43] Douglas Grant finds it difficult to explain why Thomson should have chosen as a patron a man whose foreign policy he was soon to attack, and he suggests Dodington may have once more been instrumental in securing for Walpole the flattery of a poet.[44] But it should be clear by now that poets, whether Thomson, Pope, or Gay, considered patronage by the government their just reward. It appears, too, that even a year earlier the pro-Walpole press was anxious to claim Thomson as their own. After the appearance of *Winter,* dedicated to Sir Spencer Compton, the *London Journal* (4 June 1726) had remarked, "It was to a Pollio and a Maecenas, that the *Romans* owed their Virgil; it was to a Somers and a Hallifax, that the present Age ow'd its Addison; and I hope, future *Ages* will have reason to say, *It was to a* W——pole or a C——ton, *that we owe a* Thomson." Three years later, however, after the publication of *Britannia,* the *Free Briton* (13 August 1730) announced that the dedication of the Newton poem to Walpole had been rewarded by fifty pounds, and it accused Thomson of being one of the ungrateful to whom Walpole dispensed happiness. If such a payment was in fact made, the present was evidently insufficient to win the poet's support for the ministry; and future ages have had no reason to say that it was to a Walpole that we owe a Thomson.

In April, just before Gay's *Fables* appeared, Swift returned to England and at once threw himself actively into the campaign of the opposition, his aloofness apparently shattered by the pressure of the vigorous paper war that spring. In May he wrote Sheridan that he and his friends had a "firm, settled Resolution to assault the present Administration, and break it if possible," and he went on to complain of the "Beasts and Blockheads" hired by Walpole to write his pamphlets and newspapers.[45] A few days later he was taking hints from Bolingbroke for his *Letter to the Writer of the Occasional Paper,* which he never completed and never published. Bolingbroke was apparently dissatisfied with it, and it is not, in fact, one of Swift's more distinguished performances. The title is misleading, for the piece is actually a letter to the *Craftsman;* far from being a contributor to that paper, Swift seems at this point not even a reader, since his

unfamiliarity with some of its recent changes caused Bolingbroke to reject his entire introduction. The burden of Swift's
Letter is ridicule of the poverty of talent demonstrated by writers
for the government: "In a word, it seems to me that all the
writers are on one side, and all the railers on the other."[46] In
particular, he protests against the abuse Walpole's writers had
been heaping upon Bolingbroke as the supposed author of *The
Occasional Writer*. He claims that the attribution of those papers
to a particular person is based only on the information of a
"certain pragmatical spy of quality," a detail supplied Swift by
Bolingbroke and perhaps referring to no less a figure than
Voltaire. With this as his base, Swift broadens out to touch on
common opposition themes—corruption at home, a disastrous
foreign policy abroad, and the failure to promote men of genius
and learning. Will any of these ills be cured by a correct
identification of the Occasional Writer?[47]

Only a few weeks after Swift and Bolingbroke were collab-
orating on the *Letter,* the hopes of the opposition were raised by
the death of George I. Bolingbroke urged Swift to stay in
England instead of going to France for his health, as the Dean
had intended, and apparently Mrs. Howard—to whom the
opposition circles attributed an influence she did not possess—
gave him the same advice. Swift would have been pleased to
obtain a living in England "without assuming a suppliant de-
pendant air," as Bolingbroke told him he might, and it seemed
certain now that Walpole would fall.[48] On the same day that
Bolingbroke wrote Swift (17 June) the *Craftsman* ran a mock
advertisement giving notice that "the celebrated Dr. ROBERT
KING, who has performed so many wonderful Cures in this
Nation, designs in a short time to retire from *publick Business,*
having acquired a *comfortable Subsistance* by his Practice." But all
these hopes were soon disappointed. Sir Spencer Compton,
supposedly the choice of George II to succeed Walpole, quickly
proved his incompetence, and Sir Robert was retained. By 5
August the *Craftsman* was reduced to running this advertisement: "Whereas it hath been falsely and maliciously reported
that the famous, new invented *Court-Ear-Knots* were going out of
fashion, and that the Gentleman, who *sold* them, had *left off his
Business;* this is to acquaint the Publick that he only *shut up his*

Shop for a few Days, on his late Majesty's Death, and hath since *opened it* again."[49]

For Swift the retention of Walpole was no joking matter. He was ill, his trip to the continent had been canceled, and he believed he had been duped by Mrs. Howard. His disgust at the turn of public events he later recorded in *An Account of the Court and Empire of Japan* (not published in his lifetime), which bitterly allegorizes the corrupt methods used by "Lelop-Aw" to stay in power. He left for Ireland in September, his last stay in England over and his one brief entry into the active political opposition abruptly ended. But his major contribution to that opposition had already been made; *Gulliver's Travels* was already being attacked by his enemies and exploited by his friends in a way that Swift perhaps did not originally intend.

Gulliver's Travels *and Partisan Politics*

Modern commentators have never taken very seriously Gulliver's declaration, "I meddle not the least with any Party." Every student of Swift is familiar with the interpretations of the political allegory proposed by Sir Charles Firth, A. E. Case, and others. But how was the book received in contemporary political circles? The question is of special interest when we realize that the publication of the *Travels* on 28 October 1726 predated by only six weeks the opening of the new propaganda campaign against the administration of Walpole, a campaign signaled by the appearance of the *Craftsman*. Indeed Sir Robert's latest biographer speaks of Swift's book as "one of the most remarkable and virulent satires ever to be written against Walpole," and John Loftis terms it one of the "propagandistic triumphs" of the opposition.[50] On the other hand, we have been assured by other scholars that Swift's fears about its reception were groundless, that the fictional framework of the satire was so diverting that the book gave no offense, and that Swift spoke sincerely when, five years later, he claimed never to have offended Walpole.[51]

Nor, in settling such a question, are the celebrated letters from Swift's friends much help. Much of the correspondence concerning the publication or reception of the *Travels* is couched

either in mysterious terms or in friendly banter, and sometimes
contradictions appear which are difficult to reconcile. Swift,
concerned about hurting his own person or fortune, had sought
a printer willing to venture his ears; but Pope, a few weeks after
its publication, reported that no "considerable man" was very
angry at the book, so that Swift "needed not to have been so
secret upon this head." At the same time he was amused to
observe "that countenance with which it is received by some
statesmen." Both Pope and Gay agreed that the book was
thought to be free from "particular reflections," but Swift wrote
from Ireland that "the general opinion is, that reflections on
particular persons are most to be blamed," and he clearly felt he
had angered the ministry.[52] None of this is particularly revealing
about the reactions of the political world to a book which,
despite changes in the text by its cautious London printer, might
well have seemed a precursor to Bolingbroke's and Pulteney's
new journal.

Much more fruitful in determining the extent and nature of
that reaction are comments in political journals, "keys," newspapers, and pamphlets in the first five years following the
publication of the book. For the sake of convenience this
evidence may be divided into three groups: comments which
dwell on the "particular reflections" or which assume Swift to be
associated with the opposition; indications that even by its genre
as a "general satire" *Gulliver's Travels* had political overtones;
and examples of the manner in which the opponents of Walpole
capitalized on Swift's book by quotation and imitation. Such
evidence indicates that, whether Swift wished it or not, his book
was received almost at once as a decidedly political document
and was both understood and used as a contribution to the
political journalism of the opposition.

In the month immediately following its publication, there was
much to support Pope's contention that no men of consequence
were angry at the book. The manner in which the *Travels* "for
their Variety of Wit and pleasant Diversion" became "the
general Entertainment of Town and Country" is well known;
harlequinades, Lilliputian odes, scandalous memoirs of the
court of Lilliput—all helped make Lemuel Gulliver as popular a
topic of town conversation as Mary Tofts the Rabbit Woman,

about whom "Gulliver" himself wrote a pamphlet.[53] Indeed, during November the world of political journalism itself seemed more diverted than vexed by the book. Mist's *Weekly Journal,* a paper usually able to turn anything (even the Rabbit Woman) against the government, merely imitated Swift's satire to ridicule the "Kingdom of Philology"—not without a few gentle hits at Swift himself (19 November 1726); whereas the violently Whiggish *Weekly Journal, or British Gazetteer* was content to print (26 November) a whimsical letter to Lemuel from his brother Ephraim Gulliver, and the *London Journal,* another supporter of the government, made incidental references to Gulliver's adventures in language either neutral or favorable (12 November, 26 November). Thus, whatever the private views of "people of greater perspicuity," as Gay termed them, public criticism in the political world was for the moment disarmed.

However, from the beginning its political allusions were obviously understood; the delight in the book expressed by the Oxford Tory Dr. Stratford and the exiled Jacobite Atterbury was no doubt matched by a corresponding displeasure in those statesmen whose faces Pope enjoyed watching.[54] From within weeks of its publication the book had been generally attributed to Swift, who was known to be on good terms with Bolingbroke and Pulteney; and during November keys and pamphlets exploiting its political meanings were probably already in preparation. Yet it was only after the inauguration of the *Craftsman* on 5 December and the beginning of a newly invigorated journalistic war that these implications became politically significant. Thus Abel Boyer, who serialized excerpts from *Gulliver* in his *Political State of Great Britain,* categorized the work as a "Romantic Satire" in his November issue but as a "Political Satyr" in his issue for December. As befitted his journal, Boyer emphasized the political passages by capital letters and other devices, but aside from suggesting that the Flying Island represents the Royal Prerogative he made no interpretations of specific symbols; indeed he argued that the "Allusions and Allegories . . . are for the most part so strong, so glaring, and so obvious" that no explanation is necessary. Nor did he accuse Swift of political malice or of alliance with the opposition, though he did identify the author as his old friend "the *Examiner.*"[55]

The *Craftsman* itself, though it was soon to praise the book obliquely, refrained from interpreting specific allusions in the way it was later to do with *The Beggar's Opera*. Instead, its issue for 16 January engages in mock disparagement of the modern tendency to turn serious things into ridicule, as exemplified by *Gulliver's Travels* and *An Enquiry into the Reasons for the Conduct of Great Britain,* the latter a defense by Bishop Hoadly of the government's management of foreign affairs. In fact, the *Craftsman* remarks ironically, the *Enquiry* is only a servile imitation which might better be entitled *"Gulliver* turn'd Statesman." Actually, the *Craftsman* had little need to point to specific allusions in Swift's work, since several other writers had been busily undertaking that task. In the first weeks of December appeared three books written to satisfy the demands of those who, like Swift's friend Erasmus Lewis, were "dayly refining" and seeking the key. Each of these volumes deserves to be considered separately.

The first is the series of four separate keys by "Signior Corolini del Marco," published by Curll. These are of some interest because not only is Flimnap identified with Walpole but Reldresal (as Case has suggested) with his brother-in-law Viscount Townshend; the identifications refer, however, only to the rope-dances in Part One and to the description of a chief minister in Part Four, and no effort is made to explain a consistent allegory. Curll's writer also explains the satiric jibes at the Orders of the Garter, Thistle, and Bath; understands the "conspiracy" against Gulliver to represent the "sufferings" of the late earl of Oxford; equates the physician in the academy of political projectors with Walpole; and sees references to the South Sea Bubble everywhere.[56] When these keys were issued in one volume as the *Travels . . . Compendiously Methodized,* they included a frontispiece showing Flimnap with his wand, looking short, fat, and curiously deformed—probably meant to be taken as Walpole—and a poem called "Verses Writ in the Blank Leaf of a Lady's *Gulliver,* as it lay open, in an Apartment of St. James's Palace." The verses tell us that despite the remote nations Lemuel visits, the "Secret" is to be found only in court, where Magna Charta is ignored, judges play at ombre, bishops are subservient to statesmen, senators purchase places, and vice triumphs: "See Wagers laid who come shall next in Play/ And read your *Gulliver* both *Night* and *Day.*" Nowhere, however, do the keys suggest Swift's book is designed for an immediate political purpose, and some of the "interpretations" they contain should perhaps be attributed to the difficulties which Curll himself was having with the government at just this time.[57] At best, these pamphlets were merely a flimsy effort to capitalize on a work which had caught the popular imagination; they deserve the contempt with which they were received by Boyer and others when they first appeared.

Of much more serious import is a tract called *A Letter from a Clergyman to his Friend,* also published in December, which indeed has the manner of a typical response to an antigovernment pamphlet. The writer conceives of *Gulliver's Travels* as a primarily political document intended to breed disharmony and "create a Dislike in the People to those in the Administration," a design especially vile "in such a Juncture as the present." Moreover, he hints that Swift is united with others in this incendiary plot, as he warns "there is no honest Man among us but would contribute the utmost in his Power to bring the Author, and *those concerned with him* to exemplary Punishment." Gulliver's description of English parliaments is objected to, but the *Letter* centers its attention upon Swift's insult to the "Family and Person of the greatest Man this Nation ever produced." Oddly enough, it is Swift's description of Flimnap as "morose" that particularly enrages the writer, who promptly unleashes four pages of impassioned panegyric of Walpole as "amiable to all," "the Delight of his Royal Master, and the Darling of the People," the preserver of the peace of Europe, and the wise statesman on whose great pattern future ministers will grow wise. But only ridicule of such a man could be expected from Dr. Swift, who now caps a career of irreligion and chicanery by "leading People into Disaffection and Disloyalty who are committed to his Care for right Information."[58]

The charge made in the *Letter* that *Gulliver's Travels* was written to support the Bolingbroke-Pulteney opposition appears also in a third pamphlet published in December, *Gulliver Decypher'd.* This book, once erroneously attributed to Arbuthnot, heaps abuse on "Peter, Martin, and Johnny" (i.e., Pope, Swift, and Arbuthnot) while at the same time it pretends to vindicate the "Rev. Dean" who has been accused as the author of the

Travels: "A Third Reason why this Book cannot be [by] the worthy D——, is the many oblique Reflections it is said to cast upon our present happy Administration, to which 'tis well known how *devoutly* he is attach'd and affected."[59] Gulliver, he admits, is no traitor, "tho' every Body says that he is disaffected." And this disaffection the writer lays squarely at the door of Swift's friends in the opposition. It is inconceivable, he argues ironically, that the Dean would act so contrary to the dignity of his character "merely to gratify a little Party Malice, or to oblige a Set of People who are never likely to have it in their Power to serve him or any of their Adherents." Moreover, he quotes the king of Brobdingnag's reflections on the management of the treasury and standing armies (both commonplace topics of the opposition) and then comments in terms that allude to the new and surprising alliance of Tories and dissident Whigs:

> Every Body knows, that all this has been a common *Jacobite* Insinuation . . . but, to our great Surprize, it is of late, very frequently in the Mouths of a quite different Set of People, discarded Courtiers some call them, of whom we may truly say—*No King can govern, nor no God can please.* For unless they are concern'd in the Administration, nothing goes right.[60]

Elsewhere, however, this tract praises the wit of the *Travels,* concluding, mildly enough, that the book is the production of two or three men of talent "who think sufficient Regard is not paid to their Merit by those in Power, for which Reason they rail at them" (p. 45). Yet even this last remark seems to respond to the charge of the decay of letters under Walpole, a motif soon to be common in opposition propaganda.

By the spring of 1727, extended political commentaries on the *Travels* had ceased to appear, but they were being replaced by an increasing number of attacks on Swift and on *Gulliver* in the paper war between opposing factions. He was, of course, thought to be contributing to the *Craftsman,* though there is no evidence that he did so; as we have seen, he had declined Pulteney's gambit as early as September 1726. But when he returned to England in April, it was to a political climate described by Bolingbroke as "boisterous" and by Pope as "very warm, and very angry."[61] In the journalistic battle the chief source of anger was Bolingbroke's *Occasional Writer,* which appeared in February and March. One of Bolingbroke's motifs in the first of these papers was that the ministry is remiss in rewarding the "brightest talents"; as might be expected the *Answer* from a ministerial defender alluded sarcastically to Swift's career under the Tory administration in 1710–14. Similarly, other replies to the Bolingbroke pamphlets drew in Swift ("your Friend *Gulliver*") and, on one occasion, Pope ("a *Coadjutor* of yours, who carries a *natural Pack* on his shoulders").[62] One such attack, ridiculing a Latin motto used by Bolingbroke, quotes the motto from advertisements of *Gulliver's Travels;* it is, he says, more venerable, but it has been "pre-engag'd by a Friend; and He the only Author who for chaste *Decency,* and severe *Veracity,* has a better Title to it than your self."[63] Even Boyer's *Political State,* which, it will be recalled, had earlier reacted to the *Travels* with neutrality if not with approval, now angrily pointed to both Swift and *Gulliver* in its efforts to counter the effect of Bolingbroke's *Occasional Writer.* It was no doubt this kind of thing which Swift had in mind when he complained to Sheridan on 13 May of the "Beasts and Blockheads" hired to write for Walpole and which, as Davis points out, helped to inspire his own *Letter to the Writer of the Occasional Paper.*[64]

Though Swift's *Letter* remained unpublished, its appearance, even with his name, would have done no more than confirm suspicions already raised by *Gulliver's Travels* about his share in the opposition. Throughout 1727 and 1728 attacks on Swift and sometimes specifically on *Gulliver* continued to appear in pro-government newspapers and in separate volumes, accusing him of disaffection and linking him with Bolingbroke and Pulteney.[65] Some of these, it is true, were simply in reaction to the appearance of the Pope-Swift *Miscellanies* and were, on the surface, nonpolitical; Smedley's *Gulliveriana* (1728), for instance, is surprisingly free of the usual political smears. But the more general view in the circles around Walpole was probably expressed in a political pamphlet appearing in May 1728, where Swift is accorded a central place in the opposition. The following passage is intended to be the judgment of a future historian on the "insolent Faction" headed by Pulteney:

This Gentleman was at the Head of the Faction; and assisted by several Persons of Wit; but they were chiefly Men of desperate Fortunes, or worse Characters; the most noted of these were an attainted Lord, who had before sacrificed his Interests with all Parties, and an *Irish* Dean, who, though one of a happy Genius, and some Learning, was such a debauched immoral Man, that whatever was known to come from him was of no Weight with the People.[66]

Why Swift should be singled out for a place of honor in the councils of the opposition is not made clear; perhaps the writer merely had in mind Swift's well-known friendship with Bolingbroke, but, perhaps too, he recalled the image of Flimnap and Reldresal cutting capers on a straight rope.

Swift may have been right in supposing that personal satire was what his book was most blamed for, but there can be little doubt that many of the general themes of the *Travels* were well suited to the purposes of the opposition. The broad indictment of human folly and corrupt institutions in Parts Two and Four (usually held to be of little political interest) were soon to be echoed in the flood of pamphlets and papers attacking Walpole. Gulliver's emotion at considering how the native virtues of English yeomen "were prostituted for a piece of Money by their Grand-children, who in selling their Votes, and managing at Elections have acquired every Vice and Corruption that can possibly be learned in a Court"[67] is hardly distinguishable from the passion expressed in scores of *Mist's*, *Craftsman*s, and tracts in 1727 and 1728. Even Swift's attack on war suited immediate partisan needs, for until the signing of the Preliminaries of Paris in May 1727, the opposition press carried on a vigorous campaign against what they pretended to believe was Walpole's war policy. Again, the marks of a bad administration listed in the *Craftsman* for 24 June 1727 would have seemed familiar enough to readers of *Gulliver*: a desire for mystery in handling public affairs, the corruption of Parliament, a vein of "Luxury" throughout the land, the manufacture of fictitious plots or conspiracies, the corruption of the law, and the failure to base preferments on virtue and merit. The last motif, the promotion of the unworthy, so frequently reiterated in the opposition press and so evidently near to Swift's heart, appears in the *Travels* less often than one might expect; but the fact that "Wit, Merit, and Learning" are not yet rewarded was singled out by Gulliver in his letter to Sympson nine years later as an example of the failure of his book to produce effects—but then neither had the "Courts and Levees of great Ministers" yet been "weeded and swept."[68]

Even in the most general sense, as an indictment of human corruption and the degeneracy of the age, *Gulliver's Travels* was useful to those who opposed Walpole, especially since this indictment is coupled with a recognizable portrait of the prime minister and with a partisan viewpoint on such issues as standing armies or a national debt. The *Craftsman* praised the *Travels* soon after its publication in terms which showed its appreciation of the political value of "general" satire. Number 20 (13 February 1726/7), attacking the decay of letters under the Walpole ministry, concludes with this ironic passage:

> I hope these dissatisfy'd, repining Spirits will at least allow that, however other parts of Learning may have been neglected and despis'd, yet no *Encouragement* has been wanting to *satirical* Writings; and if they do not soon produce some excellent pieces of this kind, I think they will be fairly left without any Excuse, and I shall be willing to give them up to all the Severity of the Patrons of the *Antients*.
>
> Indeed, we have had some very good specimens of this sort of writing already publish'd; *one* of which seems to lash mankind in too severe and general a manner; however, as there is a great deal of *Wit* in that book, so I am sorry to say, for the Sake of human nature in general, and of my own Country in particular, that, I am afraid, there is *too much Truth in it.*

As I have indicated earlier, general satire could also be linked to the familiar idea that the head of a state is responsible for the moral health of the body politic. As the *Craftsman* (24 February 1727/8) puts it, when corruption is placed "on the Pinnacle of Power, in the very Heart of a first *Minister,* it will no longer be contained within any bounds; the Contagion will take and spread, and the whole Country become infected." Swift himself, at Bolingbroke's suggestion, makes much of this "transference" in his *Letter to the Writer of the Occasional Paper,* and the medical metaphor in which it was usually expressed is carried to its literal extreme by the "Ingenious Doctor" in the School of Political Projectors in Lagado, who cures public diseases by applying private remedies to politicians. (Curll's *Key,* incidentally, rather perversely finds that this doctor suggests "a country Practiser [near Lynn, Regis, in Comitatu Norfolciae] who is a much greater Adept in this Science," i.e., Walpole;[69] and the "universal Resemblance between the Natural and the Political Body" was doubtless responsible for the frequency with which Walpole was satirized in these years as a quack doctor.)

Thus, by a reversal of this traditional motif, general satire which laid bare the defects of existing institutions could have political implications. It may be helpful to recall a poem by Swift which exploits this idea for the purpose of ridiculing Edward Young. "Satire the Last" (1726) of Young's *The Universal Passion* was dedicated to Walpole and included a passage which shows Young is aware that satirizing a "flood of *British* folly" while simultaneously praising those in power may seem a bit paradoxical. He addresses Sir Robert directly:

> Nor think that Thou art foreign to my Theme;
> The *Fountain* is not foreign to the *Stream*.
> How all mankind will be surpriz'd, to see
> This flood of *British* Folly charg'd on thee?[70]

His escape from this difficulty is to argue, not too convincingly, that the folly of the English is the bad effect of a good cause, the success of their rulers in making Britain a land of wealth and peace. Swift, however, mocks the inconsistency of separating fountain from stream; "On Reading Dr. Young's Satires" (written 1726) reminds Young that he cannot have it both ways; either the satire is false or the dedications to those in power are hypocritical:

> If there be Truth in what you sing,
> Such Godlike Virtues in the *King,*
> A *Minister* so filled with Zeal
> And Wisdom for the Common-Weal . . . .
> If this be Truth, as you attest,
> What *Land* was ever *half* so *blest?* . . .
> For, such is good Example's Pow'r,
> It does its Office ev'ry Hour,
> Where *Governors* are good and wise;
> Or else the truest Maxim iyes:
> For this we know, all antient Sages
> Decree, that *ad exemplum Regis,*
> Thro' all the Realm his *Virtues* run,
> Rip'ning, and kindling like the Sun.

But, Swift continues, let us suppose your satiric depiction of Britain is an accurate one:

> Or take it in a diff'rent View;
> I ask, if what you say be *true,*
> If you allow the present Age
> Deserves your *Satire's* keenest Rage; . . .
> If these be of all Crimes the worst,
> What *Land* was ever *half* so *curst?*[71]

It is small wonder that Young judged *Gulliver's Travels* to have little wit "of that Kind which I most like."[72]

Such, then, was the way in which general satire like that in the second and fourth parts of the *Travels* could be linked with the political opposition. Sometimes, though infrequently, attacks on general satire pointed directly at Swift's book. Thus the *British Journal* on 29 April 1727 printed, without acknowledgement of source or author, an essay by James Arbuckle which had appeared in the *Dublin Journal* in March.[73] Here we find the usual disparagement of those satirists who murmur against the age and who even depict mankind as less excellent than the brutes; given the date, that the allusion is to Swift seems fairly certain. The essay supplements the attack with an optimistic appraisal of the age: are not commerce and learning flourishing? Have not increased trade and riches made Britain a nation of peace and plenty and not, as some claim, of "Luxury and Prodigality"? The political turn to what begins as a literary-philosophical comment would have been unmistakable to a contemporary reader. Even more pointed is a passage in a short-lived government paper called the *Senator* (1728). In the second issue of that journal (13 February 1727/8) its author begins with a defense of the integrity of Parliament, rails at those who would spread discontent with the administration, and advances to this general conclusion:

> To attack Government, to debase Humane Nature, and to undermine Society, is the whole Secret of Popular Writing. The Delicacy of Satyr, the old Attick Poignancy, are no longer studied. Dullness pointed with Malice passes very well for Wit; and he that is revenging his own private Misfortunes upon the publick Tranquility, is to all Intents and Purposes, *A Patriot.*

That the writer has *Gulliver's Travels* particularly in mind is
indicated by the following issue (16 February), where a letter
supposedly from a reader complains that the *Senator's* first two
papers have been insufficiently specific: "You . . . have glanc'd
your Resentment rather against the Immoral Sentiments of
Gulliver and the Political Sophistries of *Cyrus*, then against the
much more dangerous, tho' perhaps at the same time much
lower Malice of the *Craftsman*."

Swift himself seems to have recognized that even the general
satire of the *Travels* could be accused of having political implications, for in his poem *The Life and Character of Dr. Swift* (written
1731) he juxtaposes the charge that he offended Walpole with
the charge that his satire reveals scenes of evil:

> But, why wou'd he, except he *slobber'd*,
> Offend our *Patriot*, Great Sir *R*——,
> Whose *Councils* aid the Sov'reign Pow'r,
> To *save* the *Nation* ev'ry hour?
> What *Scenes* of Evil he unravels,
> In *Satyrs, Libels, lying Travels!*[74]

Swift's defense here is, of course, to cite the moral end of his
satire; but perhaps more appropriate to the theme we have been
examining is his ironic disclaimer in the *Letter to the Writer of the
Occasional Paper:* "Supposing times of corruption, which I am
very far from doing, if a writer displays them in their proper
colours, does he do any thing worse than sending customers to
the shop? Here only, at the sign of the Brazen Head, are to be
sold places and pensions: beware of counterfeits, and take care
of mistaking the door."[75]

In the period 1726–31 there are a few notable instances of the
third way in which *Gulliver's Travels* proved helpful to the
opposition: by summary, quotation, and imitation. Thus the
Craftsman (5 September 1730) asserts that the principal journalistic device of the government papers is evasion: "This Rule is
admirably explain'd by that ingenious Traveller, Captain *Lemuel
Gulliver* where he gives his Master the *Houyhnhnm* an Account of
the *Lawyers* of a certain Country." And there follows a summary
of that section of the *Travels*. A more interesting example of the
method of adapting Swift in an opposition paper, however,
occurs in *Fog's Weekly Journal* for 25 July 1730. This essay first

strikes a pseudo-literary note; *Gulliver's Travels,* claims the writer, has suffered unduly from the tendency of guilty men to take innocent remarks as a personal affront:

> Thus, if a Writer animadverts upon some fashionable Piece of Roguery, many a Man whom the Author never thought of understands the whole Satyr to be leveled at him. . . .
>
> It is for this Reason, perhaps, that some People feel a Satyr in Captain *Gulliver's* Travels, while the Rest of the World can read them over and over, without finding the least Sting in any Part.
>
> I am one of those that can discover no latent Meaning, and yet conceive there is good Instruction to be gather'd from many of those singular Remarks he makes upon the strange Regions he visited.

After this ironic passage, reminiscent of the ballad "When you censure the age" in *The Beggar's Opera, Fog's* proceeds to quote lengthy excerpts from Gulliver's visit to Glubbdubdrib. In the passages quoted Swift is attacking the corruption of Parliament, the base methods by which men become great and wealthy, the preferment of the unworthy, the corruption of a kingdom by luxury, the selling and buying of votes, and so on—all themes, of course, which readers of *Fog's* would at once apply to Walpole, despite *Fog's* claim that Swift is merely giving us an instructive account of past ages. The whole essay is convincing testimony to the ease with which the *Travels* was read politically as well as to the obvious similarity between Swift's techniques and the necessarily oblique methods of opposition propaganda. The following month (in the issue for 29 August) *Fog's* again quoted a long passage from Part Three of the *Travels,* this time on the usefulness of fabricated plots and the arbitrary methods of deciphering political messages. Though on this occasion *Fog's* failed to identify the *Travels* as its source and referred to Swift merely as a "modern Author," the use of such excerpts in an opposition journal may help to explain why Swift, the following year, singled out Part Three as the section of the *Travels* likely to be "Offensive to a *Loyal* Ear."[76]

Imitations of the *Travels* for political purposes arose naturally enough; even the government writers succumbed to the temptation. *A Cursory View of the History of Lilliput* appeared in August 1727, by which time it was becoming obvious that opposition hopes of supplanting Walpole after the death of George I were to come to nothing. This pamphlet, in the guise of describing Big-Endians, Tramecksans, and the like, gives a history of English politics from the Reformation to the accession of George II, a history which ridicules the opposition for their false expectations, which assumes all Tories are Jacobites, and which even suggests allegorically that Queen Anne conspired to bring in the Pretender. It is dull stuff, but it reflects, I think, the degree of understanding with which the political allusions in the *Travels* must have been read, for the *Cursory View* is apparently designed to turn the tables on Swift by using the symbols of his political allegory to exult over a Walpolean triumph and mock his friends. "Gulliver's" knowledge of human affairs must be limited, says the author, since the heir to the Crown did *not* have a hobble in his gait (that is, the Prince of Wales did not lean toward the opponents of Walpole, as events have shown).[77]

On the opposition side, too, *Gulliver* was subject to direct imitation. Thus the *Craftsman* (17 May 1729) conflates Swift and Montesquieu in a "Persian Letter," in which Gulliver tells the traveler Rica of a strange land fallen into evil days because its public funds have been intrusted to "Shamgrigg" (Walpole). But the best example is *A Voyage to Cacklogallinia* (August 1727), by "Captain Samuel Brunt," who has traveled to a land of giant cocks and hens. Though there are a number of objects of derision here, the book in my view is almost certainly intended primarily as an attack on the administration.[78] The prime minister of Cacklogallinia, "Brusquallio," clearly corresponds to Walpole in every physical and spiritual detail. The satiric method, though, is an interesting variation on Swift's. In his conversation with Brusquallio, modeled on Gulliver's conversation with kings and masters, Brunt paints a glorious picture of English life while the prime minister cynically reads him a lesson on power politics and government by corruption. The political bitterness of this imitation of the *Travels,* like the excerpts quoted in opposition journals, must have strengthened the impression of Swift's satire as a "party" document.

In the *Letter to Sympson* added to the *Travels* in 1735 Swift has Gulliver complain of the "Libels, and Keys, and Reflections, and Memoirs, and Second Parts; wherein I see myself accused of reflecting upon great States-Folk . . . ."[79] How, he protests, could what was said so long ago and at such a distance be applied to "any of the *Yahoos*, who now are said to govern the Herd"? Despite the irony of that passage, Swift might not have been particularly pleased by the political applications; in the summer of 1727 he might even have been embarrassed by anything of his which could be construed as a libel on the court.[80] Moreover, as he coldly informed the Abbé Desfontaines, his book was not written for only one city, one province, one kingdom, or even one age, since the same vices reign everywhere. But, whatever Swift's feelings on the matter, the evidence shows that those *Travels* intended to mend the world were also of some service to an immediate political cause with which he was fully in sympathy.

3

THE TRIUMPHS
OF WIT,
1728–1730

IN MAY OF 1728 the exiled Bishop Atterbury was doubtless cheered to read in a letter from his son-in-law that though "Sir Robert is as absolute in power at present as ever," Pulteney "pushes him hard" and "he drives too fast, not to be thrown at last." Such optimism, though, was ill founded. In the first few years of the reign of George II, Walpole quickly consolidated his position, winning the affection of the new king and keeping the affection of his most powerful advocate, Queen Caroline. Pulteney was able to do little pushing in the Commons, since the election of 1727 had gone heavily in the ministry's favor. The uncertainty in England's relations with Spain had been exploited by the opposition for the past two years, but this uncertainty seemed on the way to being resolved by the Congress of Soissons. Only a month later Atterbury was informed, "Nothing will be able effectually to shock the Great Man, if affairs go on successfully at Soissons."[1] When peace was finally brought by the Treaty of Seville (November 1729), the position of the Great Man seemed very firm indeed.

Outside the House of Commons, however, the paper war went on unabated, and in that arena the opposition seemed much more impressive. The *Craftsman* continued in irony or fable to attack Walpole's "system" of corruption, while the progovernment papers defended the ministry with arguments as fascinatingly forthright as this one: "Men are always corrupt, and must often be manag'd . . . . Corruption is good or bad in its Effects as good or bad Governors apply it."[2] Nathaniel Mist was forced to flee the country after printing a Jacobite allegory by

"Amos Dudge" (the duke of Wharton?) in his journal for 24 August 1728, but his place was supplied a month later by *Fog's*, which carried on its campaign against the government with more moderation and more wit.[3] In April 1728, Sir John Gonson charged the Grand Jury of Westminster to prosecute the authors of indirect and oblique libels, and in his charge voiced the official dismay at the ubiquity of opposition propaganda:

It is a Shame to our Nation that there should be any Persons . . . so little sensible of the Happiness which we enjoy as to libel and disturb such a King, and such an Administration; yet this Offence is now grown so common, that if a Man goes into a Coffee-House, it is uncertain whether he lays his Hands upon a News-Paper or a Libel.[4]

The intensity of political rhetoric was so great that when Henry Baker's *Universal Spectator* began in the autumn of 1728 it was proudly advertised as the only newspaper "Free from Politicks or Raillery, religious or party Controversy and Contention." Even the death of Richard Steele in 1729 became the subject of political contention, with the government papers praising his political writings and the *Craftsman* both applying those writings against the present government and charging Walpole with neglect of their author.[5]

Indeed, nothing seemed too trivial for political comment. When a translation of Tacitus by Thomas Gordon, supervisor of the government press, appeared in 1728, it was dedicated to Walpole and absurdly advertised as "The Annals of Tacitus. Vol. I. Containing the Annals." Mist, who was not the man to let pass a blunder of this magnitude, promptly printed the following epigram, addressed "To the Translator of *Tacitus*":

> G——rd——n in Print has made it plain,
> That Annals, Annals must contain;
> For fear his Readers should mistake,
> And Annals not for Annals take;
> And unassisted by his Notes,
> Think 'em Gazettes, or Plays, or Votes:
> Annals are Annals now we see!
> What else, dear Critick, should they be?

If thy fam'd Author does appear,
Throughout, so unperplex'd and clear,
Who for a Guinea would not strain,
To view the *Roman* made so plain?
And in each learned Page commend
Religion's Guardian, *Walpole*'s Friend.[6]

The *Craftsman* (20 April, 27 July) then continued the joke by quoting sections of Tacitus dealing with corruption, with standing armies, and with debasement of the Roman senate under tyrants, blandly asserting that Gordon's translation must be believed because of his undoubted affection to the present government and the encouragement of this very work by Sir Robert Walpole. It is against the background of this kind of political byplay, then, that one must view the appearance in these years of *The Beggar's Opera*, *The Dunciad*, and *Polly*.

Gay the Hare and Bob, the Poet's Foe

When the lists of court appointments were published after the coronation of George II, John Gay found himself appointed gentleman usher to the two-year-old Princess Louisa. He promptly refused the post, explaining to his friends that he was too old to accept such a position and consoling himself that he could no longer be beguiled by false expectations. Swift and Pope were outraged by the indignity of the appointment, and both wrote to Gay in strong terms condemning the court and congratulating Gay on his new-found freedom. Pope contrasted his friend with the "mean, servile, flattering, interested, and undeserving" who did gain favor from the court, and Swift blamed both Mrs. Howard and Walpole for Gay's disappointment. He wrote Lord Carteret, "Your friend Walpole hath lately done one of the cruellest actions I ever knew, even in a minister of state, these thirty years past." Swift's suspicions were based on the talks he had held with Walpole the year before, when he attempted to persuade the minister that false accusations against Gay of writing political libels should not endanger his chance of preferment; but Walpole, according to Swift, pretended to believe that the Dean was apologizing for his own writings during the Oxford-Bolingbroke ministry: "Mr. Walpole knew well enough that I meant Mr. Gay."[7] It is doubtful, however, that this incident was responsible for the insult to Gay; as W. H. Irving points out, Walpole was well aware of Gay's closeness to the managers of the *Craftsman,* and no one sponsored by Mrs. Howard was likely to gain favor from Queen Caroline.[8]

A question more interesting than why Gay was offered such a poor post is why he expected a better one. However much its satire may have been sharpened in the following months, *The Beggar's Opera* was well under way while Gay was still expecting a respectable place; he had that same year published the *Fables,* critical enough of courts and courtiers; and at no time did he make any secret of his friendship with Bolingbroke, Pulteney, and other opponents of the administration. Why, then, were he and his friends so shocked at finding the hare not taken up, as the queen had promised, but ungently let down? The answer seems to be, once again, that as "men of wit" they regarded patronage as their due and honestly expected those in power to support them regardless of "party," and as humanists they expected poets, the teachers of virtue, to play some role in the circles of power. At the same time, they were unwilling to conform to the wishes of men in power and fearful that such support would endanger their independence. Thus it ought to surprise us neither to find so outspoken an enemy of the administration as Swift soliciting both Dodington and Carteret on behalf of Pope, nor to find Pope proudly—if forgetfully—proclaiming, "I never thought myself so warm in any Party's cause as to deserve their money." When a man like Gay was refused encouragement while those less worthy gained it, his friends could only view the episode as an affront to all men of letters and as a symbol of the intellectual corruption of the court and the ministry. Pope promised that his *Dunciad* would soon show what a "distinguishing" age they all lived in, and years later Swift was still moralizing about the incident in general rather than personal terms: "however insignificant wit, learning, and virtue may be thought in the world, it would perhaps do government no hurt to have a little of them on it's side."[9]

In his poems, too, Swift pursued the same theme. *Directions for a Birth-day Song* (1729) parodies the nauseous flattery which a poet must engage in if he is to receive favor from a court, and *To*

Mr. Gay (1731) moves from an expression of disgust at Gay's treatment by *"Bob,* the Poet's Foe" to a vicious personal attack on Walpole the nation's foe. *A Libel on Dr. Delany and a Certain Great Lord* (1730) examines the whole degrading relationship between poets and politicians. Congreve, Steele, and Addison are given as instances of mistreatment of literary figures by politicians, and Gay's own sorry experience is also depicted:

> Thus *Gay,* the *Hare* with many Friends,
> Twice sev'n long Years the *Court* attends,
> Who, under Tales conveying Truth,
> To Virtue form'd a *Princely* Youth,
> Who pay'd his Courtship with the Croud,
> As far as *Modest Pride* allow'd,
> Rejects a servile *Usher*'s Place,
> And leaves *St. James*'s in Disgrace.

After praising Pope—not quite accurately—for refusing to "lick a *Rascal Statesman*'s Spittle," Swift gets to the heart of the matter; poetry and learning, he says, are too frivolous and insignificant to interest the Walpoles of the world:

> True *Politicians* only Pay
> For solid Work, but not for Play;
> Nor ever chuse to Work with Tools
> Forg'd up in *Colleges* and *Schools.*
> Consider how much more is due
> To all their *Journey-Men,* than you.
> At Table you can *Horace* quote;
> They at a Pinch can bribe a Vote:
> You shew your Skill in *Grecian* Story,
> But, they can manage *Whig* and *Tory*:
> You, as a *Critick,* are so curious
> To find a Verse in *Virgil* Spurious;
> But, they can *smoak* the deep Designs,
> When *Bolingbroke* with *Pult'ney* Dines.[10]

That such disparagement of the world of letters typified the Walpole government was, as we have seen, one of the popular motifs of opposition propaganda, but it was also a conviction deeply felt by men like Swift, a conviction which the disappointment suffered by Gay could only reinforce.[11]

But Gay was not to suffer long, for on 24 January 1728 *The Beggar's Opera* began its long and successful run. About the political implications of Gay's satire there can, of course, be no question. Even as a general satire on courts and courtiers it might, like the *Fables,* have given some offense, but contemporary audiences saw specific allusions to Walpole in a number of different characterizations—in the corruption-ridden pair Peachum and his "brother" Lockit, who could be taken as Walpole and Townshend or as Walpole and Horatio; in "the great man" Captain Macheath, with his "gang"; and in "Robin of Bagshot, alias Gorgon, alias Bluff Bob, alias Carbuncle, alias Bob Booty," who "spends his life among women." Macheath's problems with Lucy and Polly were also suggestive of Walpole's marital infidelity, and the song "When you censure the age" was so clearly a reference to the government's sensitivity to criticism that the audience supposedly stared and laughed at Walpole in his box when it was sung.[12] Small wonder that Swift wrote Gay: "Does W—— think you intended an affront to him in your opera. Pray God he may."[13]

The opposition papers naturally made the most of the opportunity Gay had provided them. The *Craftsman* for 17 February 1727/8 produced one of its finest ironic essays, pretending to attack *The Beggar's Opera* as "the most venomous *allegorical Libel* against the G——t that hath appeared for many Years past." Even the satire on Italian operas is seditious, says the *Craftsman* writer ("Phil. Harmonicus"), since everyone knows they are favored by the royal family. Of course, he continues, the players will claim their satire is general, but there are innuendoes throughout which belie their claim—innuendoes which he then proceeds to explain in detail. He takes Macheath to be representative of Walpole, though he admits some argue for Lockit because as *"prime* Minister of *Newgate"* he appears on stage as a corpulent man and his brother Peachum as a slovenly fellow (the usual depiction at the time of Sir Robert and Horatio Walpole). The following passage is an example of the kind of "innuendo" he obligingly unravels: "Again, says He [Peachum], *can it be expected that we should hang our Acquaintance for nothing, when our* Betters *will hardly* save *theirs without being paid for it*—*Innuendo* that *some Persons* have been well paid for *saving* or *Screening* their *former Acquaintance"* (a common charge against Walpole since the

South Sea Bubble). Irving is correct when he says the essay
"overemphasized" the political implications of the play,[14] but the
overemphasis is deliberate and humorous: the *Craftsman* simultaneously points to the political satire clearly present in the text,
satirizes Walpole further by enlarging in a farfetched manner
on hints in the play, and effectively parodies the tendency of the
government press to overread plays, poems, or the *Craftsman*
itself by the "doctrine of innuendoes."

The *Craftsman* essay was printed separately as a "Compleat
Key," and other political pamphlets, essays, and poems similarly
exploited the popularity of the opera. Several ballads addressed
to Polly Peachum and printed in the *Craftsman* made the most of
the parallel between Macheath and Walpole; a letter to the same
journal even suggested jokingly that Gay was "secretly set to
work by some Person [Walpole], whose *Circumstances* made him
wish that a *Plunderer of his Country* might, for the future, be
esteemed a less *infamous Character*."[15] One of the papers seized by
government agents in a raid on the *Craftsman* offices in 1730 was
a long letter, never printed, defending *The Beggar's Opera* on
purely literary grounds; its editor, Amhurst, did not, apparently, think a nonpolitical account of the play worth using.[16] Mist,
too, found the play helpful in his campaign against the government, and Swift wrote for the *Intelligencer* a highly disingenuous
defense of his friend in which he managed a few hits of his own
at court and ministry.[17] The *Craftsman* reported on 18 May that
pamphlets on *The Beggar's Opera* abounded and took pains to
puff *Memoirs Concerning the Life and Manners of Captain Mackheath,* an anonymous piece which used the "history" of the
Captain to develop a thin allegory on the "plunders" of Walpole
and to sound all the customary notes of opposition propaganda
on luxury, the South Sea Bubble, the decay of learning, and
bribery and corruption. It was this sort of by-product that
helped make Gay's opera a political touchstone to an extent he
doubtless had not intended; even a year later the *Universal
Spectator* (16 May 1729) gave as proof of its success in avoiding
politics, "I have not even nam'd the *Beggar's Opera*."

What was the government's response to all this? The reaction
in government circles has, I think, been exaggerated in some
accounts of the play. *The Beggar's Opera* did not, as D. H. Stevens
suggests, result in an intensification of government propaganda

and an increase in the number of Walpole's newspapers.[18] Such an increase occurred, but both the new journals and the government's efforts to prosecute printers of opposition papers grew out of the virulent journalistic campaign against Walpole at the end of the decade, a campaign carried on at a level somewhat below that of the "polite and witty" world that attended *The Beggar's Opera* and read *Gulliver's Travels.* Thus Edward Roome's *Senator,* a paper begun on 9 February, did not have as its major purpose to combat the political satire of *The Beggar's Opera,* as has been claimed, but to combat the more direct and more dangerous attacks on the government in the *Craftsman* during the current session of Parliament; Gay's opera is alluded to only a few times in its entire run of thirty-two issues, and then it is in terms which attack not the play itself but its exploitation in anti-government papers and pamphlets. The *Craftsman* was the irritating thorn in the government's side, and it had to be answered; about this time Walpole considered a plan to stop its circulation at the post office.[19] At this point, at least, the outpourings of the opposition press concerned the government more than a popular dramatic satire, the first of its kind. Newspapers were expensive to operate, and Robert Walpole did not start them for a song.

But if it is claiming too much to attribute a train of prosecutions and new journals to the effects of *The Beggar's Opera,* this does not mean that the government press ignored it altogether. Walpole's writers approached it, however, with some caution; after all, one did not simply label as a seditious libel a play that was the sensation of the town and that had been attended not only by Sir Robert but by the king and queen. Their method, then, was not to attack its political satire—which they pretended was entirely the invention of malcontents—but to decry its literary and moral deficiencies. In March Dr. Thomas Herring, preacher at Lincoln's Inn, preached against the play, and though his attack was on its supposed immorality it was doubtless no accident that such a sermon came from a "Court Chaplain." Swift, in his defense of Gay, called Herring a "prostitute" divine, and Atterbury's son-in-law reported: "The Court espoused his election as Preacher at Lincoln's-inn . . . and probably he will gain further advantages from the Court."[20] In the same way, the *London Journal* in its issues for 20 and 30 April accused the opera of debauching the nation's morals and encouraging the proliferation of robberies. As a matter of fact, there *was* an increase in street robberies in the months following the opening of the play (or at least an increase in the reports of such robberies in the press), so that Mist on 2 March was forced to counter this argument by attributing the rise in crime not to the "Pleasure the Town takes in the Character and Impunity of Captain Mackheath" but to the "general Poverty and Corruption of the Times, and the Prevalency of some Powerful Examples."

In other attacks, the government papers denounced the play for its low humor and took its success as a sign of the degeneracy of British taste.[21] But, as far as I know, not a single government newspaper condemned it as politically motivated or libelous; indeed, the *Senator* described Gay as the "innocent" author whose work had been "explained into a *Libel*" by the opposition. Instead, the pro-Walpole paper suddenly began echoing the complaints that their opponents had been making for two years about the decay of taste and the decline of letters in England. What really lay behind this approach, though, is indicated by pamphlets like *The Twickenham Hotch-Potch,* by "Caleb D'Anvers," which, before denouncing the play for its low humor and the town for its corrupt taste, accused Gay of ridiculing "the MINISTERS of our most August *Monarch,* and those whom he has invested with Posts of the greatest Office and Trust . . . under the prime Characters of a *Thief-Catcher,* a *Jaylor,* and a *Highwayman.*"[22] It is clear, I think, that the moral and aesthetic arguments against Gay's opera expounded by the government press were a mask for objections that were primarily political.

It is also interesting to find *The Twickenham Hotch-Potch* and other pamphlets in these months citing not only Gay but Pope, Swift, and Arbuthnot as *evidence* of the sad state of English letters. To think that the country of Bacon, Milton, Spenser, and Dryden should now be sunk to praising the work of "an impertinent *Scotch*-Quack, a Profligate *Irish*-Dean, the Lacquey of a Superannuated Dutchess, and a little virulent Papist"![23] Such attacks were the result of the third volume of the Pope-Swift *Miscellanies,* published on 9 March. As Pope intended, this volume, containing *Peri Bathous,* drew the fire of all those dull writers soon to be demolished in *The Dunciad.* Though most of the attacks thus provoked dealt only with the literary quarrel, a few took pains to connect the Scriblerians with the political opposition. Thus a poem in the *Flying Post* linked Pope, Swift, and "Polly Peachum" with "Squire D'Anvers" (meaning Pulteney, in this instance), and another work included the royal family and the "present Ministry" in a list of those libeled by Pope and Swift.[24] At the same time, abuse of the opposition by government writers was now more likely to include Pope and Swift; a mock notice in the *Flying Post,* for example, suggested allegorically a correspondence between the Pretender and "William Squab" (Pulteney), "Henry Gamble" (Bolingbroke), "the *Irish* Dean, and the *Poet-Laureat,* or undertaking Poet of Twickenham."[25]

One of the attacks evoked by the *Miscellanies* deserves special attention, since it provides an excellent example of the intermingling of literary and political matters in the year of *The Dunciad.* Called *An Essay upon the Taste and Writings of the Present Times* (May 1728), it so piqued Pope that he sent it to Walpole in an unsuccessful effort to discover from Sir Robert himself the identity of the author. The pamphlet adopts the tone of pseudo-impartiality common in such productions; it pretends to be a serious, objective assessment of the literary world, but its judgments are all along party lines. Swift, Pope, and Gay are contrasted with writers of real merit—Addison, Steele, and Edward Young. Though this piece purports to be a response to the *Miscellanies,* it actually says little of them except to defend Booth, Wilks, and Cibber at some length. Moreover, the *Essay* is dedicated to Walpole, who is praised for labors not his own—the elevation of letters and learning, the placing of all great geniuses "round the Throne of a most gracious Monarch," where they flourish under the royal sunshine. At the same time, however, the text of the pamphlet laments the decay of taste in England and, just as the government newspapers were doing, cites as evidence the popularity of Gay's opera:

> If a Writer had an Inclination to quarrel with the present Age, he could not write a more severe Satire upon it, than transmitting the *Beggar's Opera* . . . down to Posterity with this plain Advertisement, *viz.* That in the first Year of the Reign of King *George* II. when all the

Works of *Shakespear, Ben Johnson, Fletcher,* and *Steele* were acted with the
nicest Judgment, . . . this Opera became the most fashionable Entertainment of the whole Nation.[26]

The criticism of Pope is personal; he is accused of trying to
elevate himself by belittling other writers, like Addison. But the
attack on Swift is completely political. The Dean is, admittedly,
unequaled in wit and humor, but he has misused his powers by
attacking the government. Swift, we are told, is a "kind of *Midas*
reversed": "he formerly proved the Duke of *Marlborough* to be
no General; and thus he now proves a *W——le* no Statesman."[27]
And Swift is further accused of joining forces with Mist and
other "Patriots," no doubt because Mist had recently been
reprinting essays from the *Intelligencer.* The last third of the
Essay is also overtly political, consisting of extended attack on
Mist and the *Craftsman* and extravagant praise of the Walpole
ministry. Despite its pretensions as a serious piece of literary
criticism, the entire pamphlet would have been recognized by its
readers as a party document in which literary judgments are
subservient to political affiliations.

Dunces and Censors

Though the *Essay* was apparently published just after *The
Dunciad,* it made no direct reference to it. Yet, had there been
time, Pope's poem would properly have found a place in this
politically motivated attack on the Scriblerian writers. The
edition published in May 1728 and the "variorum" *Dunciad*
which appeared in April 1729 are works which both in general
theme and particular detail exhibit a definite political bias,
especially when viewed in the light of opposition propaganda
and the increasing hostility of the government press to the
Scriblerian group since *The Beggar's Opera.* One should not be
misled by the pretended impartiality of the poem or by Pope's
efforts to secure court approval by presenting the poem to the
king through the good offices of Robert Walpole. As was so
often the case in those years, what appears to be an exclusively
literary event or literary quarrel inescapably assumes political
overtones, though to be sure the political ramifications of Pope's
mock epic are not as blatant or as important as those of Gay's

mock opera. But even though *The Dunciad* is a great deal more
than the sum of its political implications, it would be a mistake to
ignore those implications or the service which the poem ren-
dered to Pope's friends in the opposition.

Like that of *Gulliver's Travels,* even the general satire of *The
Dunciad* might well have been offensive to supporters of the
government. As Aubrey Williams puts it, the poem offers a
vision of "England on the verge of a cultural breakdown," a
vision arising from a sense of threat to traditional values.[28] As we
have seen in some detail, just such a vision is presented in scores
of opposition pamphlets and papers. A few weeks after the
publication of the poem, for example, the *Craftsman* (8 June
1728) wrote ironically, "I have often wonder'd, that our *British
Poetry* should be at so low an Ebb, under the Administration of
GENTLEMEN, who have so distinguished themselves in nothing
more remarkably than their Encouragement of *Arts* and *polite
Learning.*" And the same issue indulges in a mock panegyric
upon the peace, prosperity, and "incalculable Blessings" of a
nation flourishing under the protection of Walpole. Although
the common identification of the court and the ministry as the
source of a moral and political infection which spread gradually
outward to encompass the nation is reversed in *The Dunciad,* the
effect is the same; for there, in Williams's words, "the commercial and middle-class standards of the City invade the aristocratic
province and corrupt the standards traditionally associated with
the king and the nobility" (p. 31). To show dullness progressing
from City to Court, and the Smithfield muses brought to the ear
of kings, is to make the same indictment of the cultural failures
of the Wapole administration that opposition papers had been
making for six years. Though the "progress" was not completed
until Pope published the final book fifteen years later, the
political implications of the broader themes in the 1729 *Dunciad*
would not have been missed by an audience familiar with the
innuendoes, charges, and countercharges of political journalism.

For most readers, of course, the personal satire of the poem
was likely to be more intriguing than its underlying themes, and
here too a political bias appears: an astonishing number of the
Dunces turn out to be government hacks or minor office-
holders under Walpole.[29] Admittedly, many of the victims of

Pope's satire are simply his personal or literary enemies, and admittedly, too, he claims to be utterly nonpolitical in his attack on dullness:

> (Diff'rent our parties, but with equal grace
> The Goddess smiles on Whig and Tory race,
> 'Tis the same rope at sev'ral ends they twist,
> To Dulness, Ridpath is as dear as Mist.)[30]

Yet Pope's cautious insistence that dullness knows no party fails, I think, to stand up to close examination. It must be remembered that the poverty of literary talent in the writers hired by Walpole had been a recurring theme in all the opposition journals and a matter of great concern to Swift on his last visit to England, when he encouraged Pope in the writing of this poem. In the poem itself these "Beasts and Blockheads," as Swift called them, nearly all find a place. Among the Dunces referred to in the text and notes of the 1729 *Dunciad*, the following are writers for the government, publishers of government papers, or minor placemen: Matthew Concanen, Benjamin Norton Defoe, "Orator" Henley, William Wilkins, John Oldmixon, Edward Webster, Leonard Welsted, Edward Roome, James Pitt, Abel Boyer, Barnham Goode, Philip Horneck, George Duckett, Thomas Burnet, Theophilus Cibber, Jonathan Smedley, Stephen Whatley, William Benson, Thomas Cooke, and Bishop Hoadly. To this list one might well add certain "well affected" literary figures like Colley Cibber, Ambrose Philips, Laurence Eusden (Poet Laureate), and—in one edition—Joseph Mitchell, known as "Walpole's poet." According to James Sutherland, the duke of Newcastle, Walpole's secretary of state, was probably the model for the portrait of the noble patron in Book II.[31] In balance against this impressive list one may put only three names associated with the political opposition: Nathaniel Mist, Charles Molloy, and Eustace Budgell. Mist is included because his journal had been printing attacks by Theobald and others on Pope; his open Jacobitism, which had resulted in his recent flight from the country, made him a natural choice for Pope in his weak effort to appear politically impartial. Molloy was doubtless included in the notes because he wrote for Mist; he became the chief writer of *Fog's* after Mist decamped, and after

1735 Pope replaced his name with that of William Arnall, one of the best paid of all of Walpole's hacks. Budgell, a cousin of Addison, bore a paranoid grudge against Walpole; his bizarre behavior before the king in 1728 had made him a laughingstock of the town and earned him a place in Pope's poem.

In short, readers attentive to the political scene could easily have thought even the first *Dunciad* a contribution to the incessant attacks on Walpole's "hireling scribblers."[32] What would have been most striking, it seems to me, is that neither the *Craftsman* nor Nicholas Amhurst is mentioned either in the text or the notes of *The Dunciad;* yet from the point of view of the progovernment press that journal was the chief villain in the paper warfare. Its omission from the section on party-writing would by itself be enough to expose the pretense of Pope's claim that the goddess of Dullness shines on all alike. When the general theme of decay of letters and cultural disintegration is coupled with the one-sided account of political writers, with the praise of Swift for his *Drapier's Letters,* and with the defense of "un-pension'd" Gay and his *Beggar's Opera,* the variorum *Dunciad* emerges as a poem which must have pleased Bolingbroke and Pulteney for more than literary reasons. George II may have been sincere when (as Arbuthnot wrote Swift on 19 March 1728/9) he called Pope a "very honest Man," but the poem which prompted the remark could be viewed in a light that would not have pleased that monarch or his ministers.

Pope could not be directly accused by his enemies of having purposely libeled the writers hired to defend the government, since a rather pointless effort was maintained to keep the identity of those writers secret. But naturally some of the attacks on *The Dunciad* revived the old charges that Pope was a political turncoat and even a Jacobite.[33] And much was made of the few lines in the poem which seemed to hit directly at the court. Matthew Concanen, himself one of Walpole's writers, undertook to show that close reading would reveal Pope's political bias. "Not long since," Concanen wrote, "Mr. *Pope* has given it under his own *Hand* in the Postscript to the Notes upon the Odyssey, that he is no *Party-Man* . . . . I am sure that Speech is no way reconcileable to several Passages in the Dunciad." As evidence he cited both the opening lines and the following passage (from the 1728 version):

Thy dragons * * and * * shall taste,
And from each show rise duller than the last:
Till rais'd from Booths to Theatre, to Court,
Her seat imperial, Dulness shall transport.
Already, Opera prepares the way,
The sure fore-runner of her gentle sway.
(III.299–304)

Concanen's explication of these lines is as follows:

Whoever considers the Insinuation which these last Verses contain,
that *Harlequinades* and *Pantomimes* shall from Entertainments for the
Rabble in Booths, become the Diversions of a Court . . . must at the
same time think of some Power able to make them so; but what that
Power is, the Poet leaves Asterisms to explain: And it is clear enough to
whoever understands the Measure of the Verse, and compares it with
the Context, that the Blanks are to be filled with Names, which of all
mortal Names ought to be the most Sacred, and the most exempt from
Ridicule in *English* Poetry.[34]

He warned Pope to fill the blanks with words "consistent with his
Allegiance," advice Pope heeded in the edition of 1729 by
substituting "Magistrates and Peers" (and not "George and
Caroline") for the asterisks. Edmund Curll complained not only
of the passage cited by Concanen but also of the line, "Still
Dunce the second reigns like Dunce the first" (I.6); both he and
Edward Ward insisted that Pope was libeling the court in a
dangerous manner.[35] Amidst such criticism one is puzzled to
find a progovernment paper apparently defending Pope: the
British Journal (28 September 1728) compares the situation of a
great poet harassed by minor literary enemies to that of a great
minister assaulted by a cabal of malcontents. The remainder of
the essay, however, indulges in the usual disparagement of all
men of letters as unfit for "business," and the reference to Pope
is probably tongue-in-cheek. For the most part, Walpole's newspapers refrained from a political reading of *The Dunciad,* just as
they had ignored the political satire of *The Beggar's Opera.*
    On the other hand, as time went on the opposition press
seized with some delight on the notion of dullness pervading
Walpole's England. Pulteney, in a pamphlet of 1731, addressed
the prime minister in these terms: "I am told that you have lately
taken the most eminent Authors of the *Dunciad* into your Pay,

and employ them in your Cause, either for Offence or Defence, as occasion requires. The *late Pieces* utter'd in your Service, seem to put this Point beyond all Dispute." As much as Walpole despises writers, Pulteney goes on, he has been forced to fly to them for protection, but none will accept his pay except his *"Dunciad Advocates."* Infuriated by this charge, the government writers replied with a simple *tu quoque*; one said he knew of no author of *The Dunciad* but Pope—"If he is taken into pay, let him . . . answer for himself."[36] Nonetheless, it became habitual for the opposition writers to call their opponents Dunces. Even as late as 1741, *Common Sense* was writing a mock panegyric upon Dullness and referring to the "Legion of Dunces" surrounding Walpole. The same charges were made in the *Grub-street Journal,* which in 1730 began championing Pope in his war with the Dunces. Though this significant periodical will be discussed later in detail, it should be noted now that its ridicule of Grub Street was political as well as literary in origin.

In other ways, too, Pope's quarrel with the Dunces was frequently drawn into the political arena. When James Moore Smythe and Leonard Welsted included an attack on Atterbury in their *One Epistle to Mr. A. Pope,* they infuriated the writer of *Fog's,* who demanded (6 June 1730) to know "what Good these Gentlemen propose to themselves by turning a poetical Controversy into a Party one." They will be disappointed, he warns, if they mean to pay court to Walpole by this lampoon, "for that Gentleman's Penetration seems to be such, that he seldom confers Favours, except when he has more solid Reasons for it than meer Genius and Capacity." Again, Paul Whitehead's poem *The State Dunces* (1733) is a clear instance of turning the poetical controversy into a political one, for Whitehead asks Pope to satirize new victims, the *"big, rich, mighty, Dunces of the State."* And in his poem the goddess Dullness shows her power most in the person of Robert Walpole, who, inspired by her, is led "blundering to the Helm of *State*" (pp. 7, 9). It did not, however, require either Welsted's attack or Whitehead's imitation to make a political application of *The Dunciad,* for the text of the poem itself invited such a reading in the turbulent political atmosphere of 1728–29.

Despite the political turn which some of his enemies gave to *The Dunciad,* in the year following its publication Pope managed to consolidate his position in circles close to the court. The king approved of the poem, and during 1729–30 Pope seemed on friendly terms with Walpole. The rest of the Scriblerians, however, were not faring so well. In March 1729 Arbuthnot reported to Swift: "As to the condition of your little club, it is not quite so desperate as you might imagine, for Mr Pope is as high in favour as I am affraid the rest are out of it."[37] By the "rest" the doctor really meant John Gay, whose play *Polly* had been suppressed by the government in December and whose subsequent activities were proving something of an embarrassment to Pope in his efforts to remain in high favor.

The story of the suppression of *Polly* is a familiar one, but some aspects of the episode need to be re-examined in a study of political-literary relations in these years. The facts are simple enough. On 12 December 1728 Gay was informed by the duke of Grafton (the lord chamberlain) that his play could not be performed; no particular reason was given by Grafton, but, according to the Preface to the printed edition, Gay was later told the action was taken because of his authorship of seditious pamphlets and his slandering of great men in this sequel to *The Beggar's Opera*. Resolved to print the play and thus vindicate himself from such charges while avoiding financial loss, Gay and his friends began soliciting subscriptions. His beautiful patroness the duchess of Queensberry entreated "every toupee and every patriot or politician for the encouragement of a guinea," as one contemporary account put it, and was banished from the court for soliciting the "very King and Queen themselves, to contribute to publish what they had before condemned." Gay, naturally, became a martyr in the eyes of those opposed to the court; by the time the play was published, Arbuthnot was jokingly referring to him as a "little Sacheverel," the "terror of Ministers," whose glory put Will Pulteney to shame.[38]

What really lay behind the government's action against *Polly* has never been entirely clear. At the time Colley Cibber was accused by some of using his influence to suppress the play in order to insure the success of his own *Love in a Riddle*, a play which was promptly hissed from the stage for "party" reasons; though Cibber ridiculed the charge in his autobiography, Gay himself seems to have thought the rival playwright responsible. But there is only hearsay evidence to connect Cibber with the affair. Some critics, too, have found the government's action puzzling because *Polly* seems too "simple and harmless" to have given offense.[39] Even at the time, opinion was divided about the satirical intention of Gay's new opera. Thomas Rundle, later bishop of Derry, expressed one viewpoint in a letter to his friend Mrs. Sandys:

> It is praised and railed at most extremely; but all people join in asking, where was the offence. The friends of the Minister's aver it is impossible that any can be so audacious as to imagine that there is the least resemblance. —But why was it forbidden? Who refused its being acted? Who exclaimed against it as an odious and plain parallel? They rightly say, they see not the least likeness;—nor perhaps can you, Madam, or I: But those that forbad it, thought they did; and it is hard, since they are willing to compliment great men with every virtue, they should deny them that perfection . . . of *knowing themselves.*[40]

Lord Hervey, on the other hand, found it "less pretty, but more abusive" than *The Beggar's Opera,* with the abuse so ill disguised that Walpole resolved not to let himself again be ridiculed in a "theatrical Craftsman."[41]

Since Hervey was later the bitter enemy of the Scriblerian group, his view need not be accepted at face value. But what of the text of the play itself? Though its satiric sections are vastly outweighed by romantic and moralistic passages, it seems to me that many lines in the play are indeed "more abusive" than the good-humored ridicule of *The Beggar's Opera,* especially when viewed in the light of popular motifs in the anti-Walpole press. Nor could Gay have been completely unaware of the danger he was running. His very denial of particular satire in his Preface reads like a passage from the *Craftsman;* and he must surely have known that when Ducat sings

> Maids like courtiers must be woo'd,
> Most by flattery are subdu'd;
> Some capricious, coy or nice
> Out of pride protract the vice;
>   But they fall,
>   One and all,
> When we bid up to their price,[42]

audiences fed on a weekly diet of charges of "bribery and

corruption" would immediately equate Ducat with Walpole. At another point, Ducat brags, "I have a fine library of books that I never read; I have a fine stable of horses that I never ride; I build, I buy plate, jewels, pictures, or any thing that is valuable and curious, as your great men do, merely out of ostentation" (I.i). Again, Gay can hardly have been ignorant of the similarity between this self-portrait and the ridicule by the opposition press of Walpole's display of rich vulgarity at Houghton; and Ducat's attempts to be unfaithful to his wife would have added one more detail to the similarity. Moreover, both the hanging of Peachum, about which Polly says "I wish all great men would take warning" (I.v), and the execution of Macheath might be looked on as seditious wish-fulfillment on Gay's part, since both had been viewed as Walpole-figures in *The Beggar's Opera*. When it is recognized that the play contains personal reflections as well as general satire on courts and politicians, *Polly* appears less innocuous than Rundle seemed to think. Perhaps no play attacking general vices like avarice and "corruption" could escape a political reading in 1729, and certainly a sequel to *The Beggar's Opera* would be subject to very close scrutiny. Gay seemed to recognize the inevitability of such criticism when he wrote Swift months later of his efforts to revise *The Wife of Bath*: "The ridicule turns upon Supe[rsti]tion, & I have avoided the very words Bribery & corruption. Folly indeed is a word that I have ventured to make use of, but that is a term that never gave fools offence."[43]

The text of the play, then, seems to support the view that more than theatrical rivalry was involved in the suppression of *Polly*; whatever Gay's suspicions about Cibber's role in the affair, there is enough political satire in the play to make credible Hervey's version, in which Walpole himself was responsible for the lord chamberlain's action. But whatever the case, it was perhaps not a wise move on the government's part to turn this dull play into a *cause célèbre*. At court a "Female Faction," as a satirical poem of that title called them, supported the duchess of Queensberry and drew part of the town with them; Rundle wrote sarcastically of the "prudence of him who advised the King, and set his wit against a woman."[44] The opposition papers, of course, made capital of the incident, since it seemed to confirm so much of what they had been saying about the administration's disregard for liberty of expression and individual property rights; the progovernment newspapers passed by the episode in silence. The *Craftsman* for 1 February gave an amusing mock-defense of the suppression of the play in a letter signed "Hilarius"—one critic thinks Gay may have written it himself—and followed up with a proposal on 8 March that Cibber and others establish an "Index Expurgatorius" to remove politically offensive passages from plays.[45] In the same way *Fog's* (26 April 1729) ironically condemned the play by citing obviously harmless lines and interpreting them as libels. Thus it was the alleged overreading of the literary text that the opposition press chose to ridicule on this occasion.

Only two weeks after the play was banned, in fact, a ballad on this theme appeared in the *Craftsman*; called "A Bob for the Court," it opens as follows:

> Ye Poets, take Heed how you trust to the Muse, *fa la.*
> What words to make choice of, and what to refuse, *fa, la.*
> If she hint at a Vice of political Sort, *fa, la.*
> *Application* cries out, *That's a Bob for the C——t, fa la.*

The very name "Macheath" must be avoided:

> If *Macheath* you should name in the midst of his *Gang, fa la.*
> They'll say 'tis an Hint you would *Somebody* hang; *fa la.*
> For *Macheath* is a Word of such evil Report, *fa, la.*
> *Application* cries out, *That's a Bob for the C——t, fa, la.*

The ballad continues in the same vein, suggesting that "application" will pervert the poet's innocent intention in his use of all such words—*Corruption, Ambition, Pomp, Pension, Soissons, Galleon,* etc. The last stanza ends the poem on a note of mock-loyalty:

> Now God bless King GEORGE; all his *Enemies* rout, *fa, la.*
> All those that are IN, and all those that are OUT; *fa, la.*
> May true, honest Hearts be his Bulwark and Fort, *fa, la.*
> And so there's an End *of a* BOB *for the C——t. fa, la.*[46]

The final line, of course, suggests by its pun on "Bob" that if true, honest hearts are depended upon, Walpole will fall. The satire of this political ballad, like that of the essays in *Fog's* and the *Craftsman*, is directed at a literary fault—"application," the particularizing of general statements—but of course this literary habit in a political context could be made to suggest overzealousness, paranoia, and guilt. Perhaps, indeed, the banning of *Polly* was more useful to the opposition than its performance on stage would have been.

As the decade drew to an end, Walpole continued in power, undismayed by the efforts of his opponents. The Treaty of Seville, concluded in November, brought peace with Spain but naturally did nothing to abate the "Prodigious clamour against Sir Robert."[47] Though the effects of the clamor were negligible in the seats of real power, like the House of Commons, the opposition seemed to have its own way in the literary world. By 1730 it was clear that the great satirists of the age were, in varying degrees and for varying reasons, contributing to the campaign of the "disaffected faction." After all, in the four years since the beginning of the Bolingbroke-Pulteney alliance England had seen the publication of *Gulliver's Travels*, *The Beggar's Opera*, *The Dunciad*, and *Polly*, each of which, however extraordinary in its own right, was also useful to the political forces who hoped to unseat the prime minister. The political involvement of Swift, Pope, and Gay was not, of course, a matter of direct contribution to political pamphleteering. It was not the same situation as it had been in 1712–14, when Swift and Steele faced each other as the principal propagandists for the Tory administration and the Whigs in the wilderness. But the literary world was no less divided along political lines now than it had been then, if one may use "divided" to describe such an unequal distribution of talent; and it was now not pamphlets on Dunkirk but works written primarily as imaginative literary art which revealed and re-emphasized the political division.

One of the few writers of note not aligned with the opposition was Edward Young. According to Welsted and Smythe, Young had been courted by both of "the great contending Powers in Poesy," but had recently shown signs of acceding to the "*Treaty of Twickenham*"; indeed, according to Benjamin Victor, Young never gained a bishopric because of a week-long visit he paid in this period to Bolingbroke at Dawley Farm.[48] Nevertheless, if

Welsted's political metaphor was meant seriously, it was notably inaccurate, for Young in his public utterances had not wavered from the course he set for himself in *The Instalment.* Though he praised Pope and attacked the party writing of both sides in *Two Epistles to Mr. Pope* (1730), his other poems in these years left no doubt that he was firmly loyal to the court interest and properly grateful for his pension. *Ocean, an Ode Occasion'd by His Majesty's late Royal Encouragement of the Sea-Service* (1728) and *Imperium Pelagi, a Naval Lyrick . . . occasion'd by His Majesty's Return, Sept., 1729, and the succeeding Peace* (1730) were doubtless among the poems Swift had in mind when he depicted Young as torturing his invention to flatter knaves. Most revealing of all, though, was *An Apology for Princes, or the Reverence due to Government,* a sermon preached before the House of Commons on 30 January 1729. Since the occasion was the anniversary of the execution of Charles I, Young would have been expected to take a political position, and he did not disappoint his audience. Despite his claim to preach "with an entire Abstinence from *Party,* without which, most Compositions would be famish'd," one quickly encounters passages like this attack on the opposition:

WHAT a world of Enemies has Power? *Great merit* is quick to take Offence; *Little merit* to fear Justice; the *Proud* think it Magnanimity to Oppose; the *Ill-natur'd,* Pleasure; . . . And what is more melancholy, Men of *Riches, Talents,* and *Birth,* are sometimes tempted to conspire with their Opposites, by thinking that Power is held by *Others,* in their own wrong.[49]

Preached as it was during the commotion over *Polly,* Young's sermon places him at a considerable political distance from his fellow poets Gay, Pope, and Swift.

Just before Young preached his sermon, another poet who had begun by flattering the ministry suddenly changed his direction. James Thomson, it will be recalled, had eulogized Walpole in the dedication to his poem on the death of Newton, but in his new poem *Britannia* he bemoaned England's timidity in the face of Spanish depredations of British ships and thus poetically echoed the opposition's attacks on Walpole's foreign policy. In its despair over the degenerate condition of Britain, its contrast between "luxury" and "liberty," its praise of patriotism, and its denunciation of the "insulting *Spaniard,*" *Britannia* was

immediately recognizable as a "party" poem, and it was duly
praised by opposition papers and pamphlets. One government
paper, the *Daily Journal*, bravely attempted to appropriate the
poem by quoting out of context a long passage eulogizing peace,
but *Fog's* quickly countered by citing lines more suitable for
opposition propaganda and more representative of the poem as
a whole.[50] What prompted Thomson's political about-face cannot be determined; the incident points up once again the
difficulty of generalizing about the political "convictions" of
eighteenth-century poets. Obviously sensitive to the charge of
apostasy, Thomson attempted to conceal his authorship of the
poem, but to no avail. A year later the *Free Briton* (13 August
1730) accused him of ingratitude to Walpole, claiming that he
had received fifty pounds for the dedication to the poem on
Newton but had nonetheless in *Britannia* libeled the ministry "in
formidable Poetry."

Though the poetry is in actuality far from formidable, *Britannia* is noteworthy for another reason. It is an early example of
what A. D. McKillop has called "dissident Whig panegyric," in
which the conventional praise of peaceful imperialism "reverts
to the contrast between the unique and glorious situation and
mission of Britain and the present state of things."[51] It was a
strain that was to become increasingly prominent in the literary
circles of the opposition, especially in those poets who were to
seek patronage from the newly arrived Prince of Wales. On the
same day that *Britannia* was published (25 January) the *Craftsman* opened its essay with the remark, "Nothing can be more
grievous to an honest Man, who has any Regard and Concern
for the Welfare and Happiness of his Country, than to find it
from a rich and flourishing Condition daily declining in its
Wealth, Power, and *Reputation.*" Given the fact that one of the
goals of opposition propaganda was to inculcate this "sense of
decline" in the popular mind, two literary methods were open to
writers sympathetic to the Bolingbroke-Pulteney interest: either
satiric exposure of the present state of affairs in the tradition of
the Tory wits or patriotic exhortation in the tradition of Whig
sentimentalism. The first four years of the new opposition were
notable for a virtual explosion of satire from the pens of the
Scriblerians, but in the decade which followed poets and dramatists began to turn more and more to the pattern of patriotic
sentiment set by Thomson's *Britannia*.

4 THE WITS AND THE GOVERNMENT IN THE YEARS OF CRISIS, 1730–1734

IN FEBRUARY 1730 Lord Bathurst wrote to Swift that the *Modest Proposal* was so reasonable it need not be confined to Ireland or to the eating of children: "For I happen'd to peep the other day into a large assembly not far from Westminster Hall, & I found them roasting a great fat fellow; for my own part I had not the least inclination to a slice of him, but if I guessed right, 4 in 5 of the Company had a devilish mind to be at him."[1] Bathurst's appraisal was too optimistic. The great fat fellow, who had just scored a diplomatic victory with the Treaty of Seville, was not to be devoured just yet. But in the first three years of the new decade, the opposition nibbled at him with increasing energy, their hopes raised by his rift with his brother-in-law, Townshend, by the success of their claims that trade had suffered under the new foreign policy, and by his increasing difficulties with the City. Walpole's narrowing majorities over the salt tax debates in 1732 raised their hopes even more, and the furor in 1733 which forced the government to withdraw the excise bills put his authority in serious jeopardy for the first time in ten years.[2]

As Walpole's difficulties increased, the paper warfare gained in intensity. Progovernment newspapers like the *Free Briton*, the *London Journal*, the *British Journal*, and the *Daily Courant* hammered hard at the *Craftsman* and at *Fog's Journal*. Francklin, the printer of the *Craftsman*, was arrested, but that paper continued its attacks on the administration and its tedious series of historical parallels to Walpole's "corrupt" government. Sir Robert rose in the House and complained of the "scurrility" leveled at him, and, indeed, the flood of satire and pamphlets reached a new

height in these years. Pulteney, in his *Proper Reply* (1731) to a
pamphlet called *Sedition and Defamation Display'd*, engaged in a
virulent attack on Lord Hervey in a passage later used by Pope
in his portrait of Sporus. Then, in *An Answer to One Part of a Late
Infamous Libel* (1731), Pulteney revealed a conversation in which
Walpole supposedly had insulted the Prince (now George II). As
a result of the first pamphlet, Pulteney fought a duel with
Hervey, and as a result of the second he was struck from the list
of privy councilors.

In a time of such political bitterness it is not surprising that
antigovernment innuendoes were again discovered in areas not
overtly political. As a writer for *Fog's* complained, "Some People
indeed will make us believe, that all the Farces in dumb Shew are
so many political Satyrs; as if the Disaffected had a Notion that
what they dare not speak they may venture to *dance*."[3] But "some
people" were quite correct in their suspicion, and the summer of
1731 saw the suppression of a number of minor theatrical
performances.[4] *Fog's* itself played the same game, pretending
that the prime minister had subscribed for thirty copies of the
ridiculous play *Hurlothrumbo* (it was actually his son who did so)
and using this in a mock defense of Sir Robert's patronage of
belles-lettres. Some of the minor skirmishes on the fringe of
political warfare seem hilarious in retrospect. The Rev. Samuel
Croxall, a minor writer and translator of Ovid, preached the
January 30th sermon before the House of Commons in 1730;
remarkably enough, Croxall chose as his text, "Take away the
Wicked from before the King, and his Throne shall be established in Righteousness" and defended in his sermon the right
of good citizens to attack both the measures and the favorites of
a king. This was a far cry from the sermon preached by the poet
Young before the same assembly on the same occasion a year
earlier, and the outraged government supporters reacted pre-
dictably. The House failed to vote him their thanks, the *Daily
Journal* accused him of acting the part of a *Craftsman* rather than
a divine, and a satiric poem depicted him as complaining to
Walpole that his literary efforts had not been rewarded by
preferment in the Church:

If a Truth may be ask'd, Sir, pray what may it mean?
My Pretensions so fair, I'm not yet a Dean?
That my *Ovid*, my *Aesop, Circassian*, and all

The gay Things I have wrote, should not merit a Stall?
When the Muse has long begg'd, that you always should slight her,
Who had Hopes of exchanging her Wreathes for a Mitre.
By your Pride or Contempt, my Laurel's ill-fated,
Translating so often—and never *translated*.[5]

By now the opposition's mock dismay at the state of literature in Walpole's England was well established as a political theme. Pulteney's claim that Walpole had taken into pay all the authors of *The Dunciad* was referred to constantly by both sides; and the failure of the ministry to support men of letters was a motif incessantly harped upon by opposition papers like *Fog's*, a motif reduced to absurdity by the *Daily Courant* (21 July 1732): "One is not fit to be a Treasurer because—*risum teneatis*—he does not write verses and play upon a Lute." Thus when Aaron Hill devoted his genteel pen to some *Advice to Poets* in 1731, he was not elevating himself above politics despite his pretension to do so. In his "Epistle Dedicatory to the Few Great Spirits of Great Britain" Hill attacks the system of patronage in exchange for flattery, demands a loftier strain of poetry which will produce a national change in the public spirit, reveres poets as true patriots, and makes broad hints about the odium into which a minister's name will fall if he neglects the works of poetic genius. Moreover, the poem which follows directly warns Walpole that his reputation with posterity will depend not on votes but on the Muse. Whatever Hill may have intended by all this, his essay and his poem could not escape the political overtones generated by similar arguments in the organs of opposition propaganda. Nor could his essay possibly have had any effect; the gap between men of letters and men of business was not to be closed again.

The Birthday Fibber and the Grub-street Journal

The treatment of literary men by the administration was a prominent theme in another affair of these years which much diverted the town. Eustace Budgell, the cousin of Addison, startled the court in 1730 by petitioning the king to redress the wrongs done him by Sir Robert Walpole. For the next few years Budgell poured out letters and pamphlets in which he blamed Walpole for all his various legal and personal problems. Some-

what to their later embarrassment, his cause was taken up by
Fog's and the *Craftsman,* who saw in him a valuable ally in their
attacks on the government, and all the government organs
accordingly mocked his evident madness. Since one of Budgell's
delusions was that he was a man of letters, Walpole's disregard
for belles-lettres became intermingled in his writings with complaints of persecution. Thus in his *Letter to Cleomenes King of
Sparta* (1731) Budgell contrasts Walpole with leaders of the past
who advanced no men to government posts who were not men
of learning, and in *A Letter to Ulrick D'Ypres* (1731) he develops a
crude allegorical caricature of Walpole as Xunchi, chief minister
in the kingdom of Tarquin, whose antipathy to "Men of *Parts*
and *Learning*" stirred up all good writers to oppose him: "The
finest *Wits* and *Pens* in Tarquin, upon all these Considerations,
added Fuel to the Resentments of the People: they drew the
Picture of *Xunchi* in its proper Colours; and their own personal
Injuries adding an uncommon *Spirit* to their writings, made the
several Pieces they published read and admired by all the
People."[6]

Naturally, *Fog's* and the *Craftsman* were quick to exploit such
attacks as these, which fit so well into their own arsenal of
propaganda. *Fog's* for 20 March 1731 took delight, for instance,
in quoting a long section from Budgell praising the late earl of
Oxford for his patronage of men of genius, in contrast to
Walpole, who is surrounded by Dunces. More quotations from
Budgell (to the same effect) followed in the issue of 1 May 1731.
The government papers, meanwhile, were devoting entire issues
both to refuting this charge and to impugning poor Budgell's
sanity. Thus the *Daily Courant* found two points in the *Craftsman*
very much open to dispute: "The one is, that no Man can be a
good Minister, who is not . . . a *Writer of Verses.* The other is, that
Mr. B——l is a Man *Compos Mentis.*" The same paper, a year
later, was still representing Budgell as blaming Walpole not only
for his own misfortunes but for "the Want of Taste for Tragedy
in these Nations, which has visibly declined, as well as all other
sound and useful Literature, since the A——n of Affairs has
been in his Hands."[7] The whole affair, which ended only with
Budgell's suicide in 1737, was pathetic and ridiculous enough,
but it may have helped the opposition cement in the public mind
the notion of "Bob, the Poet's Foe."

The real men of letters, of course, had no part in all this, though Swift was distressed when Budgell sought his aid. They were, instead, amazed by a more remarkable instance of the government's insensitivity to the literary world, the appointment of Colley Cibber as poet laureate. The incumbent, Eusden, had died at the end of September 1730. Between that time and Cibber's appointment on 3 December, the press was filled with speculation about the choice of a successor, with possibilities including Dennis, Theobald, Duck, and Cibber. Swift reported the rumor that "Duck is absolutely to Succeed Eusden in the Lawrell, the contention being between Concannan or Theobald, or some other Hero of the Dunciad."[8]

Stephen Duck, the Thresher Poet, to whom Swift referred, would have been a choice only slightly more ridiculous than Cibber. He had been patronized by Queen Caroline, and, according to Gay and Pope, was the favorite poet of the court. Moreover, this "Phenomenon of Wiltshire," as Pope called him, was puffed in publications ordinarily devoted to giving political support to the administration. Thus the *British Journal* for 10 October 1730 ran a long essay praising his purity of thought and language in contrast to Pope's, and the *Political State of Great Britain,* which almost always eschewed anything remotely literary, printed eighteen pages of poems by Duck in its issue for October.[9] Dr. Alured Clarke, who seems to have been instrumental in sponsoring Duck at court, also thought him a superior genius to Pope, but advised Duck to pay compliments to Pope despite the fact that Pope "deserves them not from anybody that has a true love for the Royal Family." Not surprisingly, Clarke also counseled Duck to avoid reading Swift or other satiric writers.[10]

Both the court's patronage of Duck and the lord chamberlain's appointment of Cibber were obvious evidence for the opposition's claims of the decay of letters under Walpole. In a letter to Gay Swift snarled about the "tasteless ungratefull court" which "deserves no better Genius's than those by whom it is celebrated,—so let the Post rascal open this letter, and let Walpole read it."[11] Many of the satiric poems and epigrams with which the press was flooded on the occasion of Cibber's appointment were, of course, merely personal satire. One example, from the *Grub-street Journal* (31 December 1730), will suffice:

> But guessing who would have the luck
> To be the *B——day* Fibber;
> I thought of DENNIS, TIBBALD, DUCK,
> But never dreamt of CIBBER.

But other poems on the same theme could scarcely avoid the implication that the choice of Cibber reflected the tastelessness of the entire age. One *Hymn to the New Laureat,* having observed that "he who such a Man could Chuse/ Ought only to be Sung by such a Muse," concludes with this ironic prayer:

> This is my sole Ambition, sole Desire,
> When I from Hence to other Worlds, retire,
> (To Mine, and to my Country's deathless Praise)
> It may be said I liv'd when *C——r* wore the BAYS.[12]

Some put the blame on the lord chamberlain, the duke of Grafton, as this epigram attests: "Tell, if you can, which did the worse,/ Caligula, or Gr[afto]n's Gr[a]ce?/ That made a Consul of a Horse,/ And this a Laureate of an Ass."[13] Swift, however, saw that the matter must be pushed farther than that; writing to Pope he admits that the court could be excused on the grounds that the laureate's place is in the lord chamberlain's gift, "but who makes Lord Chamberlains is another question. I believe if the Court had interceded with D. of Grafton for a fitter Man, it might have prevailed."[14] Opposition papers like *Fog's* were only too happy to make political capital out of the episode. *Fog's* for 2 January 1730/1, for instance, printed an epigram in which Dennis protests to Grafton that he can never be praised by a poet who cannot write, to which Grafton responds that he never meant to *do* what deserved to be praised. *Fog's* then goes on to make the usual link to Walpole: "Nay there is not, I believe, a surer Way to judge of a Minister's Character, than (abstractedly from the Attacks and Defenses of Faction) to examine *How far He enquires out, and distinguishes, Men of Letters.*"

Thus the "advancement of a Person to the Throne of Wit, who has generally been look'd on but as a *Defiler* of it's Footstool" is added by the opposition to its list of Walpole's blunders. An epigram in the *Grub-street Journal* similarly puts the affair in a political context:

In ancient days, when pensions, bribes, and screens
    Were things unknown in Senate, and at Court;
Then was the glorious time, when Kings and Queens
    For pride kept Poets, and kept Fools for sport:
But now frugality, which bears such rule,
    Joins pride and sport, a POET and a FOOL.[15]

The allusions to "pensions," "bribes," and "screens," of course, makes the application to Walpole unmistakable. *Fog's* went so far as to insinuate that Cibber (here called "Keyber" to point up his loyalty to the Germanic royal family) was to be a new partner of Walpole's two chief political propagandists who wrote under the pseudonyms of "Osborne" and "Walsingham":

We are informed that *Keyber* comes on pretty well in his *Spelling*, and by that Time he begins to *read* a little, he will be initiated into the Society of Political Authors, and join'd to *Messieurs Osborn and Walsingham*, in order to form a worthy Triumvirate; and, as he has the Happiness to be provided with all the *Paraphonalia* of a *Whig Hackney*, in every Body's Opinion, he will do his Patron as much Honour and Service as the best of them.[16]

Though this is meant humorously, Cibber was also treated as one of Walpole's political hack writers in the mock epic *Verres and his Scribblers* (1732). Through his New Year's odes and his odes on the king's birthday, Cibber seemed an absurd apologist for the health of England under Walpole; *Fog's* (22 January 1731/2) spoke sarcastically of "what a Satisfaction it must be to all Lovers of the *Belles Lettres* to see the Laurel placed upon such an Head. What an excellent Celebrator of the Actions of Great Men is this excellent Poet." It is the laureate's task, according to a poem in an earlier issue of *Fog's*, to show that trade flourishes as never before and that under Walpole the nation "slumbers in peace." These are the themes he must sing as he thrums his "venal Lyre" (15 January 1731/2).

Obviously, any writer required by his position to celebrate the court would have aroused the ire of an opposition paper like *Fog's*, but that it should be celebrated in "Keyberian" verse seemed doubly an affront to the wits of the day. "The Millenium of dullness seems to be fast approaching," wrote the poet

Thomson to a friend, and in Pope's view "the whole age seems resolv'd to justify the Dunciad."[17] But apologists for the government were careful to set matters in an entirely different light. An ode to Walpole on New Year's Day, 1731, written just as Cibber became poet laureate, can still praise him as a guardian of poetic taste:

> Thee, the sacred Muses hailing,
>   Dullness seal'd in Slumber lies;
> Arts and Wealth thro' thee prevailing,
>   Faction far confounded flies.[18]

Since poems ridiculing Cibber were printed on the same page of the *Gentleman's Magazine* as this poem, the lines must have seemed to some readers beautifully ironic.

The *Grub-street Journal*, which was unfailing in its satiric jibes at Cibber, provides another significant example of the almost inevitable connection between the literary and political worlds as the decade of the 1730s opened. Ostensibly this paper, which from its first issue in January 1730 established itself as the wittiest and most urbane journal in London, was politically neutral. As early as the third paper the "Grubeans" declared that they would steer clear of party squabbles, and J. T. Hillhouse, who has made the only modern study of the paper, has taken at face value the notion that the *Journal* "eschewed politics." But a pretense of impartiality was the most common gambit of political propaganda, and it was not likely that a paper so constantly embroiled in the literary and journalistic disputes of the day could really have no political bias, especially since its satiric victims were so often the heroes of *The Dunciad* and the hacks writing for Walpole. Hillhouse admits that insofar as the *Journal* had political leanings they were Tory and Jacobite.[19] This is, I think, an understatement; the *Journal* showed a constant bias against the administration and spoke directly on many occasions about political issues, particularly when they involved the City of London. Even if it had confined itself to literature, its constant defenses of Pope and Swift would have involved, necessarily, a political as well as a literary bias.

Certainly some readers of its early issues assumed that the *Grub-street Journal* was anti-Walpole. The *British Journal* of 21

November 1730 coupled an attack on the *Craftsman* with a sideswipe at the *Journal*, and the progovernment *Daily Courant* in its issue of 11 June 1731 printed an epigram which identified "D'Anvers, Fog, and Grub" as the three "Sons of Dullness" who "in Factions Course most stupidly engage." The *Journal* promptly responded with an epigram ridiculing the *Courant*, the *London Journal*, and the *Free Briton*, but a few months later was again required to respond to a letter in the *Courant* linking it with the opposition. As early as 24 September 1730, the *Journal* was forced to defend itself against the charge of "favouring one Party and some particular Persons, more than others," a charge which it answered with the weak excuse that "whatever appearance there may be of this, it has been all accidental." But its protestations were not taken seriously. One writer in a pseudo-Quaker magazine called *The Friendly Writer and Register of Truth* accused the *Journal* of Jacobitism and of accepting "Nothing but Ironies against the Governors of the People"; and in December of 1733 Eustace Budgell, whom the *Journal* had been attacking, argued that there was no difference between his politics and those of Russel, the editor of the *Journal:*

> Your *Principles* . . . are said to be against the *present Ministry,* so that nothing but *rank Malice* and *Envy* could have made you fall upon Mr. *Budgell* in so *barbarous* a manner; since it is pretty well known that he *agrees* with you in having no great Opinion of the present Measures."[20]

Thus, if the *Grub-street Journal* "eschewed politics," that fact was not obvious to many of its contemporaries.

Nor is it obvious to any careful reader of the paper, since from the spring of 1730 on, the *Journal* heaped ridicule on the newspapers supporting the administration. Of course, one must understand that the premise of the entire paper is a mock defense of Grub Street hacks and thus its satire on the men writing for Walpole is often in the form of ironic praise. In the issue for 21 May 1730 (No. 20), for instance, "Mr. Pamphleteero" argues that the ancient society of Grub Street is "extremely well affected to his Majesty, and the present Ministry" and that members of the society "have brought . . . unanswerable arguments in defence of Places and Pensions," as was justly pointed out in a recent letter in the *Craftsman.* Two issues later

(No. 22, 4 June 1730), the *Journal* attacked the *London Journal,* defended the exiled Bishop Atterbury, and quoted from *Fog's.* No. 38 (24 September 1730) printed a poem ridiculing the governmental writers with lines like, "Write not like Drapier, or John Bull;/ But Ministerial be, and Dull"; the poem is printed with the protestation that the editors *"differ in sentiment from the author,"* a protestation unconvincing in the light of the constant stream of such sentiments in the editors' pages. Again, No. 47 (26 November 1730) contains a long essay apparently defending the Grubeans who write against the opposition but actually attacking the "indulgences" such writers receive from the Treasury and the post office. The same issue, in fact, prints a poem satirizing the *Free Briton.* One final example of the *Journal's* war on Walpole's political writers is the poem in No. 140 (7 September 1732) laughing at the preferment of Matthew Concanen to the post of attorney general of Jamaica; it opens, "Come, *Dunciad* Authors, come to dinner all,/ C———'s made Attorney General." What is especially amusing about this example is that a writer in *Fog's* a week later (16 September) accused the *Grub-street Journal* of altering the epigram in such a way as to make it a panegyric, declared that Russel and his cohorts were turncoats, and wished a *"certain Person"* joy of his new allies.

But the "certain Person" was not likely to receive much joy from this witty paper, not only because of its reiterated satire on his "hireling scribblers" but also because of its occasionally open and direct hostility to his government. In November and December of 1731, for example, the *Journal* vigorously attacked the *Free Briton* for its aspersions on the common council and lord mayor of London, and throughout its life it defended Tory interests in the City in opposition to Walpole. Sometimes even the news columns were used for political jokes, as in the item reporting that a certain jury—by implication the jury which had convicted the printer of the *Craftsman*—supped after the trial "very elegantly upon a Calves-head, and other curious dishes," an allusion to the violently Puritan "Calves-head Club."[21] Or again, an outspoken epigram on Walpole was printed on 30 July 1730, early in the paper's history:

> To banish far an English Bishop hence,
> ——— himself descends to Evidence;
> Who, against *Chartres* swear, he highly blames,

> And Knighthood's shield protects the *Squire of Dames.*
> Say, where is most his *matchless Virtue* seen?
> As then th' Informer, or as now the Screen?

This epigram, which Hillhouse dismisses as "cryptic," is actually taking Walpole to task on two counts, his having given evidence before the House of Lords in 1723 against the Jacobite Bishop Atterbury and his "screening" or protecting Colonel Francis Charteris, who was pardoned for rape in April 1730. Such an open sneer at the "matchless virtue" of the prime minister could not go unanswered, and the *Free Briton* (6 August 1730) promptly printed a poetic reply based on the dubious premise that rape is preferable to treason. Nor did the *Journal* confine itself to personal satire on Walpole; No. 62 (11 March 1731) catalogued a series of instances in which the public is told the exact opposite of what everyone knows to be true: that trade is flourishing, that reflection on the minister is attack upon the king, that standing armies are the best guardians of liberty, and that bribery and corruption are essential for the public good—all, of course, government "lies" harped on constantly by the opposition. Finally it should be noted that in 1733 the *Journal* consistently attacked Walpole's excise scheme, abandoning all pretense of political impartiality and increasing its attacks on the progovernment journalists. In one of its early issues of that year, moreover, it managed to combine political and literary satire by including in its annual ridicule of Cibber's New Year's Ode a parody in which the laureate himself defends the excise bill (8 February 1732/3).

For all this, the *Grub-street Journal* remained more interested in literary than political satire. I have stressed its hostility to the administration to show that its political orientation was in accord with its literary biases. In the early 1730s a paper which entered so vigorously into literary and journalistic quarrels would inevitably be drawn into political squabbles as well, and a journal which made its reputation by ridiculing Cibber, Duck, and the lesser dunces while defending Pope and Swift would be especially suspect in the eyes of supporters of the administration. With the *Journal*, though, the matter goes farther; the evidence indicates clearly that its literary and political prejudices reinforced each other, that in fact its literary judgments were at least in part colored by political considerations. Paradoxically, the best illustration is its hostile reception of Henry Fielding. Though Fielding was eventually to become a prime force in the literary opposition to Walpole, in his early career his politics were more problematic.

Fielding's Early Plays

Those who regard the literary figures opposed to Walpole as motivated by fixed principles or operating from a common ideology must have great difficulty with the career of Henry Fielding. It is well known that in some of his plays of the mid-thirties (especially *The Historical Register*) Fielding satirized Walpole to a degree that would have satisfied any opposition politician and that after the Licensing Act of 1737 forced him to leave the stage he carried on a journalistic campaign against the ministry, possibly in *Common Sense* and certainly in the *Champion* (1739–40). It has also been made clear in recent studies that after he left the *Champion* Fielding's politics underwent a shift, a shift which was made obvious in his pamphlet *The Opposition: A Vision* (1741) and which was a response either to money from Walpole or to a growing disillusionment within some factions of the opposition.[22] As I will indicate in Chapter 7 his change of politics in this later period must give pause to biographers seeking to establish Fielding's political "integrity" or ideological consistency.

But just as problematical though less well studied are Fielding's relations with Walpole in the years with which we are immediately concerned, 1730–34. On the one hand we are faced with his early plays, in some of which (especially *The Author's Farce, Tom Thumb, Rape upon Rape,* and *The Welsh Opera*) many scholars have detected sharp satire directed at Sir Robert. On the other hand we have a body of evidence which shows Fielding by no means unwilling to align himself with the ministerial forces before 1734. A detailed review of this evidence and a close examination of the early plays will reveal, I think, considerable tergiversation on the part of the young playwright in the uncertain political climate of the early thirties. There may, in fact, be more than political malice behind the charges later made by his enemies that he accepted favors from Walpole before and during his career as a dramatist and had thus been "bought off" at least once before the better-known shift of political allegiance in 1741.

The most recent evidence to come to light about Fielding's political attitudes at the outset of his playwriting career is an unfinished burlesque epic written in his hand and preserved among the papers of his cousin, Lady Mary Wortley Montagu. Isobel M. Grundy, who discovered the three cantos of this poem, dates their composition at 1729; as she points out, they represent a bid for Lady Mary's patronage "and perhaps, through her, for that of Walpole," who is warmly praised in the course of the poem.[23] The poem, in fact, is an inverted *Dunciad;* Pope, Swift, and Gay are depicted here as the sons of Dullness, in league with "Caleb" (the *Craftsman*) and with other forces of sedition, all bent on defeating wit and learning by defeating Walpole. George II and Caroline are "Wit's brightest Patrons," but Caleb assures his fellow writers that a Jacobite victory will restore the realm of dullness. He addresses the cabal of Scriblerians as follows:

> Were Popery once Master of the Ball
> How soon must Learning, Wit, and Knowledge fall
> Wit (like a Summer Flower) can only thrive
> By Liberty's warm Beams preserv'd alive
> And should the Star of Popery arise
> The Star of Liberty must quit the Skies
> But ah! it labours to ascend in Vain
> By G—— depress'd beneath an Iron Chain.
> So Satan—as the Sacred Stories tell
> Howl'd vainly, by th'almighty chain'd in Hell
> Then knows not Ilar [Gay] to what mightier End
> All my seditious, Lieing Writings tend
> Look through the long Record of Ages past
> The M—— first falls the K—— at last
> The Counsellors from M——y to drive
> Is an old Game by Me still kept alive.[24]

Not only does Fielding attack Pope, Swift, and Gay as seditious dullards, he praises Walpole and the court as the bulwarks both of liberty and of learning; and thus he neatly reverses a pet theme of the opposition. Grundy's important discovery clearly reinforces the notion that Fielding was bidding for Walpole's favor at this time and simultaneously renders suspect any "anti-Walpole" reading of his plays written in 1730, only a year after these verses.

A similar difficulty for such a reading is posed by his two facetious poetic epistles to Walpole, dated by Fielding as "Written in the year 1730" and "Anno 1731" when they appeared in his *Miscellanies* (1743). Both are addressed to Sir Robert, and both jokingly compare the poet with the statesman. Though a shortened version of the first appeared in 1738 in the *Gentleman's Magazine,* they do not seem to have been published in the years Fielding ascribes to them, but of course there is the possibility that they were conveyed privately to the minister by Lady Mary or by Fielding himself. The first opens with a mixture of flattery and banter:

> While at the Helm of State you ride
> Our Nation's Envy, and its Pride;
> While foreign Courts with Wonder gaze,
> And curse those Councils which they praise;
> Would you not wonder, Sir, to view
> Your Bard a greater Man than you?[25]

He continues with a tongue-in-cheek "proof" that he, the bard, is as great as the statesman and with a mock equation of the minister's levee and the bailiffs at the poet's door. But he will come down from his window at Walpole's bidding "into whatever Place you please," though he is fittest, he says, for a sinecure. The second epistle is in the same vein, making much of the comparison between the levee and the creditors. H. K. Miller suggests that these poems reflect Fielding's own experience in waiting upon the great and that he may not have been completely joking when he asked the prime minister for a place.[26] Though another critic has suggested that the poems are ironic attacks on Walpole and should be dated much later, there is, in my view, not the slightest reason for doubting the dates Fielding assigned them or for reading them satirically.[27] In manner they are much like the insolent, bantering "poetical petitions" which Joseph Mitchell, "Walpole's Poet," sent to Sir Robert asking for favors, even for a sinecure.[28] And they accord well with the burlesque cantos of 1729 and with other evidences of Fielding's approaches to the minister in these early years.

Some of this further evidence, though more circumstantial,

points to Fielding's reputation in the first few years of the decade as a writer who had benefited or was seeking to benefit from Walpole's patronage. In an epigram in the *Grub-street Journal* (26 September 1734), for instance, he is included, along with Pope, Young, Welsted, Thomson, and Frowde, in a group under obligation for the "indulgence" of the "Primier with the staff." Again, Mitchell, in *A Familiar Epistle* to Walpole printed in 1735, writes as follows:

> Your Praises who has better sung?
> —Pardon is begg'd of *Messieurs* YOUNG,
> TIBBALD and WELSTED, FIELDING, FROWDE,
> And fifty more who round you crowd.[29]

Of course, both these references postdate the time of *Tom Thumb* or *The Welsh Opera,* but they may well refer to events occurring in that period. They could not have been written if Fielding had achieved any reputation for satirizing Walpole in his early plays. Nor, in fact, are there any references in either anti-Walpole papers or prominiterial organs which link Fielding with the opposition in these years. Indeed, in April 1731—the same month as Fielding's *Welsh Opera*—the opposite sort of signal was given, for, as Charles Woods has shown, at that point Fielding wrote an epilogue for Theobald's *Orestes,* a play dedicated to Walpole with his permission and thanking the minister for the "generous Encouragement which the politer Arts" have received from him. And Woods concludes that at this time Fielding probably was thought to belong to the "outskirts" of Walpole's camp.[30]

Nine months later, in January 1732, such a reputation would have been enhanced, I think, by the fact that Fielding wrote an epilogue to *The Modish Couple,* a play supposedly by a Captain Bodens but actually by Lord Hervey and the Prince of Wales.[31] This play was violently attacked by all the opposition journals, who sneeringly accused its author of writing "like a Courtier," who ridiculed its "Keyberian" style, and who complained of a "standing Army" being placed on stage to prevent its being criticized. Though Fielding's share in this enterprise was not directly mentioned in the attacks, his contribution must have been noticed. The condemnation of *The Modish Couple,* as

Charles Woods says, "shows how deeply the spirit of party had penetrated into the social and theatrical life of Walpole's London."[32] In such an atmosphere Fielding's epilogue for "Bodens," like his help to Theobald, would have constituted a clear sign that he was ready to align himself with the court party or that he had already done so. As we shall see, the final and most explicit signal came the very next month, when Fielding's own play *The Modern Husband* was printed with a dedication to Sir Robert Walpole, the "wise Statesman" and "generous Patron."

Against this background, then, of a mock epic praising Walpole and ridiculing his enemies; two friendly poetic epistles to Walpole; contemporary references to help from Walpole given or sought by Fielding; an epilogue contributed to a play dedicated to Walpole; another epilogue contributed to a play castigated for political reasons by the enemies of Walpole; and finally Fielding's dedication of *The Modern Husband* to Walpole— against all this we must set those plays performed at the Haymarket in 1730–31 which presumably satirize Walpole: *The Author's Farce*, *Tom Thumb* and its revision as *The Tragedy of Tragedies*, *Rape upon Rape*, and *The Welsh Opera*, together with its printed revision *The Grub-Street Opera*. In considering the presence or absence or degree of that satire we should keep in mind that there is not the slightest scrap of evidence which suggests that the first three of these four plays were read or viewed at the time as satirizing Walpole, though it was obviously not a time when public comment was lacking about plays considered politically suspect. All the evidence is internal, and in our evaluation of it we must remember the background of external evidence I have sketched, a background indicating at the least a political naiveté incredible in a supposed satirist of the government and at the most overtures, perhaps successful ones, on Fielding's part for the favor of that government. But let us examine briefly the plays in question.

In *The Author's Farce*, the first of the plays to be acted at the Haymarket in 1731, political satire seems to have remained undetected until 1962, when Sheridan Baker published what is perhaps an overingenious explication of it.[33] Though admitting that it is all rather innocuous, Baker believes that even this first version of the play (as distinguished from Fielding's revision of it in 1734) employs a series of symbols and commonplaces, such as the parallel of the stage and the state, which act as satiric vehicles against Walpole. His readings are sometimes quite unconvincing; consider, for example, this conversation between Bookweight (Edmund Curll) and one of his hack writers:

> *Scarecrow.* Sir, I have brought you a libel against the ministry.
> *Bookweight.* Sir, I shall not take anything against them—(*aside*) for I have two in the press already.
> *Scarecrow.* Then, sir, I have another in defense of them.
> *Bookweight.* Sir, I never take anything in defense of power.[34]

Baker calls this the "first open slur Fielding ever made at the Walpole ministry," but it is difficult to see how such conventional ridicule of party writing of any kind can be construed as a slur on the government. As for Baker's suggestion that Punch is Walpole or that the marital battle between Punch and Joan is symbolic of Walpole's troubles with his wife, Charles Woods is surely correct when he points out that "there seems to be little political satire in the 1730 text, and if Professor Baker's line of reasoning were followed, every stage production of the Walpole era that presented Punch and Joan or Harlequin would be politically suspect."[35]

On the other hand, *The Author's Farce* does contain a cynical song (Air VIII) with the refrain "When you cry he is rich, you cry a great man," an unmistakable jibe at the Great Man even if pointless in context. And it does attack some of the literary figures whom the opposition press loved to ridicule: Cibber (here again called "Keyber"), Curll, Orator Henley, Samuel Johnson of Cheshire and his *Hurlothrumbo,* and other such sons of dullness. Though Baker does not comment on it, I think Witmore's speech decrying the state of letters may have more political significance than most of the passages allegedly containing personal satire:

In an age of learning and true politeness, where a man might succeed by his merit, it would be an encouragement. But now, when party and prejudice carry all before them, when learning is decried, wit not understood, when the theaters are puppet shows and the comedians ballad singers, when fools lead the town, would a man think to thrive by his wit? If you must write, write nonsense, write operas, write entertainments, write *Hurlothrumbos,* set up an *Oratory* and preach nonsense,

and you may meet with encouragement enough. If you would receive
applause, deserve to receive sentence at the Old Bailey; and if you
would ride in your coach, deserve to ride in a cart. (I.v)

This passage could have come from *Fog's* or any other opposition journal. Though ridicule of people like Henley and Cibber
was by no means restricted to opposition writers, the parallel
between the state of letters and the state of politics had obviously
been exploited by Fielding to vilify Pope and Swift in the
burlesque cantos of 1729, and it may also have been in his mind
in constructing this play; here, however, the realm of dullness
and its constituency are in accord with those described by the
Scriblerians themselves. Even though we must reject the view
that *The Author's Farce* contains personal satire on Walpole and
accept Woods's conclusion that the play is "generally non-politi-
cal," we should realize that Fielding's *literary* satire here was
similar to that exploited by opposition propaganda and would
not have been displeasing to an anti-Walpole audience.

Even more innocent of political innuendo, I think, is Fielding's second play at the Haymarket, *Tom Thumb*, which may be
considered together with its revision a year later as *The Tragedy of
Tragedies*. Once again, though, some critics have found it full of
suspicious details. One recent editor, for instance, suggests that
Huncamunca's gross appetite and her "pouting Breasts" may be
satiric cuts at the corpulent princess royal, Anne. When the King
in *The Tragedy of Tragedies* welcomes Tom with the line, "What
Gratitude can thank away the Debt,/ Your Valour lays upon
me?" (I.iii) the same editor, with the zeal of a Walpole agent,
claims the word *Debt* "probably referred to Sir Robert Walpole's
handling of public funds."[36] By this critical method, of course,
any single word in the text can be juggled to refer to some aspect
of the prime minister or the royal family. More interesting than
this kind of overreading of specific details is the generalized
interpretation of Tom Thumb the Great as the Great Man,
Walpole, cut down to size. Such an interpretation is appealing,
but by the same token Lord Grizzle, described in the dramatis
personae as "Extremely zealous for the Liberty of the Subject,"
and Foodle, "A Courtier that is out of Place, and consequently of
that Party that is undermost," can be said to ridicule the
opposition and to do so in a fairly damaging way, since these
characters incite rebellion in the course of the play.

Cross, who believed the play reduced the prime minister to pygmy size, credits the subtlety of the satire with warding off government interference: "No one could quite say that Tom Thumb was intended for Walpole, so perfect is the irony."[37] Indeed, so perfect is the irony that it has escaped detection until the twentieth century, for in the 1730s the ridiculous figure Tom merely seemed to cut down to pygmy size the heroes of pretentious tragedies. Even a sophisticated politician like John Perceval, first earl of Egmont, failed to note any hint of political satire in either *Tom Thumb* or *The Author's Farce,* both of which he saw on 24 April 1730; his account of them refers only to their "ridicule on poets, and several of their works."[38] His diary, it might be added, is at this point full of rumors about the possibility of Walpole's fall from power, and he was hardly a man insensitive to political implications. Moreover, it has not been sufficiently emphasized that the opposition press, far from capitalizing on the popularity of a play satirizing the prime minister as it did with *The Beggar's Opera,* actually used *Tom Thumb* as evidence for the decay of literature in Walpole's England. Thus *Fog's* (1 August 1730) ironically cites Walpole's attendance three times at the play in a mock defense of Sir Robert's love of belles-lettres, and the *Craftsman* (22 August 1730) echoes this theme; neither takes the play as in any way satirical of the government or the prime minister, and both speak of it mockingly in the same vein as they do *Hurlothrumbo.* In response to this tack, one progovernment journal gives an ironic list of the trivial "crimes" the opposition had to dredge up against Walpole and includes this item: "That he subscrib'd for *Thirty Books* of *Hurlothrumbo* and was present *Three* several Nights at the Tragedy of *Tom Thumb.*"[39] Even three years later (10 March 1733) *Fog's* was still alluding to *Tom Thumb* as a supremely innocent and frivolous exercise. In the absence, then, of convincing political readings or supporting external evidence, it seems safest to take this delightful play at face value, lest we fall into that category of critics ridiculed by *Fog's* for taking even farces in dumb show as so many political satires.

There is a similar lack of contemporary comment about political implications in the third play of this period, *Rape upon Rape.* But here I think the problem is more complicated, for in this play Fielding expounds upon a serious social theme which is in some contrast to the burlesque frivolities of *Tom Thumb* and

The Author's Farce. And it is a theme then being given prominence by the opposition because of a contemporary scandal which itself lies in the background of the play. The title *Rape upon Rape* was soon changed to *The Coffee-House Politician,* and one might expect some political satire in the ramblings about specific contemporary events indulged in by the foolish father, Politic, who neglects his daughter while he reads his papers. But those scenes are completely innocent; the real satiric force of the play, as the Prologue forewarns us, is directed at the corrupters of justice, the "champions, whom the public arm/ For their own good with power" but who betray their trust. It has not, I think, been recognized that Fielding's general satire here arises from a particular case with political overtones, that of the notorious Francis Charteris, "Rapemaster General of Great Britain."

Charteris (or Chartres), whose name dots the pages of Swift and Pope, had been found guilty in February 1730 of a rape on his maidservant, had forfeited vast sums of his fortune, and had been committed to Newgate. In April 1730, however, just two months before Fielding's play, Charteris "received his Majesty's most gracious Pardon; the Merits of his Case being fully represented to his Majesty in Council by the Judges, who tried it at the *Old-Baily,* it appeared in such different Light from what the Jury were pleased to take it in, that there appeared very just Ground to soften the Rigour that was expected by the common People."[40] Indeed the common people did demand rigorous treatment of Charteris, and his pardon, though not unexpected, produced the usual complaints that robes and furred gowns hide all. "Does not Chartres misfortunes grieve you," wrote Gay to Swift just after the trial, "for that great man is like to save his life and lose some of his money, a very hard case!"[41] The *Political State of Great Britain* protested (without irony) that Charteris's burden was made heavier by satires, banter, and raillery, and many of these, of course, developed the theme that it is "more difficult to get a rich man hanged, than to save a poor fellow from the gallows."[42]

Given this atmosphere in the spring of 1730, I think there can be little doubt that audiences at the Haymarket in June would have immediately connected Fielding's *Rape upon Rape* with the Charteris affair. In its slightly misleading title, its preoccupation with the subject of rape, and especially in its attack on bribery and corruption in the administration of justice, the play seems hardly distinguishable from other comments on the case. Consider, for instance, this conversation between Justice Worthy and Isabella on the prevalence of rape:

> *Worthy.* Sure modesty is quite banished from the age we live in. There was a time when virtue carried something of a divine awe with it, which no one durst attack; but now the insolence of our youth is such, no woman dare walk the streets, but those who do it for bread.
> *Isabella.* And yet our laws, brother Worthy, are as rigorous as those of other countries, and as well executed.
> *Worthy.* That I wish they were; but golden sands too often clog the wheels of justice, and obstruct her course: the very riches, which were the greatest evidence of his villainy, have too often declared the guilty innocent; and gold hath been found to cut a halter surer than the sharpest steel.[43]

The satiric point is put in general terms, but surely no one could have missed its particular application to the most famous rape case of the day.

There may be more to this particular application than a mere allusion to a specific miscarriage of justice, for the Charteris case had decidedly political overtones. Charteris was, apparently, one of the "Runners" for Walpole, and it has been said that the frequent attacks upon him by Pope and Arbuthnot were politically motivated.[44] Swift called him "that continual favourite of Ministers" and in *Verses on the Death of Dr. Swift* depicted him "at Sir *Robert's* Levee" informing the prime minister of the Dean's death.[45] At any rate, the opposition certainly made political capital out of his pardon. In August 1730, the *Craftsman* called Sir Robert the "Friend, Confident, and Patron" of Charteris, and Pulteney forthrightly accused Walpole of having saved Charteris from the gallows.[46] A typical antigovernment ballad, "On Colonel Francisco Rape-Master General of Great Britain," made the same charge, with allusions both to Walpole and to his aide, Sir William Yonge:

> But when Verdict was past, he was down in the Dumps,
> And for Shifts and Excuses Sir *William* he pumps;
> Ay, and BOBBY the *Screen* too was put to his Trumps,
>   Which nobody can deny.[47]

Moreover, the parallels between Walpole and Charteris, both wealthy "great men," proved irresistible; Pulteney, a year after the pardon was issued, pointed to the similarity of their "characters and circumstances," and a government paper listed "Col. Charteris" as one of the names the prime minister was most frequently called by the *Craftsman*. The same parallel, of course, lies behind the ironic comment in Arbuthnot's famous epitaph of Charteris that the Colonel, even without trust of public money, had managed to acquire a "Ministerial Estate."[48] In 1731 the political exploitation of the Charteris case appeared on the stage when the crudely propagandistic play *The Fall of Mortimer* alluded to the incident. Mortimer, the Walpole figure, is told that "Sir Maiden Battery" awaits him; he remarks, "What does this Bullet headed Knight want now? I saved his Life but t'other Day, for which I had 20000 Marks—I hope 'tis in danger again." There follows a scene in which Sir Maiden again makes payment to Mortimer, who assures him, "You may depend upon me on the like, or any other occasion."[49]

Compared to such direct and obvious linkings of Walpole and Charteris, *Rape upon Rape* seems innocent enough. Yet in June 1730, while the case was still causing an uproar, a play with such a title and with the corrupt administration of justice as its theme might have appeared politically motivated. It should be noted that in *Rape upon Rape* the crime of rape is treated lightly and wittily; Fielding's satire is directed not at the rake, Ramble, but at the hypocritical justice, Squeezum. And the prologue points the way to a political interpretation of that satire. In Ancient Greece, Fielding tells us, "No grandeur could the mighty villain screen/ From the just satire of the comic scene:/ No titles could the daring poet cool,/ Nor save the great right honourable fool." But now, he says, vice has "grown too great to be abused;/ By power defended from the piercing dart." Satires are quashed; his Muse is "heroic" because it dares to attack the misapplication of public power:

> Vice, clothed with power, she combats with her pen,
> And, fearless, dares the lion in his den.
> Then only reverence to power is due,
> When public welfare is its only view:
> But when the champions, whom the public arm

> For their own good with power, attempt their harm,
> He sure must meet the general applause,
> Who 'gainst those traitors fights the public cause.[50]

The use of words and phrases like "screen" (always associated with Walpole in this period) and "Vice, clothed with power" suggests a dramatic intention that may go beyond general ridicule of hypocritical justices of the peace. Indeed, the prologue's promise of bold satire and artistic courage seems almost irrelevant if the play is taken at face value. But in the context of opposition propaganda in 1730, especially its exploitation of the Charteris case, a line like "he is the greatest of villains, who hath the impudence to hold the sword of justice while he deserves its edge" might seem bold enough.[51]

To some extent, too, an attack on corrupt justices, even if taken literally, suited the needs of the anti-Walpole faction. In *The Fall of Mortimer*, for instance, the group of patriots protest that magistrates and other officers of the law are only the "creatures" of Mortimer; and in 1732 the *Craftsman* (5 August) echoed the charge when it called for some of the "modern Farce-writers" to divert the town with the "Humours of a *Mock-Magistrate* and his *Clerk*," adding "When *Men in Office* are thus suffer'd to make a *Trade* of their *Duty*, They will be oblig'd, in Return, to become the *Tools* of a *Minister*, whose Creatures They are, by making use of their Authority to influence *Elections*, or carry on any other *dirty Job*, which his Service requires." Perhaps, then, Fielding has gone beyond the incorporation into his play of a common complaint about life under Walpole, for corrupt administration of justice may also be taken as a metaphorical representation of the corrupt administration of all the functions of government. At one point Justice Squeezum asserts that the "makers of laws," as well as the executors of them, should be "free of them; as authors and actors are free of the play-house," and the Prologue, as has been indicated, speaks of "power" in general rather than justices of the peace in particular.

On the other hand, the play can be taken simply as an attack on the perversion of justice, the theme of so many of Fielding's later works. Despite the opposition's exploitation of the Charteris case, there is obviously no way to prove that Fielding intended to merge his general social theme with an attack on the administration, nor is there any evidence that the play was so regarded at the time. The most that can be said, I think, is that this play, like *The Author's Farce,* suited the needs of the opposition without indulging in obvious personal satire of Walpole and without forcing upon its author a political commitment he was not ready to make.[52]

After *Rape upon Rape,* Fielding's activities are obscure until March of 1731, when he produced *The Tragedy of Tragedies* and *The Letter Writers,* a play unsuccessful at the time and free of any hint of politics. But in April came *The Welsh Opera,* of which the very substance was politics and scandal. For the first time Fielding unambiguously jeered at politicians and court figures, reducing them to the level of a Welsh family with its domestic squabbles. As many scholars have pointed out, the allegorical characters of *The Welsh Opera* were easily identifiable: Squire Apshinken and his wife as George II and Caroline, Master Owen as the Prince of Wales, Robin the butler as Walpole, Sweetissa as Molly Skerrit (Walpole's mistress), William the groom as Pulteney, and so on.[53] Begun as an afterpiece, *The Welsh Opera* was so successful that its performance was abandoned while Fielding revised it as a full-length piece, *The Grub-Street Opera.* This new play, in turn, was first scheduled for 11 June, then postponed for a few days, and then deferred until further notice. As far as is known, it was never performed.[54]

Though *The Grub-Street Opera* was not literally suppressed by the government, as is sometimes said, there can be little doubt that it was dropped because of the "prevailing influence" spoken of in the preface to the first printed edition of *The Welsh Opera,* an edition not authorized by Fielding. The spring and summer of 1731 were not healthy times for plays with political themes, and no doubt the fact that *The Welsh Opera* was produced as an afterpiece to *The Fall of Mortimer* with its scathing attack on Walpole helped bring it into disfavor. The government seemed determined to bring an end to the company acting *The Fall of Mortimer,* and after *The Grub-Street Opera* was withdrawn constables arrested the actor playing Mortimer along with other performers. A few weeks later a performance of *Hurlothrumbo* was broken up because the company had refused to close up shop.[55] Amidst all this hubbub Fielding's good-natured satire made a very slight noise indeed. Neither *The Welsh Opera* nor its promised revision was mentioned in all the furor in the press over these incidents, nor did the pamphlet warfare which raged over *The Fall of Mortimer* take any notice of Fielding.[56] And unlike *The Fall of Mortimer* and other anti-Walpole works, his plays are not included in the list of "false and scandalous Representations" by "State-Incendiaries" drawn up by the grand jury of Middlesex in July.[57]

Indeed, compared to such works *The Grub-Street Opera* is innocence itself, and it is absurd to speak of it as "violently pro-opposition."[58] Its most recent editor suggests that it was probably the scandalous satire on the royal family rather than the hits at the prime minister which caused the government to put pressure on the play.[59] Moreover, though Walpole and the royal family bear the brunt of the satire, Pulteney and the opposition are also laughed at; and in a world where "down from the beggar, up to the great man/ Each gentleman cheats you no more than he can," Walpole comes off worse than other politicians only as a result of his superior position. As Puzzletext says, "If Robin the butler hath cheated more than other people, I see no other reason for it, but because he hath had more opportunity to cheat" (III.xiv). And so, in the words of Air LX, they are "rogues all" and "Bobs all," and one's final impression of the play is more that of political cynicism than political commitment.

What, then, may be concluded about Fielding's relations with Walpole in 1730–31? Though obviously more daring than any of the previous plays, *The Welsh Opera* and *The Grub-Street Opera* still did not link Fielding with any political group and need not be considered hopelessly inconsistent with the bantering epistle Fielding addressed to Walpole in 1731, though they are certainly inconsistent with the eulogy of the minister in the cantos of 1729. None of the plays before *The Welsh Opera* show more than the mildest satire of the government, if even that, and Fielding did not develop the reputation of a writer hostile to Walpole. He was out to amuse the town; he did so in a way occasionally pleasing to the opposition while at the same time making occasional bids for Sir Robert's patronage. *The Welsh Opera*, after all, appeared in the same month as Theobald's *Orestes*, with its dedication to Walpole and its epilogue by Fielding. But others had been less discreet, the stage was coming under closer scrutiny from the government, the company at the Haymarket was breaking up, and Fielding apparently became alarmed. Edgar Roberts speaks of Fielding's strange silence after the withdrawal of *The Grub-Street Opera* when one might have expected him to capitalize on the "suppression" as Gay had done with *Polly*. Roberts concludes that Fielding "saw his best interest in ending the play's life and in concealing or obscuring his reasons for doing so."[60] Instead, his best interests led him to arrange by December of 1731 for his plays to be performed at the "establishment" Theatre-Royal at Drury Lane. There, in short order, he wrote the epilogue for *The Modish Couple,* a play damned by politically biased audiences for its association with the court, and in the following month (February 1732) dedicated *The Modern Husband* to Sir Robert Walpole.

The dedication to Walpole, which some have seen as ironic, is a conventional request for the minister to act as the protector of literature; its praise is typical of such dedications and is close in thought to the dedication Theobald had just published with *Orestes*.[61] Fielding calls on Walpole to protect "an Art from which You may promise Your self such notable Advantages; when the little Artifices of Your Enemies, which You have surmounted, shall be forgotten, when Envy shall cease to misrepresent Your Actions, and Ignorance to misapprehend them."[62] Given the circumstances leading up to Fielding's change of theaters and given the language of the dedication itself, there is not the slightest reason to suspect irony here unless we are so intent on showing a political consistency or growing political involvement on Fielding's part from 1730 to 1737 that we ignore all evidence to the contrary. It is worth noting that a few months after *The Modern Husband,* the progovernment *Daily Courant* issued a warning to all anti-Walpole playwrights but excepted the players at Drury Lane, who, it says, have performed with great decency. As John Loftis reminds us, Fielding's shift to Drury Lane means that his dedication to Walpole represented a sincere bid for patronage.[63]

Whether Walpole's patronage was bestowed in tangible form despite the barbs of *The Welsh Opera* is not known, but two later attacks on Fielding's political trimming do seem to have reference to this period of his life. The *Historical View of the Political Writers in Great Britain* (London, 1740) speaks of Walpole giving money to Fielding despite Fielding's authorship of a libelous satire, and the events discussed are said to have occurred *before* Fielding "set up for a Play-Writer" (p. 50). More significant is an attack in the anti-Pelhamite journal *Old England* (1749). This essayist gives a summary in conditional mode of Fielding's career as a mercenary writer, with one passage perhaps relevant to the events of 1731–32:

> If there be such a Wretch, who, having wrote a Farce of personal Ridicule against a Minister and all his Family, finds Means to insinuate to them, by the Canal of a credulous Agent, that the dirty Work being extorted from him by griping Want and Penury, he was desirous to, and afterwards actually did, suppress it for a small Consideration of *Relief;* and if, after he had run thro' his Subsidy with an Extravagance of Voracity, he should threaten to revive the abusive Scenes of Scurrility, unless he was purchased a second Time into Silence . . . .[64]

Since the only "farce" by Fielding we know which both ridicules Walpole's personal life and was voluntarily suppressed is *The Grub-Street Opera*, it seems reasonable to nominate it for the play in question. These passages are far from conclusive. But the fact remains that, whether he was bought off or was simply cautious, in the move to Drury Lane, the dedication to *The Modern Husband,* and the epilogue to *The Modish Couple* Fielding unmistakably and publicly aligned himself with the Walpole camp.

This move brought upon him the wrath of the *Grub-street Journal;* almost immediately that most urbane of newspapers unleashed an attack on the playwright which continued almost unabated for some three months. As both Wilbur Cross and John Loftis have pointed out, the motivation for the attack was surely political.[65] The *Journal*'s bias against both Walpole and Drury Lane made an obvious target of Fielding, whose earlier plays the "Grubs" had ignored. It is thus, in Loftis's words, "scarcely coincidence that this hostility coincided with Fielding's bid for Walpole's patronage."[66] In fact, I think, the case could be put much more strongly. In the course of its attack on Fielding, the *Journal* took care both to link *The Modern Husband* with *The Modish Couple* and to speak insinuatingly of the "tyrannical" imposition of bad plays on the town (22 July 1732). Moreover, Fielding was defended by Thomas Cooke in the *Comedian*, a periodical which intermingled comment on the stage with praise of Walpole and defense of his policies; the ensuing quarrel between the *Grub-street Journal* and the *Comedian* may have been based as much on political association as on any real disagreement about the merit of Fielding's play. The only obstacle in the way of a political interpretation of this critical dispute has been the identification of "Dramaticus" (the *Journal* writer who took the lead in the attack on Fielding) as Sir William Yonge, a Commissioner of the Treasury and an invaluable henchman of Walpole; but that identification, as I have shown elsewhere, is incorrect.[67]

Fielding himself, I think, hints in his next play at the political motivation of the *Journal*'s critical assault: his "prolegomena" to the printed version of *The Covent Garden Tragedy* first links the *Journal* with the *Craftsman*, the leading paper of the opposition, and then puts in the mouth of a typical *Grub-street Journal* critic the following complaint:

> The first five Lines are a mighty pretty Satyr on our Age, our Country, Statesmen, Lawyers, and Physicians: What did I not expect from such a Beginning? But alas! what follows? No fine Moral Sentences, not a Word of Liberty and Property, no Insinuations, that Courtiers are Fools, and Statesmen Rogues.[68]

All these themes—the praise of general satire, the speeches upon liberty, and the attack on statesmen and courtiers—are, of course, commonplaces of opposition propaganda; *Liberty and Property*, in fact, was the title of a volume published that year by Eustace Budgell, who by this time was a laughingstock of the progovernment press. That Fielding should insert such a speech in a piece of criticism which he labels "originally intended for the *Grub-street Journal*" clearly reveals his belief that the *Journal*'s criticism of him was more political than literary.

For the next few years Fielding produced his plays at Drury Lane and kept his work free from politics. In 1734, for whatever reason, he revised *The Author's Farce* in a way which permitted a few satiric hits at Walpole.[69] In April of that year, as I will explain in the next chapter, his return to the Haymarket with

Don Quixote in England signaled a move toward the opposition as clearly as his earlier change of theaters and dedication to Walpole had signaled a move toward the court party.[70]
  I have considered this portion of Fielding's life and works in perhaps burdensome detail, but I think that when all the pieces of the puzzle are assembled—the cantos, the ambiguous plays, the poetic epistles, the epilogues and dedication, the later rumors of ministerial favors—the picture which emerges is illustrative of the real relations between politics and literature in this period. It is not a portrait of a writer gradually but consistently moving toward a set of firm political principles, still less of an ideologue burning with conviction and defying the forces of power and corruption, but of a popular playwright cautiously seeking his advantage wherever it lay. He could not avoid politics, any more than could other literary figures of his time; his problem, then, was to please a portion of his audience hostile to the government without burning his bridges to the sources of power. When his first attempt at open political satire brought difficulties for him, he retreated quickly to the company of Colley Cibber at Drury Lane and, perhaps, to the patronage of Robert Walpole. Both his predicament and his response are humanly though not ideologically understandable, and we may so regard them while indulging in neither the accusations of some of his later enemies nor the apologetics of some of his later admirers.

Swift's Final Poems

  While Fielding spent the opening years of the decade first in political tergiversation and then in political silence, the older group of wits, the Scriblerians, continued their loose confederation with the leaders of the opposition. Swift, in Ireland, wrote optimistically to Gay of his comfort at seeing patriots of all denominations, Whig and Tory, high church and low, united by a common dismay at the corruption of the government. And he added, "If this be disaffection, pray God send me allways among the disaffected."[71] His contributions to the cause of the disaffected were by this time limited almost completely to poems,

though some of these came closer to bringing him into difficulty
with the authorities than *Gulliver's Travels* ever had. His bitter
attack on Walpole in *A Libel on Dr. Delaney and a Certain Great
Lord,* for example, almost provoked the government to action
and was attacked in the progovernment *Daily Journal.*[72] The
attitude with which those close to the court regarded the great
satirist at this time may be measured by this comment from Lord
Hervey on some unnamed piece by Swift:

> Whatever one may think or venture to say in private company, sure
> no man ought to be suffered to write and print a ridicule upon the
> established religion or an invective against the established Government
> of any society of which he is a member, and under whose protection he
> lives in ease, affluence and liberty. The inclosed, and the *Tale of a Tub*
> are indisputably written with a vast deal of spirit and vivacity; but I
> think he deserves to be hanged for one, and to have his gown pulled
> over his ears for t'other.[73]

Hervey's distinction between private thought and public utterance is one which Swift himself would have drawn in different
circumstances, but he nonetheless continued to maul the established government in both letters and poems throughout the
early 1730s. In his correspondence in these years Swift speaks
contemptuously of an England governed for twelve years by a
dunce, congratulates Pulteney on defeating the excise bill, and
maintains his close friendship with Bolingbroke. His continuing
hostility to Walpole is revealed also in several poems written in
the period 1730–34 but not published until later. In *To Mr. Gay
on his being Steward to the Duke of Queensberry,* for instance, Swift
again blames "Bob, the Poet's Foe" for having humiliated Gay by
offering him an unworthy post at court, and the poem then
develops an ironic contrast between Gay's position as steward of
the duke's accounts (a position he did not in fact have) and
Walpole's management of the nation. The attack is in terms
made familiar by the *Craftsman* but used more openly and
bitterly than even that paper ordinarily dared to do: Walpole is a
bloated monster, an avaricious steward enriching himself at the
expense of his master, a corrupt state-physician, and a highly
placed version of the notorious moneylender, Peter Walter. The
final verses recount the uncertainty about Walpole's future at

the time of the succession of George II, and here again we find
Swift ringing changes on the conventions of opposition propa-
ganda, from the epithet "brazen" to the pun on "Robbing" and
"Robin":

> I KNEW a *brazen* Minister of State,
> Who bore for twice ten Years the publick Hate.
> In every Mouth the Question most in Vogue
> Was, *When will* THEY *turn out this odious Rogue?*
> A Juncture happen'd in his highest Pride:
> While HE went robbing on; *old Master* dy'd.
> We thought, there now remain'd no room to doubt:
> *His Work is done, the Minister must out.*
> The Court *invited* more than One, or Two;
> Will you, Sir *Sp*[ence]*r*? or, will *you*, or *you*?
> But, not a Soul his Office durst accept:
> The subtle Knave had all the Plunder swept.
> And, such was then the Temper of the Times,
> He ow'd his Preservation to his Crimes.[74]

The same strain of invective appears in Swift's poem congratulating Pulteney for having been struck off the list of privy
councilors (1731) and in his vicious "Character of Sir Robert
Walpole," the "Cur dog of Brittain & spaniel of Spain." The
famous *Verses on the Death of Dr. Swift* (1731) is less openly
political, but the ethos created is unmistakably hostile to the
government and the court; Swift takes occasion to celebrate not
only himself but Bolingbroke and Pulteney, and to ridicule the
"Fools with Stars and Garters,/ So often seen caressing *Chartres*."
When a country squire asks Lintot for the works of Swift, he
finds in their place only the fruits of Walpole's patronage:
Cibber's birthday poems, Duck's odes upon the queen, pamphlets against the *Craftsman*, vindications of Sir Robert, orations by
Henley, and free-thinking tracts of the kind most favored by
court ladies. The satire is less directly political, but Swift's
version of the Walpolean literary pantheon is the same as that in
countless pieces of opposition propaganda.

This set of poems had no immediate political impact, for the
verses addressed to Gay and to Pulteney did not appear in print
until 1735 and the *Verses on the Death of Dr. Swift* awaited publication until 1739, when it was printed first in a version which

eliminated most of the politically dangerous material.[75] Though
it has been thought that Swift's "Character" of Walpole was not
published in his lifetime, it was in fact printed in 1739 in an issue
of the antiministerial journal *Common Sense* (14 April), but
without Swift's name attached in any way; the "Character" also
seems to have circulated in the court circle in 1731, though again
apparently without being attributed to Swift.[76] In 1733, however, two of Swift's most impressive attacks on the administration, *Epistle to a Lady* and *On Poetry: A Rapsody*, received immediate publication in London, and the government took immediate
action. Printers and publishers were arrested, as was Mrs.
Barber, who had brought the manuscript over from Dublin.
According to Sheridan's *Life of Swift*, Walpole ordered a warrant
for Swift's arrest but withdrew it upon being told an army would
be required to arrest Swift in Ireland.[77] Although those arrested
were eventually released without being brought to trial, these
two poems must have been offensive indeed to officers of the
government, and they help explain why Swift continued to be an
occasional target of the prominsterial press.[78]

  The *Epistle to a Lady* begins innocently enough, as the poet
banters with a lady who had asked him to write verses about her
in heroic style. But as Swift explains his refusal to ascend to the
sublime, the banter gives way to an assault on king and minister,
and in the second half of the epistle the lady is left far behind.
His proper mode, the poet says, is to smile while lashing, to
scorn rather than hate evil ministers, and to laugh at the vices of
a court: "Shou'd a Monkey wear a Crown,/ Must I tremble at his
Frown?" The spectacle of Walpole's enriching himself while
wrecking the ship of state merely makes him merry. Let D'Anvers, Pulteney, and Bolingbroke scourge the villains; his own
task will be merely to expose them:

> Let me, tho' the Smell be Noisom,
> Strip their Bums; Let CALEB hoyse 'em;
> Then, apply ALECTO's Whip,
> Till they wriggle, howl, and skip.
> (Lines 176–80)

In a fit of passion the poet proclaims himself dispassionate and
celebrates the value of raillery over railing, sneering over

scolding. So the lady cannot hope to escape his satire, since those
in higher places have had to suffer it:

> Can you put in higher Claims,
> Than the Owners of *St. J*[ame]*s.*
> You are not so great a Grievance
> As the Hirelings of *St. St*[ephen]*s.*
> You are of a lower Class
> Than my Friend Sir *R*[obert] *Br*[as]*s.*
> None of these have Mercy found:
> I have laugh'd, and lash'd them round.
> (Lines 241–48)

The poem concludes with a return to its ostensible subject, levels
of poetic style, but neither the government nor anyone else
could have felt that literary theory was primary in Swift's mind
here.

On Poetry: A Rapsody, like the *Epistle to a Lady,* makes its
political attack under the guise of discussing literary matters, but
here the presumed subject is itself that favorite theme of opposition propaganda, the state of letters under the regime of Robert
Walpole. In such a world poets can expect no preferment, the
opening lines tell us; even beggars and pedlars are better qualified by fate to rise in church or law or politics. But if one persists
in a poetic career, the only hope for success is to dismiss all
thoughts of fame and sell one's meager talents to those in power:

> The vilest Verse thrives best at Court.
> A Pamphlet in Sir *Rob*'s Defence
> Will never fail to bring in Pence;
> Nor be concern'd about the Sale,
> He pays his Workmen on the Nail.
> (Lines 186–90)

But the aspiring poet must heap his praises only on living kings,
for dead ones are forgotten or castigated. Here Swift pauses
momentarily to portray a dead monarch and his ministers, still
scheming and bribing in the midst of hell; the lines brilliantly
juxtapose the somber personages of the classical underworld
with the grubby trappings of Walpole's administration:

And lo, his Ministers of State,
Transform'd to Imps, his Levee wait.
Where, in this Scene of endless Woe,
They ply their former Arts below.
And as they sail in *Charon's* boat,
Contrive to bribe the Judge's Vote.
To *Cerberus* they give a Sop,
His triple-barking Mouth to Stop;
Or in the Iv'ry Gate of Dreams,
Project [Excise] and [South-Sea Schemes]:
Or hire their Party-Pamphleteers,
To set *Elysium* by the Ears.
(Lines 207–18)

The poem's extraordinary strength derives not from occasional sallies at political schemes like the general excise but from the persistent depiction of the intellectual and literary decay of Walpole's world, where Smithfield drolls or Punch's booth or the bards of Wapping and Kentish Town are the true recipients of poetic fame. And, as in *The Dunciad,* the Smithfield muses assault the ears of kings:

Harmonious *Cibber* entertains
The Court with annual Birth-day Strains;
Whence *Gay* was banish'd in Disgrace,
Where *Pope* will never show his Face;
Where *Y*[oung] must torture his Invention,
To flatter *Knaves,* or lose his *Pension.*
(Lines 304–9)

In the final section of *On Poetry,* the political theme reaches a climax as Swift presents a sarcastic "model" eulogy of George II, Caroline, and the "Remnant of the Royal Blood." His account of this "Constellation" concludes, unsurprisingly, with an ironic rhapsody on the virtues of Robert Walpole:

Now sing the *Minister* of *State,*
Who shines alone, without a Mate.
Observe with what majestick Port
This *Atlas* stands to prop the Court:
Intent the Publick Debts to pay,
Like prudent *Fabius* by *Delay.*

> Thou great Viceregent of the King,
> Thy Praises ev'ry Muse shall sing.
> In all Affairs thou sole Director,
> Of Wit and Learning chief Protector;
> Tho' small the Time thou hast to spare,
> The Church is thy peculiar Care.
> Of pious Prelates what a Stock
> You chuse to rule the Sable-flock.
> You raise the Honour of the Peerage,
> Proud to attend you at the Steerage.
> You dignify the noble Race,
> Content yourself with humbler Place.
> Now Learning, Valour, Virtue, Sense,
> To Titles give the sole Pretence.
> *St. George* beheld thee with Delight,
> Vouchsafe to be an azure Knight,
> When on thy Breast and Sides *Herculean,*
> He fixt the *Star* and *String Cerulean.*
> (Lines 441–64)

In the guise of praise, these lines systematically enumerate the conventional topics of ridicule on Walpole: his marital difficulties, his obesity, his sinking fund for retiring the public debt, his contempt for wit and learning, his indifference to the church, and his habit of promoting the unworthy; it is for all these, the conclusion seems to say, that he was awarded the Order of the Garter. The quality of irony in this poem is unsurpassed anywhere else in Swift's verse, and it is only slightly astonishing to hear from Dr. William King that after its publication Swift received the thanks of the royal family. King then remarks, "This I can easily conceive, as irony is not a figure in the German Rhetoric. . . . The Rhapsody would probably have continued to Dr. Swift the favour which it had acquired him, if Lord Harvey had not undeceived Q.C. and taken some pains to teach her the use and power of the irony."[79] In order of composition, *On Poetry* stands as his last significant poem; as Pope was later to do in the final book of *The Dunciad,* he completes his poetic career with a vision of the supremacy of the inferior and the advancement of the unworthy, a vision in which the double themes of literary decay and political corruption are inescapably intertwined.

Pope's Deepening Commitment

The circle of Swift and Pope was saddened by the death of Gay in 1732. Shortly before his death Pope advised him to write verses flattering Queen Caroline on the occasion of her Royal Hermitage, adding that "one should not bear in mind all one's life, any little indignity one receives from a Court." But Gay replied, in the last letter we have from him, in a manner worthy of the author of *The Beggar's Opera:*

As to your advice about writing Panegyric, 'tis what I have not frequently done. I have indeed done it sometimes against my judgment and inclination, and I heartily repent of it. And at present as I have no desire of reward, and see no just reason of praise, I think I had better let it alone. There are flatterers good enough to be found, and I wou'd not interfere in any Gentleman's profession. I have seen no verse upon these sublime occasions, so that I have no emulation. Let the patrons enjoy the authors and the authors their patrons, for I know myself unworthy.[80]

The court which Gay in his last months refused to flatter paid him no more attention dead than it had paid him alive. His death, however, created a stir in the literary world accompanied, as one contemporary account has it, by "some shrewd Hints aimed at the Superiors, for not regarding the Merit of so valuable a Person." When his opera *Achilles* was performed posthumously in 1733, a letter in the progovernment *Daily Courant* attacked it severely, accusing it rather absurdly of containing political allegory and chastising the Scriblerians as a "*Motley* Committee of *Half-Politicians* and *Half-Wits.*"[81] But the flurry over *Achilles* was only a gesture, for the opera was innocent of political overtones; Gay's final fling at the government was to come six years after his death with the publication of the second volume of his *Fables.*

We should not be surprised to find Pope advising Gay to try once more to ingratiate himself with the court, for at the opening of the decade Pope was still attempting to maintain friendships on both sides, despite the political overtones of *The Dunciad.* In 1730, for instance, he was embarrassed by Swift's description of him in *A Libel on Dr. Delany* as too greathearted "to lick a *Rascal Statesman*'s Spittle." Sherburn points out that when

the poem appeared, Pope, through the influence of the Burling-
tons, was on better terms with the court than at any time in his
career, and he wrote at once to Fortescue, his main link with
Walpole, to disclaim the import of Swift's lines:

> I've had another Vexation, from the sight of a paper of verses said to
> be Dr Swift's, which has done more by praising me than all the Libels
> could by abusing me, Seriously troubled me: As indeed one indiscreet
> Friend can at any time hurt a man more than a hundred silly Enemies.
> I can hardly bring myself to think it His, or that it is possible his Head
> should be so giddy.

To Swift, of course, Pope expressed himself very differently. A
few months later we find Bathurst gently chiding Pope for being
too busy at court to write a "Poor Country Gentleman" and Pope
excusing himself to Gay for his attendance at court. In 1732
Pope can still claim to Swift that he has no taste or talent for
politics, though the world minds nothing else: "I have personal
obligations which I will ever preserve, to men of different
sides."[82]

But even by the time that letter was written Pope had already
been drawn into politics. In the exacerbated political atmosphere of the 1730s the pose of impartial littérateur became as
untenable for Pope as it had been in 1713, and by the middle of
the decade he was established in the eyes of the public as a writer
firmly in the camp of the opposition. Not that the public could
ever have had much doubt about Pope: his intimacy with
Atterbury, at whose trial he had testified; his friendship with
Swift, Gay, Arbuthnot, Bathurst, and Pulteney; his ridicule of
government hack writers in *The Dunciad*; his connection (as it
was thought) with the *Grub-street Journal*; and above all his
closeness to Bolingbroke—all these had already caused Pope
long ago to be identified with the "disaffected wits" opposed to
Walpole and the court. When Burlington, Cobham, and Chesterfield went into the opposition as a result of the excise affair of
1733, Pope's natural loyalties were reinforced; and his personal
feud with the court wits Lord Hervey and Lady Mary had
inescapable political overtones. It may well be, as Maynard Mack
has argued, that Pope and Walpole approached the world with
such fundamentally different values that they were destined

almost inevitably to be "mighty opposites"; but it was surely the
fact that Pope's "personal obligations" were predominantly to
men of *one* side only that led him into warfare, at first covert but
eventually open, with Sir Robert's administration.[83] He could
not have been insensible, either, to the claims Pulteney kept
making that all men of wit were joined together against the
ministry or to the fact that, as Mack points out, the methods of
opposition propaganda—innuendo, allusion, catch-words, epithets, and the like—consituted a satirical instrument made to
order for his verse.[84] In his poems of the early thirties Pope
increasingly turned this instrument against the government, and
it is worth tracing briefly how he slowly began to gain the reputation of a participant in the party broils he had sought to avoid.

As I have indicated, Pope's name was drawn into the disputes
of the political papers in 1730, when Welsted's satire *One Epistle
to Mr. A. Pope* included an attack on Bishop Atterbury in a way
that would give point to the line, "And Wit's made Treason by
the *Popian* Law." Letters to two successive issues of *Fog's* protested the gratuitous insult to the exiled bishop, arguing that no
good can come to the author from "turning a poetical Controversy into a Party one" since Walpole "knows the Value of Places
and Pensions too well to part with them for a *Song*."[85] But
poetical controversies had a habit of turning into party ones
when Pope or Swift was involved, and Pope's efforts to remain
apolitical were not helped when *Fog's* printed a poem called
Dawley Farm in its issue for 26 June 1731; this poem, eulogizing
Bolingbroke and the "sweet Recess" of his country estate, was
attributed to Pope by at least one government hack and was
violently attacked in an "answer" in the *Gentleman's Magazine*.[86]

The publication in December 1731 of Pope's *Epistle to Burlington* also created a furor with some political overtones. The
portrait of Timon in that poem as the embodiment of wealthy
bad taste was widely identified as representing the duke of
Chandos, a friend of Burlington's, and Pope was enraged to find
himself accused of ingratitude. Kathleen Mahaffey and Maynard Mack have argued at length that Pope in fact intended
Timon and his villa to represent Sir Robert Walpole and his
sumptuous Norfolk estate Houghton Hall. It was Walpole's
agents, they believe, who deflected the impact of the satire by
spreading the report that Pope was maliciously attacking Chan-

dos.[87] Though the points of similarity they note between Timon's villa and Houghton are not, I think, compellingly convincing, there can be no doubt that Pope himself attributed his difficulties over the *Epistle* to figures associated with the government party. In *A Master Key to Popery,* a prose satire on his critics which remained unpublished, he ironically rehearses the interpretations of the poem held by such court wits and ministerial hacks as Lord Hervey, Lady Mary, Bubb Dodington, Leonard Welsted, Matthew Concanen, Colley Cibber, and Sir William Yonge. Though most of these perversely insist that Timon must be identified with Chandos, the supposed "author" of the *Master Key* has doubts; Pope, he says, may be attacking a man in power, for he has already been severely satirized for "adhering to some Folks in their Exile, to some in their disgrace, & others in their Imprisonment" (i.e., Atterbury, Harley, and Bolingbroke). Sir William Sweet-Lips (Yonge) then is credited with the view that Timon represents Walpole, citing as his chief arguments that it would suit Pope's impudence to abuse a place he'd never seen (Houghton) and that "unless Sir Robert be abus'd here, he is not abus'd in the whole Poem, a thing which he thinks altogether Incredible."[88]

Even if one does not go so far as Mahaffey and read this *Master Key* as Pope's effort to point the Timon sketch back in the direction he had intended all along, it is at least evidence that Pope saw the handiwork of Walpole's forces in the embarrassment which the poem caused him. Bolingbroke, too, seemed inclined to that view: "By the authority that employed itself to encourage this clamor, and by the industry used to spread and support it, one would have thought that you had directed your satire in that epistle to political subjects, and had inveighed against those who impoverish, dishonor, and sell their country, instead of making yourself inoffensively merry at the expence of men who ruin none but themselves."[89] There was thus a political twist to the brouhaha over the *Epistle,* but the political element was kept behind the scenes. One published "key" to the poem (*A Miscellany of Taste*) did find Walpole attacked therein (though as Sir Shylock rather than as Timon), but otherwise the journals and pamphlets ignored the possibilities of the Timon portrait. As accustomed as opposition papers were to complaining of Walpole's ill-got wealth and the extravagance of his life at

Houghton, none of them turned the poem to their own uses whether Pope originally intended to satirize Walpole as Timon or not. If Mack is correct in seeing the *Epistle to Burlington* as Pope's declaration of war on Walpole, the opening shot of that war seems to have escaped the notice of the troops already engaged in battle—a fact not surprising in the case of the government papers, in view of the strategy which Mack ascribes to them, but less easy to understand in the case of *Fog's* and the *Craftsman*. But to such organs of opposition propaganda Pope's poem might have seemed innocuous in contrast, say, to *Verres and his Scribblers* (February 1732), an anonymous mock heroic with overtones of *The Dunciad* ridiculing Walpole's army of journalists and depicting in apocalyptic terms the triumph of moral and political corruption; to puffing that poem, *Fog's* gave over its whole leader in its issue of 26 February 1732. As far as the town at large was concerned, then, the *cause célèbre* created by the *Epistle to Burlington* was more literary than political.

Pope's *Epistle to Bathurst* (January 1733) makes no direct allusion to Walpole, but again the climate of the poem is similar to that of opposition propaganda. Probably no satire of this time directed at the corrupting power of money or exposing bribery and financial skulduggery in high places could be considered politically innocent. When Pope says of Sir Balaam, "In Britain's senate he a seat obtains,/ and one more Pensioner St. Stephen gains," or when he ironically praises "Paper-credit! that advanced so high,/ Shall lend Corruption lighter wings to fly," many a reader nurtured on a steady diet of *Craftsman*s must have felt at home. No doubt, then, Earl Wasserman is well justified in saying that the entire poem is an attack by indirection on Sir Robert, whose figure hovers in the background.[90] But, again, the poem aroused little notice in the political journals, and one must be careful about pushing such arguments too far. Pope's own political attitudes are indeed made clear for audiences accustomed to the allusive technique of antiministerial propaganda, but to say that is *not* to say that the *Epistle* was recognized as a political poem or that it made any real impact on the world of party journalism or that it was even understood as a literary contribution to opposition propaganda. Such propaganda was much less circumspect than Pope still chose to be, and the *Epistle* is mild compared to Swift's *On Poetry* or to Whitehead's *State*

Dunces, both of which appeared about the same time.

In the next few months, however, Pope's circumspection virtually ceased, and his political alliance with the opposition became much more evident to the town. His first Imitation of Horace, *The First Satire of the Second Book*, published in February, was bolder in its satire on court and government than anything he had published so far and brought attack upon him from the same government papers that had remained silent about the political implications of the poems to Burlington and Bathurst.

After the appearance of Pope's first Imitation, Bathurst wrote Swift, "It is time for him to retire, for he has made the town too hot to hold him."[91] The poem, indeed, is noteworthy for a great deal more than the attack on Hervey as "Lord Fanny" and the notorious couplet on Lady Mary. Its central theme, the moral freedom of the satirist, not only fit Pope's case after the outcry over Timon—as Bolingbroke reminded him it did—but echoed arguments the critics of the government had been making for years.[92] Moreover, Pope here undisguisedly mocks the royal family in irony reminiscent of Swift's *Rapsody*; praises Bolingbroke in lines borrowed from the poem *Dawley Farm* in *Fog's*; lampoons the usual butts of opposition jokes such as Cibber, Charteris, and Peter Walter; aligns himself with "Statesmen out of Place"; casts a gratuitous bouquet to the old Jacobite Shippen; touches on conventional opposition themes like attacks on standing armies or complaints that "Caesar" scorns poetry; and closes with an ambiguous reference to Sir Robert's approval of his verse that also manages to imply that Walpole alone controls the courts of law and letters. Mack, who has analyzed at length the political innuendoes of the poem, concludes: "In no other poem before 1738 does Pope engage the activities and personalities of the regime with such peculiarly personal intensity and (possibly reflecting the confidence of early 1733, when it seemed that Walpole's removal might be imminent) a tone that so clearly blends ridicule with threat and both with a parade of strength."[93] For the first time Pope had produced a poem with a predominantly political atmosphere, one which the town could accordingly respond to in political terms. There is no talk here of landscape architecture or the Man of Ross; the poet boldly defends himself as "To Virtue only and her Friends a Friend," and few readers could have been in doubt that Virtue's friends are statesmen out of place. One wretched response, for instance, immediately took issue with Pope's claim that he was no "Spy of State" by claiming that the poet had acted in precisely that capacity for Pulteney and had written the character of the "Norfolk Steward" for the *Craftsman*.[94] But a more serious reply was to come which linked Pope with Paul Whitehead, whose *State Dunces* could almost be viewed as a tribute to Pope's new role, though that role is nowhere acknowledged in Whitehead's poem itself.

The State Dunces appeared anonymously in June, four months after Pope's Horatian satire and two months after Walpole's withdrawal of the excise bill. Whitehead deliberately linked his poem to the work of the Scriblerian circle by choosing as his epigraph Swift's lines "I from my soul sincerely hate/ Both [Kings] and Ministers of State" and by dedicating the poem to Pope. The opening lines, in fact, are addressed to Pope, who is asked to turn his attention from "the dull *Parnassian* Sons of Rhyme" to new objects of satire, the Dunces of the State: "Shall *Ralph, Cook, Welsted,* then engross thy Rage,/ While Courts afford a *H*[ervey], *Y*[orke], or *G*[age]?"[95] The body of the poem is then an adaptation of the paraphernalia of *The Dunciad* to the political scene; Appius (Walpole) seeks solace from the defeat of the excise scheme among his journalistic hacks, but the goddess Dullness revives and comforts him with a display of all her sons in high places: Newcastle, Horatio Walpole, Yonge, Pelham, Hervey, etc. A parade of dukes, bishops, politicians, and Grub Street hacks appears, all dedicated to preserving the reign of Walpolean Dullness, as the goddess proclaims: "Lo! On thy Sons alone my Favours shower,/ None share my Bounty that disdain thy Power."

Whitehead's crude mock epic, coming as it did when Walpole seemed on the run after the defeat of the excise scheme, provoked the kind of response which Pope's subtlety enabled him to avoid. Budgell puffed and quoted it in the *Bee*, taking occasion to insist yet once more that all the wit was on the side of the opposition, and several poems were published as replies.[96] Though the poetic replies slashed at Whitehead, Pulteney, Bolingbroke, and the opposition journalists, none of them referred even obliquely to Pope or to Whitehead's efforts to enroll him in the antiministerial cause. But on 16 June 1733, a full-fledged attack on both Whitehead and Pope was printed in the *Daily Courant*, a paper, of course, heavily subsidized by the government and a prime outlet of pro-Walpole opinion. The attack is in the form of a poem prefaced by a short passage in prose signed "Britannicus," which reads in part as follows: "If any think I have been unkind to Mr. *Pope,* let them remember that if his Friendship to *B——ke* be not a Matter of Censure, his recommending such a Man to the Publick as a Friend to Virtue may justify some Animadversions." To Whitehead, he says, some may feel he has been *too* kind; yet that poet's youth may offer some excuse for his folly. The poem itself is in the form of an apostrophe to Prejudice; both Pulteney and Pope have yielded to her baneful influence:

> See *Pope* to thy almighty Influence bend;
> To *Virtue* and to *Bolingbroke* a Friend:
> Unequall'd Bard; yet still with mortal Mind,
> Or false to Freedom, or like Bigots blind.
> Can Sires of Slav'ry cheer a *Briton's* Bowl?
> Can St. John's *Treasons* feast a Patriot-Soul?

The echoes of Pope's Horatian Imitation (Sat. II.i) continue as Bolingbroke is attacked in ritual fashion as the Satanic figure corrupting innocent friends:

> When will thy Crimes be full, thou *false to All!*
> Still Envy, Malice on thy Aid will call.
> Still with a Pulteney join, a Pope commend;
> *To Virtue only and her Friends a Friend.*

Pope is then exhorted to use his genius to heal rather than exacerbate the divisions of the nation:

> Could I, *Dan Pope,* once reach thy lovely Strain,
> No more should Party Rage that Word prophane;
> Then should my Verse the Words of Treach'ry heal,
> And Faction's Brood to ev'ry Eye reveal.

The rest of the poem is a diatribe against Whitehead in terms that could not be said to avoid "Party Rage"; Pope, interestingly,

is said to have been abused and injured by the fawning of
Whitehead, who is left finally to dine at Dawley with Walpole's
foes.

I have described the *Daily Courant*'s poem at some length
because, to the best of my knowledge, it is the first attack on
Pope by one of Walpole's propaganda organs for the new strain
of politics in his verse. It is possible that Pope saw Hervey's hand
in this poem, for in his *Letter to a Noble Lord* he speaks of Hervey's
willingness "to cast a few conceits, or drop a few antitheses, even
among the dear joys of the *Courant*."[97] In any event, the tone of
the attack is significant; Pope is still the supreme poet, essentially
nonpolitical, and he is chided in sorrow rather than anger for his
misguided venture into politics. Though the poem makes plain
that it is Pope's first Horatian Imitation that has prompted a
response, it is only the praise of Bolingbroke which is objected
to; the other satiric thrusts of that poem—even the vicious lines
on Lady Mary—are passed over in silence. Indeed, the criticism
of Pope is tentative, almost apologetic, in contrast to the attack
on Whitehead—as Pope's poem had been oblique and reserved
compared to Whitehead's. It may be, as Mack has argued, that
from 1733 on Pope is "to be regarded as spiritual patron of the
poetical Opposition to Walpole," but it was to be some time
before Walpole's own press was to recognize him in that role.[98]

About Pope's private commitment from this point on, however, there can be little doubt. After the first Horatian satire, his
quarrel with Lord Hervey and Lady Mary reached its peak, and
though its details need not be rehearsed here we should note
that this quarrel was political as well as personal. Walpole
himself became involved at one point, in an effort to remove
Pope's offensive couplet or at least to forestall further attacks on
his faithful adherent, Lady Mary.[99] And Lady Mary's poems
ridiculing Pope made much of his association with Bolingbroke,
as did Fielding's mock epic written under her patronage. Hervey's *Epistle from a Nobleman to a Doctor of Divinity* (November
1733), in cataloguing the mental furniture of a witling like Swift
or Pope, adds a passage in the same vein:

> And when this catalogue he has run o'er,
> And empty'd of whipt cream his frothy store,
> Thinks he's so wise no *Solomon* knows more:

> That the weak texture of his flimsy brain,
> Is fit the weight on *W*——'s to sustain;
> In *Senates* to preside, to mould *the State*,
> And fix in *England's* service, *Europe's* fate.[100]

Here, again, in other words, is the connection made between the political opposition and the Swift-Pope circle of wits, as well as the contempt customary among Walpole's adherents for the pretense of mere literary men that they are fit for "business." *Tit for Tat*, a poem answering Hervey, puts the other case, with lines contemptuous of illiterate ministers and secretaries.[101] All this goes beyond Pope's personal relations with Hervey and Lady Mary into arguments about the role of wit in the body politic, arguments that had filled the public arena for years. Little wonder that in his own unpublished prose response to Hervey, *A Letter to a Noble Lord* (November 1733), Pope took occasion once more to declare that he "never wrote a line in which the religion or government of his country, the royal family, or their ministry, were disrespectfully mentioned."[102]

Such a protestation, if he had not been persuaded (apparently by Walpole) to suppress the *Letter*, might have raised at least a few eyebrows, for in his remaining poems of 1733–34 he continued to hit out at the administration, albeit obliquely and casually. His version of Donne's *Fourth Satire*, published anonymously in November 1733, depicts an infected court world, where the foppish courtier himself is allowed to voice typical charges against "the *Great Man*": "He names the *Price* for ev'ry Office paid,/ And says our *Wars thrive ill*, because *delay'd*;/ Nay hints, 'tis by Connivance of the Court,/ That *Spain* robs on, and *Dunkirk's* still a Port."[103]

Pope's hand in this poem may not have been recognized; but in January 1734 he reiterated his political feelings by addressing his Epistle *Of the Knowledge and Characters of Men* to Viscount Cobham, who had voted against the excise bill, been subsequently deprived of his regiment, and gone into opposition; readers would not have missed the significance of the dying words Pope predicts for him: "Oh, save my Country, Heav'n! shall be your last." In May came the collected edition of the *Essay on Man*, where for the first time Bolingbroke is identified on the title page and in the text as the Friend to whom the poem was addressed and whose praises are sung at the beginning and end of the last epistle. Pope's political critics were always irked the most by his adulation of Bolingbroke, who had just been denounced in the House of Commons by Walpole himself during the debate on the Septennial Bill and whose continuing importance to the opposition was just then being underlined by his *Dissertation upon Parties* appearing in the *Craftsman*.[104] Finally, in his second Horatian Imitation (Sat II.ii), which appeared in July, Pope made a few more slighting references to standing armies and the excise scheme and developed further his image of the simple life of the "Country Party," a life in contrast to the wealthy corruption of a court. None of these poems attracted the attention of the government journalists in the way that the first *Imitation of Horace* had; but Pope's stand had been taken, and his complete emergence four years later as the leading literary spokesman for the opposition could have come as no great surprise to careful readers.

The years we have just surveyed, the years of Pope's deepening political commitment, of Fielding's hesitancy, and of Swift's final political poems, were also the years of greatest crisis for Walpole. The excise affair marked a significant defeat for him—one which, however, the disunited, diverse elements of the opposition were unable to use to their advantage. Walpole, in fact, survived the parliamentary elections of 1734 with only a slightly smaller majority in the House of Commons. Plumb writes of this period as follows:

The years 1733 and 1734 form the watershed of Sir Robert Walpole's career: yet the slope towards defeat and retirement was so gentle that few of his contemporaries perceived it. To his royal masters, to the members of the cabinet, to his family and friends, to the public at large, and even to the opposition, his authority after the election of 1734 seemed as great as ever.[105]

Without question Walpole's indifference to public opinion and his insensitivity to the public mood were instrumental in the defeat of his excise bill. As is well known, the opposition propaganda organs were successful in playing on popular fears and arousing popular anger against the supposed "tyranny" of the scheme. One progovernment pamphlet speaks of the

"Reams of Paper that have been prostituted by the Anti-minis-
terial Writers on this Occasion" and the "Vast Inundation of
Words with which they have lately overflowed the Country."[106]
The flood took the form not only of *"Craftsmen, Considerations,
Remarks, Observations, Seasonable Animadversions, &c"* but of bal-
lads, satires, and cartoons as well. Yet, as far as we know, no
writer of any significance took part directly in this torrent of
propaganda; there were no pamphlets by Swift, no plays by
Fielding, no poems by Pope or Thomson assaulting the "Excise-
Monster" or celebrating the "City Triumphant." Ford wrote
Swift, "While the Excises were depending, you were expected
every day, for it was said, why should not he shew as much
regard for the Liberty of *England,* as he did for the Money of
Ireland?"[107] Swift may have been expected, but he did not
appear; there was not to be another *Conduct of the Allies* or
Drapier's Letters. The literary opposition, as diverse and heterogeneous a body as its political counterpart, typically remained
aloof from the rough world of political journalism or pamphleteering on immediate issues. They were content, instead, to
embody political themes in literary form, to ridicule corruption
and the misuse of power in their larger aspects, and to project
abstract images of liberty and patriotism. The day-to-day ma-
neuvering in the House of Commons was of concern to them
personally, but it touched their imagination less than the more
general themes, and less than their overriding fears for the
survival of literature itself in a new world apparently hostile to
its values.

5 THE PRINCE AND THE POETS, 1734–1737

THE ELECTIONS of 1734 provided Walpole with a majority which firmly reestablished his control, and for the next few years the hydra-headed opposition seemed to flounder helplessly. Bolingbroke, despite the excitement generated by his *Dissertation upon Parties*, gave up the fight and returned to France in 1735; and Pulteney, the same year, wrote to a friend, "I am determined to give myself less trouble in parliament than hitherto I have done. . . . It is vain to struggle against universal corruption, and I am quite weary of the opposition."[1] In the following year, as the conclusion of peace in Europe allowed Walpole to reduce the military forces, he did, in fact, absent himself much of the time. By the autumn of 1736 the feeling was common that the antiministerial forces were in disarray, with even a congratulatory poem addressed "To Sir R. W. on the Abatement of the Opposition."[2] *Fog's*, the liveliest of the opposition journals, first turned nonpolitical and then expired, apparently as a result of the government's negotiation with Nathaniel Mist, its proprietor in exile.[3] The government, as though to solidify its mastery of the domestic scene, combined all its subsidized journals into the *Daily Gazetteer*, which from 1735 onward was the sole propaganda organ for Walpole.

But the opposition was not long in abatement. In 1735 it mustered 185 votes against the Address to Vote Military Supplies, a "vast minority" which must have worried the government, and it continued to bring in place bills and to make the most of popular discontent over such issues as the Gin Act of 1736.[4] There were new faces and new forces in its confused ranks, those of Chesterfield, Cobham, and the "Boy Patriots" or "Cobham's Cubs," a family group consisting of George Lyttelton, the two Pitts, and Richard Grenville, all acting under the direction of Lyttelton's uncle, Lord Cobham. The demise of *Fog's* was balanced by the beginning of a new journal, *Common Sense,* in 1737. The death of Queen Caroline in 1737 also gave them fresh hopes. Most importantly, the opposition by 1737 had succeeded in "capturing" Frederick, Prince of Wales, in whose questionable figure they found not only a patron and head for their activities but one who would remove from them any further taint of Jacobite disloyalty.[5]

As the parliamentary opposition rekindled its fires in the years 1734–37, so too did the poets and writers hostile to the administration. This was the period in which Lyttelton gathered around Frederick a circle of "Patriot Poets"; in which Fielding's plays became openly satirical of Walpole; in which the Licensing Act was passed to regulate the stage; and in which Pope became increasingly bolder in his political satire. Each of these developments must receive separate discussion, but two points are worth making at the outset. First, despite the increase in volume and intensity of antigovernment literature, it was still not quite the result of an organized, directed program; "the literary opposition," before 1737, is a term for activities and personalities as heterogeneous as those of the political opposition. What, after all, do Fielding's *Historical Register* and Thomson's *Liberty* have in common but their hostility to Walpole's government? Secondly, opposition to the administration was by this time obviously the cause which any self-respecting writer would take, at least if he were at all susceptible to the influence of literary fashion.

In 1734, for example, Pulteney, in a pamphlet addressed to the new members of the House of Commons, took pains to remind them that their support of Walpole would impugn not only their probity but their "parts": "Would you make any Figure in the *gay,* the *polite,* and *witty Part of the World,* you must not unite yourselves to *Those,* who have so long been the Objects of their *Mirth.*"[6] Pulteney goes on, of course, to give other arguments for opposing Sir Robert's measures in the House, but this one seems especially to have infuriated the author of an "official" answer in the *Daily Courant* (21 January, 1734/5):

He very graciously promises, the present *House of Commons* . . . that they . . . shall be made capable of being admitted into that generous Fellowship of *Patriots,* consisting of all the *gay,* the *polite,* and *witty Part of the World,* who, having nothing to do with the Management of *publick Affairs* themselves, laugh at all those that have, whose Credit and Influence can make any Man pass for a *Wit* and a *Patriot,* and whose *Resentment* and *Displeasure,* can fix upon any Man, the *indelible Character* of a *Scoundrel* and a *Blockhead.*

From his repetition in the rest of his essay of the terms "gay," "polite," and "witty" it is obvious that this government writer was extremely annoyed by the assumption of intellectual and social superiority on Pulteney's part. But he puts on a contemptuous front; Pulteney, he says, would have us believe that the polite, gay, and witty "are all engaged in a Faction against the government. And it is very possible that they may be . . . in the Sense that he understands *Politeness, Wit,* and *Gaiety,* and yet no great Discredit to the Government not withstanding, to be opposed by such Adversaries."

As this exchange indicates, the charges of Walpole's philistinism and contempt for men of letters were still a vital part of antiministerial propaganda. The association of the Goddess of Dullness with ministerial hacks was commonplace, and epigrams on the decay of letters under Walpole abounded.[7] When Richard Savage took the minister to task in "A Poet's Dependance on a Statesman," he may well have intended only to express his own private and unjustified disappointment, but his complaint reiterated one of the most common themes in antigovernment journalism.[8] "How can it be expected," complained the *Craftsman* (13 August 1737), "that we should have *good Writers,* while Things stand as they do at present? For all Arts are kept up by the Encouragement which is given them." In the face of this prevailing attitude, no writer of any merit in the middle of the decade would look to the court or the government for encouragement. Politics had drawn a firm line between men of wit and men of business; and it was surely not simply their political attitudes about Walpole but also their consciousness of the appreciation which the "country party" accorded men of wit that drew the writers of this generation to Chesterfield or Lyttelton rather than to Walpole or Sir William Yonge.

Lyttelton and the Patriot Poets

But one group of literary men who emerged in this period in support of the opposition was neither very gay nor very witty— the so-called "Patriot poets," including such writers as Thomson, Mallet, Glover, Akenside, and Brooke. The theme of opposition propaganda which they embodied was well characterized by a government pamphleteer in 1735; arguing that one can determine by his style whether an opposition writer is a Tory or a Jacobite, he concludes as follows: "But if every *Period* ring with *Liberty;* if every *Prince* be represented as a *Claudius* or a *Nero*; if every *Minister* wear the Habit of a *Sejanus* or a *Wolsey*," then the work in question is only the ravings of a "discontented Whig."[9] In their glorification of British liberty, their fusion of chauvinism and sentimentality, these poets continued the tradition of Whig panegyric verse described by C. A. Moore.[10] And in their glorification of the English past, especially the reign of Elizabeth, they echoed the Whig interpretation of English history then being given prominence in the opposition press. They represented, in fact, a new and powerful force in the literature of the opposition; though Thomson had turned the tradition of Whig panegyric against Walpole with *Britannia* in 1729, only in the middle and late 1730s did antigovernment literature come to be dominated by these notes of enthusiastic nationalism. Hortatory rather than satiric, rhetorical rather than realistic, their poetic campaign against the government seems far removed from the acerbic wit of *Gulliver's Travels* or *The Beggar's Opera*. Reading their verse or their plays, one can only sympathize with the prominsterial writer who remarked rather plaintively, "'Tis to be hoped that the Pulse of this Nation will ever beat high for Liberty; not so high however as to border upon Lunacy."[11] Yet their efforts may have had more effect in rousing public opinion, especially on matters of foreign policy, than the antigovernment satires which, of course, continued to appear throughout the decade.

In some ways it is misleading to think of them as Whig poets, since to do so is to use a party label which they themselves would have questioned. "It may be difficult to define 'Tory,' " writes John B. Owen of this period; "it is impossible to define

'Whig.' "[12] In 1734, for instance, William Talbot, son of the lord chancellor but himself an opposition Whig M.P. for Glamorgan, argued in a letter to a friend that the nominal distinction between Whig and Tory ought to be abolished, since "a Ministerial Whig and a State Tory, when in power, are so exactly alike in their conduct, that my discernment is not sufficient to distinguish one from the other." The principles of a "real Whig" in his account turn out to be a mixture of general Lockean doctrine and particular themes dear to the opposition: the limited prerogative of the Crown; free elections; freedom of the press; encouragement of trade; and firm opposition to ministers who govern by corruption, who develop a parliamentary influence by places and pensions, or who allow British merchants to be plundered on the seas. What he calls "Tory Sentiments" include, again, general principles like placing the prince above all laws or restraining freedom of thought and specific political sins attributed to Walpole by opposition propaganda. It is the Tory, he says, who believes

that whatever reflects upon the character of a man in power is a libel; that even the public spirited sentiments of a patriot, delivered on the *Stage* in the character of a BRUTUS, or a CATO, may be injurious to the peace of the nation; and villainy made odious by the representation of a SEJANUS or a BUCKINGHAM, may by popular malignity be interpreted to reproach those at the helm of affairs with the like dispositions; that therefore the *Stage* ought to be under the immediate directions of a Court Officer.[13]

In the ideology of this member of Parliament, then, a real Whig is one who will "indiscriminately oppose the measures of Sir Robert Walpole." All of this sounds like Bolingbroke, whose *Dissertation upon Parties* argued that Whig and Tory are extinct terms and that the only real division is that between the country party and the adherents of a single minister controlling Parliament by corruption. The *Dissertation*, which appeared first in the *Craftsman* and was published in 1735 with a satiric dedication to Walpole, had a pronounced effect on Lyttelton, the chief patron of the Whig poets; and Bolingbroke's extension of these ideas in *The Idea of a Patriot King* became crucial in the literature of the last years of the decade, as the opposition looked—or pretended to look—to Frederick as the patriot hero who would bring the nation together and rid England of the spirit of party. In that work, written late in 1738, Bolingbroke proclaimed that only a virtuous prince could reform a corrupted Britain and restore the free constitution of the glorious English past: "The true image of a free people, governed by a Patriot King, is that of a patriarchal family, where the head and all the members are united by one common interest, and animated by one common spirit." Only in the reign of Elizabeth has England had such a wise and good monarch, who "united the great body of the people in her and their *common interest*" and "inflamed them with *one national spirit*." Bolingbroke's program, seeking its cure for a sick nation in moral regeneration rather than in a change of political institutions, was to have a profound appeal to the imagination of the later Patriot poets.[14]

No doubt the poets who denigrated Walpole by praising liberty and flattering the Prince of Wales formed something of a coterie in which Lyttelton was an instrumental figure; at the same time, it is far from clear that at this stage they acted as an organized unit, as has sometimes been claimed, or that their literary activities, especially before 1737, were the result of anything like a group plan. Lyttelton, who became an influential favorite of Frederick in 1732 and his secretary in 1737, certainly thought of himself as a patron and urged the silly and ineffectual prince to give to men of letters the rewards they could not obtain from Walpole. An aspiring writer himself, a schoolmate of Fielding's at Eton, a close friend of Pope, of Glover, and of Thomson, he was recognized at the time as a would-be Maecenas whose political efforts were dedicated not simply to opposing Walpole in the House of Commons, but to rallying promising writers around the prince, especially after Frederick went into open opposition in 1737.

Yet the significance of his role as patron can easily be overstated; as Rose Mary Davis points out, during the period of his connection with Prince Frederick, Lyttelton's efforts brought material reward only to Thomson, Gilbert West, and possibly Mallet. Indeed, his uncle Cobham may have been more effective as a patron, and Stowe became a favorite gathering-place for opposition poets and politicians alike.[15] But there is no evidence to suggest that behind these efforts at patronage or the writings of any of the poets in question was a preconceived political plan,

such as winning Frederick away from the influence of Pulteney.[16] In encouraging men of letters the leading figures of this
segment of the opposition, such as Cobham, Chesterfield, and
Lyttelton, were satisfying their personal taste while simultaneously pointing up the persistent opposition theme of the
court's indifference to literary merit. Some of the poets thus
patronized, like Thomson, had been hostile to Walpole well
before "Cobham's Cubs" came into opposition; and others, like
Glover, found their meager talents well suited to express the
spirit of patriotism which then seemed to pervade the literary
world as the most popular of themes. They did not write by
direction; but they naturally looked for support and possible
reward to those politicians and that prince whose cause they
celebrated and who, unlike Robert Walpole, did not seem to
scorn poets or fear playwrights.

Lyttelton's most important contribution to the opposition as a
writer, rather than simply as a politician and a patron, was *Letters
from a Persian in England to his Friend in Ispahan,* published in
1735 in the same month that he first became a member of
Parliament. The *Letters,* written in frank imitation of those of
Montesquieu, are not dominated by politics; most of them are
given over to romance or to lighthearted social satire using the
familiar device of a foreign observer whose native values provide the "distance" needed for satiric comment. Thus Selim in
London writes to Mirzah in Ispahan of British operas and
gaming tables and lovers. But in a series of eleven letters
Lyttelton doubles the "distance" by continuing Montesquieu's
history of the Troglodytes, a thin allegory of the development in
England of government by a wicked minister who is "not afraid
of being obnoxious to the *Spirit of Liberty.*" Other letters in the
volume, without resort to such additional fictional devices,
openly warn against the dangers of a bad administration, defend
the freedom of the press as a check against corrupt ministers,
praise a great English poet (Pope) for daring to praise men out
of power, give a Bolingbrokean analysis of political parties which
calls for the abolition of Whig and Tory and the erection of one
"national standard," and sketch in a concluding series the
history of British government from Saxon times onward. The
theme of this historical sketch is the spirit of liberty, a spirit
which is embodied in the ancient constitution, which flourished

in the reign of the model monarch, Elizabeth, and which can be endangered only by a minister who induces a prince to influence or corrupt the election of a free Parliament. The Revolution of 1688 settled the government upon a firmer foundation, but the constitution is now *"ill secured, the sword being only in the hands of the king:* to which is added a vast increase of the *wealth* of the crown,"* an increase in public debt, new taxes, and "a prodigious multiplication of *officers* wholly dependent upon the court." And in his final letters Selim expresses wonder at a people who *"profess* TO MAINTAIN LIBERTY BY CORRUPTION."[17]

All of this, of course, is very much the language of opposition journalism. It may be, as Rose Mary Davis has argued, that when he wrote the *Letters* Lyttelton was not yet as fully committed to the opposition as he was to become later, but whatever hesitation he may have felt was certainly lost on his first readers. For the government press made it clear at once that they regarded the *Letters* as simple propaganda. Lyttelton was attacked immediately in the *Daily Courant,* and his *Letters* were still being ridiculed even a year later in the *Daily Gazetteer.*[18] A pamphlet called *The Persian Strip'd of his Disguise* (1735) correctly identified many of the ideas as Bolingbroke's and betrayed the usual antiliterary, pragmatic bent of government writers as it complained that no practical advice on reducing taxes or improving commerce can be found in the *Letters;* it is too bad, laments this pamphlet, that Lyttelton, with his talent for fiction and romance, should essay political writing, which requires truth and argument.[19] Moreover, Lyttelton's volume was not only attacked in the ministerial press but touted by the *Craftsman,* which reprinted some of the letters in its issues for 12 April and 19 April 1735; a reply from a ministerial writer went so far as to accuse Lyttelton of writing the commendation in the *Craftsman* himself and urged the young man in contemptuous terms to "confine his elegant *Genius* to *Poetry* and *Inscriptions,* and harmlessly amuse the *World* with *Tales* of his *Uncle's* fine *Gardens,* and the wonderful Qualities of his *Italian Greyhound."*[20]

In the same year as the *Letters from a Persian* was published, Thomson began his publication of *Liberty: A Poem,* the first three parts appearing early in 1735 and the remaining two in January and February of 1736. But whereas Lyttelton's volume drew upon him the widespread attacks of the government press,

Thomson's poem excited hardly a ripple in the world of political journalism. Yet there was much there to have drawn fire, and the poem has long been regarded as to some extent a partisan document. Thomson dedicated it to the Prince of Wales, whose patronage he seems to have sought as early as 1732. In a letter of that year to Lady Hertford, he thanks her for presenting his book to the prince and refers to Frederick's approbation of a "first Imperfect Essay," presumably, as McKillop suggests, *Britannia*. Thomson goes on to express his hope "of seeing the fine arts flourish under a Prince of his so noble equal humane and generous dispositions; who knows how to unite the soveraignty of the prince with the liberty of the people."[21] Lady Hertford thus seems to have acted as an intermediary between the poet and the prince; Dodington's friendship with Thomson could also be counted on to recommend him to Frederick. There is no evidence that any leaders of the active political opposition were privy to the composition of the poem, though Pope may have seen a portion of it as early as 1733. Lyttelton by this time was equerry to the prince, but his acquaintance with Thomson did not begin until 1737.[22]

As a "progress" poem detailing in lengthy terms the history of liberty and the history of culture, *Liberty* meets all the criteria of Whig panegyric, with its climactic moment the Revolution Settlement. It is about this poem in particular that Samuel Johnson passes judgment on the form which Whig tradition now assumed: "At this time a long course of opposition to Sir Robert Walpole had filled the nation with clamours for liberty, of which no man felt the want, and with care for liberty, which was not in danger."[23] A. D. McKillop, in his detailed study of the poem, shows that it incorporates the ideals of "Gothic" liberty and the fear of "luxury" traditional in Whig history; though both parties accepted these ideals, he says, the opponents of Walpole tended to stress the dangers to Britain's heritage and his adherents the gains made since the Revolution rather than Britain's early liberties. Of course, the poem's extensive inveighing against luxury and corruption is of general application, but, as McKillop points out, it is also consistent with the usual line of opposition propaganda, and he demonstrates in some detail the parallels between the view of English history in *Liberty* and that in the *Craftsman* or in the *Craftsman*'s favorite historian, Rapin. Indeed, as Isaac

Kramnick has demonstrated, the political press in just these
years was reviving a seventeenth-century debate over the English past, with opposition writers adopting the Whig view of an
ancient constitution with its roots in the distant past and with
Walpole's writers, remarkably enough, adopting the historical
analysis of seventeenth-century Tories in order to date the birth
of liberty in 1688.[24] To readers of the *Craftsman* and the *London
Journal*, then, Thomson's historical panorama might have
seemed not only familiar but politically motivated.

That survey of English history occurs in Parts IV and V of the
poem, and indeed by 1736 when those two parts appeared
Liberty had both lost readers and taken on a more obviously
partisan demeanor. Consider, for example, the lines describing
the barons and King John:

> "Pressed by a band
> Of Patriots, ardent as the summer's noon
> That looks delighted on, the tyrant see!
> Mark! how with feigned alacrity he bears
> His strong reluctance down, his dark revenge,
> And gives the charter by which life indeed
> Becomes of price, a glory to be man.
> "Through this, and through succeeding reigns affirmed
> These long-contested rights, the wholesome winds
> Of opposition hence began to blow;
> And often since have lent the country life.
> Before their breath corruption's insect-blights,
> The darkening clouds of evil counsel, fly;
> Or, should they sounding swell, a putrid court,
> A pestilential ministry, they purge,
> And ventilated states renew their bloom."[25]

Or again, we may note the section in Part V (ll. 304-66) in which
Thomson, like Lyttelton and others in the band of Patriot
writers, puts the danger to British liberty in the darkly conditional future; *should* the times arrive when Britons are defeated
by "corruption's soul-dejecting arts," when Britannia's laurels
yield to "slily conquering Gaul," when "shameless pens" (the
"hired assassins of the commonweal") plead openly for corruption, when public virtue grows "the public scoff," *then* all parties
must be cast aside and the nation unite under one standard.
Moreover, Part V includes a lengthy warning that neglect of the

arts will result in the nation sinking into oblivion, like another
Carthage (ll. 374 ff.). Thomson had touched on that theme
earlier in his praise of Frederick as a patron of the arts
(I.369 ff.), as well as in his letter to Lady Hertford, but in the
admonitory context of Part V it immediately brings to mind the
countless demonstrations in opposition journalism that arts and
letters under Walpole are in ruinous decay.

In short, it may be true, as McKillop has indicated (p. 88), that
on the evidence available we cannot determine the poet's exact
political intentions; but surely no man in 1735 could have
written passages of the sort cited above without the certainty that
they would be given particular, specific, immediate political
application. Yet it seems to have been evaluated on its literary
merits rather than on its propagandistic value. Dr. Alured
Clarke, a Whig clergyman and no friend to the opposition, saw
the first part before its publication and commended it to Lady
Sundon, though admitting that the poetry did lie open to some
objections. Sir Thomas Robinson, writing to Lord Carlisle in
January 1735, referred to the poem only in literary terms,
though in the preceding paragraph he described several "virulent" antiministerial pamphlets. Budgell, in the *Bee*, listed proministerial and opposition pamphlets published in recent
months and then went on to praise Thomson's poem, but, again,
he made no political application of it at all.[26] And Thomson's
friend Aaron Hill praised the second part of the poem and its
sermon "against *Corruption*" in the *Prompter* (14 February
1734/5), a journal which was so far from being a friend to the
opposition that its preceding issue had been devoted to answering the charge that it was prominISTERIal.

Despite its partisan passages, then, the poem in its vague loftiness seems to have passed above the grubby world of practical
politics. The *Craftsman*, to be sure, puffed the poem in its issue
of 16 August 1735, well before the publication of the more
openly political Parts IV and V, and McKillop (p. 98) speaks of
the *Craftsman* essay as openly espousing the poem as an opposition utterance. But, in actuality, the *Craftsman* stops far short of
such open espousal, merely taking the poem as a starting place
for a discourse on "independency" and the "passion for Liberty"
and exploiting it as that journal was wont to do with more
innocent works of history or literature; its essay on Thomson

was not answered by the newly begun government organ, the *Gazetteer*. In fact, the absence of government reaction to *Liberty* is itself significantly pointed up by the *Craftsman*: "The *Poem* . . . has pass'd uncensur'd, and the *Author* unblemish'd; but it seems to be the only Exception to that unlicens'd Abuse, which has been thrown upon every Man, who has express'd his Fear for the *Publick*, or his Concern for the Welfare of it."

Why, we may wonder with the *Craftsman*, did an important poem so open to a partisan reading escape "uncensur'd"? Two answers may be suggested, I think, one literary and the other political. Since the poem, in Dr. Johnson's language, is "an enumeration of examples to prove a position which nobody denied"[27] and since it sought, as McKillop puts it, to "evade revolution and extremism in terms of some vaguely conceived ideal of inclusion and harmony" (pp. 104–5), it was difficult to charge it with narrowly partisan aims despite the many passages which could be taken as inflammatory—passages pointed up, incidentally, by some of Thomson's revisions in preparation for the second edition of the poem in 1738.[28] As time went on the government writers learned to cope with this difficulty in their responses, but in 1735–36 the flood of Patriot poems and plays was only beginning to seep across the land. Walpole's writers were also generally more slow to attack poets of considerable reputation like Pope or Thomson than they were to maul the minor figures in the literary opposition. The political explanation is simple enough: *Liberty* was dedicated to the Prince of Wales, whose virtues are sung in the course of the poem, and in 1735–36 the prince was not yet openly at the center of the opposition. His difficulties with the king and queen were already apparent enough, and he was being wooed by the politicians of the opposition, but at the same time the goverment was seeking to conciliate him so as to prevent the issue of his increased allowance from coming to a head.[29] Walpole's journalists would thus have been hesitant about attacking verse patronized by Frederick.

The situation certainly was different in September 1737, when Thomson published a poem addressed to the prince and celebrating the birth of the Princess Augusta. By that time Frederick had moved into open opposition; in February Pulteney had brought in a motion for settling an increased allowance on the prince, and in July Frederick had precipitated a crisis by carrying the princess, in labor, away from Hampton Court, an action which his parents took as a final insult. From that point on, Frederick's court became the center of the Patriot opposition. Thomson's poem six weeks later sounds all the patriotic notes on the occasion of the princess' birth: while hostile nations gather round and Britannia droops, while "on our vitals selfish parties prey/ And deep corruption eats our soul away," the poet's heart is gladdened by the contemplation of the prince's progeny and the prospect of new Edwards, "New Henries, Annas, and Elizas." In the "promised glories" of Frederick's reign he foresees a "recovered Britain" when "France insults, and Spain shall rob no more."[30] Though its patriotic sentiments are no different from those expressed in *Liberty*, about the partisan interests of this five-stanza poem there can be no doubt, given the changed political circumstances of the prince. Thomson himself wrote Millar, his publisher, to suggest that it be printed in the *Craftsman* or in the new opposition journal, *Common Sense*.[31]

On this occasion Walpole's press showed no reluctance to attack the poet. The *Gazetteer* of 6 October summarizes the ode as a performance "in which the Writer first, like a *true Patriot*, laments very much the miserable Condition of his Country; and secondly, like a *true Poet* prophecies all shall be well again, as soon as his *Royal Highness* shall ascend the Throne." The writer of the *Gazetteer* then takes a remarkable tack; he claims he has no idea who the "Thomson" person may be but is certain the prince will never accept such a compliment. The author is "some ignorant, insignificant, officious little Fellow" hardly worth attention, but the "versifying, rhyming Tribe" must be censured when they produce libels on the administration. All this is accompanied by a detailed analysis of the poem, which is objected to on literary as well as political grounds. That the *Gazetteer* should have ignored *Liberty* but have devoted an entire issue to assaulting these brief lines can only be indicative of the political significance which panegyric of the prince had now assumed. The *Gazetteer* of 31 October, incidentally, makes it clear that the ministerial writer's uncertainty about the identity of Thomson was only sarcasm, for that issue refers to Patriotism having been recommended "by Mr. *Leonidas*, in an Epical

Encomium, and by Mr. *Manyweathers* in a *North British* Ode," the
epithet "Manyweathers" alluding not only to the poet of *The Seasons* but also, I think, to Thomson's political turnabout in 1729.

   The *Gazetteer*'s reference to *Leonidas* is to a nine-book epic
poem which, with good reason, has remained unread since the
eighteenth century, but which created a stir in the last part of the
decade. It provides an excellent example of how poetic value
could be subordinated to political utility by the literary fringe of
the opposition. Richard Glover, its author, was not the figure
one would expect to find lionized by the hangers-on of the
Prince of Wales; yet, though a city merchant and virtually
unknown as a writer, he was on close terms with Lyttelton and
had visited at Stowe with the other poets and politicians of the
Cobham circle. *Leonidas,* on the surface, seems devoid of
political overtones. In blank verse of extraordinary flatness and
a laconic style which he must have thought suitable for a Spartan
hero, Glover celebrates the heroic self-sacrifice of Leonidas at
the Pass of Thermopylae. The theme is the patriotic stand for
"Liberty against a tyrant's pride."[32] There are no passages
indicating specific parallels to current events, and relatively few
passages rhapsodizing over liberty, but in April of 1737, two
months after the motion for the address on increasing the
prince's allowance, the subject of a patriot king was enough to
make a poem a political as well as a literary document. The
opposition writers loved to dwell on the patriot king's self-abne-
gation,[33] and with Leonidas that attitude is carried as far as it can
go. Moreover, the poem was dedicated to Cobham, as one to
whom "a poem, founded on a character eminent for military
glory, and love of liberty, is due from the nature of the
subject."[34]

   Lyttelton, who had apparently seen the poem in its early
stages, addressed a poem to Glover, dated 1734, which indicates
clearly the usefulness of such an epic to the opposition. It is in
vain, he says, for Glover to hope to inspire Britain by Sparta's
example, for Britain has been corrupted by wealth, by luxury, by
"Eternal taxes, treaties for a day,/ Servants that rule, and senates
that obey." But yet Britain must be roused by such as Glover to
the danger that threatens: "Lo! France, as Persia once, o'er every
land/ prepares to stretch her all-oppressing hand."[35] The story
of Leonidas and his three hundred Spartans is thus to be read as

an indirect contrast to Walpole and his corrupted Britons. The *Craftsman* had devoted three issues to the theme of Greek liberty (16, 23, 30 September 1732), and the implications of Glover's epic were clear to everyone even in the absence of pointed remarks within the poem.

Given these overtones, the poem's instant popularity is not surprising. Swift wrote Pope asking who Glover was and reporting that the epic had "great vogue" in Dublin.[36] The poem went through several editions, and it was so cried up by the Patriots that even other poets opposed to Walpole, like Thomson and Mallet, were inclined to ridicule its fame. Thus Richard Savage speaks sarcastically of "the sublime Leonidas—Leonidas! who has left David, Homer, Virgil, Spenser, and Milton, as far beneath him as the eagle in her flight does the wren."[37] Savage's sarcasm was probably directed specifically at the fantastic puff of *Leonidas* which Lyttelton wrote for *Common Sense* (9 April 1737). Posing as an old man unacquainted with the poet, Lyttelton makes a virtue of Glover's epic faults, praising lavishly the simplicity of diction and the absence of supernatural machinery. He congratulates his age on having produced two poets comparable to Milton, i.e., Glover and Pope. Most of his discussion is confined to literary matters; no explicit political application is made, though of course he points to the defense of a free state against oppression as a subject relevant to England. Indeed, he congratulates Glover on having avoided the imputation of writing for a party, adding ironically that the poet "has gone so far as Greece to find a story which will not bear the least suspicion of a parallel to any circumstance or character of these times. . . . None can say that he meant it against them, unless by declaring that they are against liberty."[38]

Such mock disclaimers were intended, of course, to point the way to a political reading of this epic on patriotism, and Walpole's press was quick to respond. Their attacks, again, were presumably concerned only with the literary quality of *Leonidas*, though behind the literary criticism on both sides were the obvious political allegiances involved. Lyttelton's exaggerated praise made an easy target; in the month after its appearance a writer calling himself "Miso-Musaeus" in several essays in the *Weekly Miscellany* ridiculed such absurd puffs of Glover, asking what sort of figure the English must make among foreigners when, instead of Milton or Shakespeare or Pope, *Leonidas* is put into their hands as the best poem England has produced. This writer adds, "For my Part, I have much wondered, what could possibly induce so many Men of Letters to expose their Judgments so Monstrously as they have done upon this Occasion."[39] What induced these men of letters to make such a judgment was clear enough, and it was made even clearer by a nicely turned parody in the *Gazetteer* for 25 January 1738:

For my own Part, upon the first Appearance of *Leonidas*, which has been so justly preferred to the *Iliad, Aeneid,* and *Paradise Lost,* I congratulated this Metropolis, and cry'd out in a fit of Rapture, "the Time is now come when City Poetry shall no longer be the Foundation of City Pyes and Custards." But, I confess, I am deceived in my Expectation. This divine Poem has not yet been honour'd with a second Edition. . . . There cannot be a greater Proof of the Ignorance and Corruption of this Age. . . . What, O ye Sons of Liberty would be your Loss, if Envy and Detraction should prevail against the Cause of *Sparta!* Be it your Comfort, that the most ingenious Patriots are Advocates for *Leonidas,* and that *Selim* the *Persian* is transformed into a *Spartan.*

The *Gazetteer* writer thus manages in one passage to identify Lyttelton as the chief sponsor of the poem, to connect the brouhaha over *Leonidas* with the political cause of "ingenious Patriots," to ridicule the glorification of the poem's literary qualities, and to sneer at Glover as a "City Poet." And, indeed, it is ironic that in this instance politics had prompted the circle of which Pope was a member to bring the Smithfield muses to the ear of princes.

By 1737, then, when *Leonidas* appeared, the tradition of "Whig panegyric" had been transformed into "Patriot poetry" and was well entrenched as a vital force in opposition literary circles. Indeed, the Patriot poets may have been able to carry on a campaign against Walpole more effective politically than that of the satirists simply because their poems had a positive, constructive theme and presented a corrective to the ills which they decried. Pope's plans in 1740 for an epic about Brutus, the grandson of Aeneas and founder of Britain, contained all the patriotic themes and would have provided his friends in the opposition with his own version of a "corrective" spirit.[40] Just as the presence of the prince in their midst relieved the opposition of charges of disloyalty or Jacobitism, the patriotic literature, positive and inspirational as it was, removed from the literary figures opposed to Walpole the stigma of negativism and irresponsible satire with which they were usually charged by the advocates of the administration. Fortunately for us, however, the Patriot poets had not usurped the whole field of opposition literature, for Walpole continued to receive the onslaught of those whose talents lay in satire and wit. During the same period in which Thomson, Lyttelton, and Glover were incorporating the commonplaces of the opposition into their works, Fielding and Pope continued to assault the prime minister and the court with the sacred weapon of ridicule.

Fielding, Common Sense, *and Pope*

Having considered Fielding's move from tentative satire of Walpole in his early plays to a bid for his patronage in *The Modern Husband,* we may review rather briefly his more familiar plays of the mid-thirties. After two years at Drury Lane, Fielding returned to the Haymarket in 1734 with *Don Quixote in England,* making what can only be described as a bid for favor from the opposition. Though there are a few scenes satirizing corrupt electioneering, the play itself is of no special interest and could certainly not have been considered anti-Walpole satire; it is the dedication to the earl of Chesterfield which reveals Fielding's new direction. In his short eulogy of Chesterfield, who was newly arrived in the ranks of the opposition, Fielding carefully sounds all the familiar notes of anti-Walpole writers: the "cause of liberty" is contrasted to the "calamities brought on a country by general corruption"; a free stage characterized by wit and humor is praised as a useful political weapon against the "powerful sons of dulness"; and "true patriotism" is said to be a word scandalously ridiculed by some but meaningful when applied to Chesterfield.[41] Two years earlier it had been Robert Walpole whom Fielding had addressed as the "true patriot" and who had been enjoined to triumph over his "enemies at home";

in neither instance, of course, should the phrase or those like it be taken at face value as the expression of Fielding's politics, but only as the conventional signals for favor customary in dedications to political figures.

Whether this particular signal was recognized in a material way cannot be determined. Cross assumes that it was not, that only in 1736 and 1737—after Fielding formed the Great Mogul's Company at the Haymarket—was an "alliance" made between the playwright and the lords of the opposition.[42] Although we have no evidence that an alliance was ever formed in quite the literal sense that Cross intends, certainly it is in two plays of those years, *Pasquin* and, especially, *The Historical Register,* that we find Fielding's most open and unmistakable satire of Walpole. Nor is that fact in the least surprising, for these plays were produced and published at a time when, as we have seen, the literary hue and cry after Walpole had reached a level that no self-respecting wit could afford to ignore if he hoped to amuse the town. Moreover, the new figures prominent in the opposition since the excise affair included not only Chesterfield but Fielding's former schoolmates at Eton, William Pitt and George Lyttelton. With them and with other young Patriots Fielding was now on close terms.[43] One need not, then, look to political conversion as an explanation of Fielding's turn to the opposition camp after a dedication to Walpole and two years at Drury Lane; neither the political nor the literary scene was the same as it had been in 1732.

Nor are the plays themselves heavily or bitterly satiric, not at least when compared to other political satires of the time. Fielding's persistent themes, aside from the perennial topic of corruption, are political motifs which have the maximum *literary* significance: that is, he is acutely sensitive to the triumph of the "sons of dullness" over men of wit and merit and to efforts to limit the freedom of the stage. In *Pasquin,* for example, it is easy to exaggerate the satiric significance of the comic play-within-the-play, since it is directly concerned with political matters. In point of fact, however, no opposition politician could take much heart from Trapwit's plot, since the courtiers, Lord Place and Colonel Promise, come off no worse than the representatives of the country party, Sir Henry Fox-Chace and Squire Tankard, who bribe indirectly but no less effectively and who go about shouting "Liberty and property and no excise." As in *Don Quixote in England,* the chief butts of satire are the venal electors, and the underlying theme cries a plague on both houses: "better herring is in neither barrel."[44]

It is in the superficially nonpolitical "tragedy" rehearsed by Fustian that Fielding makes his real comment on the administration, and he does so in a way made familiar both by *The Dunciad* and by countless essays in opposition journals decrying the decline of taste and learning under Walpole. The conquest of Queen Common-sense by Queen Ignorance, the neglect or scorn of men of superior sense, and the corrupt practices in law, medicine, and religion are all given political twists by innuendo and allusion. The parallel between the theater and the state was well established, as was the use of Harlequin to represent Walpole.[45] Moreover, Fielding's audience would surely have noticed that the play which Queen Ignorance commands to be performed is *The Modish Couple,* a work which had been damned because of its connection with the court and for which Fielding himself had written the epilogue. At any rate, Common-sense's dying speech foretelling the reign of Ignorance makes the political application explicit:

> Places, requiring learning and great parts,
> Henceforth shall all be hustled in a hat,
> And drawn by men deficient in them both.
> Statesmen—but oh! cold death will let me say
> No more—and you must guess et caetera.[46]

The extension of ignorance to the political arena is made explicit by these lines, but they are hardly necessary; the decline of culture and the triumph of dullness could hardly be talked about in 1736 without political overtones.

For all that, *Pasquin* contained nothing overtly objectionable to the government, and its popularity was not attributed at the time to any satire on Walpole which might have been suspected. The papers sympathetic to the opposition gave it no support and made no effort to capitalize upon it, with the *Grub-street Journal,* in fact, launching its first full-scale attack on Fielding in several years. The *Journal's* criticism, the opening section of which Cross and Loftis have mistaken for praise, was directed at Fielding's cynical indictment of *all* parties as equally corrupt and at the very generality of his satire on lawyers, physicians, and divines.[47] At the end of its critique, the *Journal* gives a clue to another motive for its view of the play by sneering at the praise which Fielding had received in the *Prompter.*

That journal, conducted by Aaron Hill and William Popple, not only was an arch-enemy of the Grubeans but was not quite so free from politics as has usually been claimed. Hill was suffered, though not gladly, by Pope and was on good terms with Thomson, but Popple in 1734 had complained that his own play *The Ladies Revenge* had been damned by the audience for political reasons. In this view, he was supported by the pro-government *Daily Journal* (8 February 1733/4), which asserted that Popple's play had been attacked only "because he had the Honour of being known and favour'd by some Persons in the Administration." When the *Prompter* began, it was puffed and reprinted in both the *Daily Journal* and the *Daily Courant* and was immediately assaulted by *Fog's,* the author of which Popple dismissed as a "Cholerick Patriot." Other jibes at the opposition press and the opposition mentality appear in the *Prompter* from time to time, and after one such sally Budgell's *Bee* remarked, "Mr. *Fog* suspected long since that the *Prompter* would at last turn out to be a *Ministerial Paper,* and, in the Opinion of many People, that Author appears now bare-faced."[48] Popple answered this charge in *Prompter* No. 27 (11 February 1734/5), protesting impartiality, and it is true that his journal for the most part devoted itself exclusively to theatrical matters; nonetheless, some suspicion about the politics of his paper must have remained. Thus its praise of Fielding's *Pasquin* and the severe criticism in the *Grub-street Journal* indicate that the play was not reviewed along party lines; even the *Daily Gazetteer* in its denunciation of Fielding the following year (7 May 1737) admitted that in *Pasquin* Fielding "was not . . . guilty of the Fault he has since committed," since in that play he had avoided personal satire and had contented himself with general ridicule of election practices. In short, there is really little evidence to suggest that *Pasquin* was regarded as the daring political satire it is now said to be, much less as a stepping stone toward a Licensing Act.

Only with *The Historical Register for the Year 1736* and its eventual afterpiece *Eurydice Hissed,* in fact, did Fielding become

so openly and obviously satirical of Walpole as to provoke
contemporary comment and bring upon him the wrath of the
government press.⁴⁹ What prompted Fielding to drop his mask
of impartiality and write, for the first time, an obviously partisan
play? Critics tend to forget that between the production of
Pasquin and that of *The Historical Register* a full year passed, a
year in which the Prince of Wales moved into an open break
with the court and became irretrievably entrenched as the
nominal head of the opposition. The entire political atmosphere
was altered in 1737, with Walpole's position weaker than it had
been for four years; and the change in Fielding's manner and
the reception accorded him, can be explained, I think, in the
same way as the change in the reception of Thomson's *Liberty* in
1735–36 and that of his *Ode* in 1737—by the bustle of opposition
activity, with Lyttelton and Chesterfield beginning *Common Sense*
in January, and Pulteney presenting in February the parliamentary motion to increase the prince's allowance. At the same time,
Fielding's company at the Haymarket began a whole series of
plays presumably with anti-Walpole satiric twists,⁵⁰ with his own
Historical Register opening on 21 March and coinciding with the
appearance of the notorious "Vision of the Golden Rump" in
two issues of *Common Sense*. *Eurydice Hissed* had its first performance in April, followed at once by the opening shot in the *Daily
Gazetteer's* war on Fielding. In that same month appeared
Glover's *Leonidas,* with its attendant puffs in the opposition
press, and in May came Pope's vicious *Epistle to Augustus.* It is
against the background of this flurry of opposition plays, poems,
and parliamentary maneuvers that we must view both the
sudden sharpness of Fielding's satire and the introduction of the
Licensing Act in late May. The government papers can hardly
be blamed for ascribing such a concentrated onslaught to the
work of a well-organized group of "patriots"; the *Daily Gazetteer*
claimed Fielding was "secretly *buoy'd up,* by some of the *greatest
Wits* and *finest Gentlemen* of the Age" only *after* his success with
the relatively innocuous *Pasquin. The Historical Register,* according to the *Gazetteer,* then appeared "under the *Patronage* of the
Great, the *Sensible,* and the *Witty,* in the Opposition," for whom
Fielding was a mere *"Cat's Paw,"* "an Engine, supported by them,
to bespatter with."⁵¹

The play which excited such invective is too well known to require much comment; suffice it to say that *The Historical Register* works into its clever fabric all the conventional opposition motifs. Fielding's ironic "Dedication to the Public," which is perhaps wittier than the play itself, warns glumly of general corruption and the loss of liberty, swipes at the government journalists and the use of the post office to propagate their wares, and ironically defends *The Historical Register* as a ministerial pamphlet and Walpole as too sensible to be the patron of the *Gazetteer*. The play which follows presents, among other things, ridicule of both Cibbers; a mock auction of a remnant of political honesty, a piece of patriotism, interest at court, and the like (reminiscent of mock advertisements in the *Craftsman*); a discovery that "men of parts" are unfit for employment by the administration; and a dance of venal patriots bribed by Quidam (Walpole). All this was familiar fare to the audiences who packed the Haymarket from March until May, but both the deftness of its methods and the open partisanship of its satire clearly suited the town in the exacerbated political atmosphere of the spring of 1737. In the afterpiece, *Eurydice Hissed*, Fielding went on to a further triumph; here the usual parallel between the "states political and theatrical" is manipulated so skillfully that Fielding is able simultaneously to ridicule the failure of his own farce *Eurydice* and the failure of Walpole's excise bill. The character Pillage is clearly both playwright and prime minister, and his levee reminds us of the parallel between statesman and poet drawn in Fielding's poetic epistles to Walpole. As the *Gazetteer* pointed out (4 June 1737), the "Drift of the Allegory throughout, is too plain to be mistaken"; in his diary the earl of Egmont both interpreted correctly the allusions to Walpole's most notorious defeat and reported that the prince applauded vigorously at the "strong passages," "especially when in favour of liberty."[52]

The image of the Prince of Wales attending Fielding's farce at the Haymarket and clapping vigorously at strong passages in favour of liberty is a crucial one to keep in mind if we wish to understand the violent attacks on Fielding in the *Daily Gazetteer*, Fielding's spirited reply in the pages of *Common Sense*, and the enactment of the Licensing Act on 21 June, an act which by closing theaters except those with royal patents and by requiring all plays to be licensed by the lord chamberlain effectively put Fielding and his company out of business.[53] That act—which provoked a controversy in the press, elicited a famous speech by Chesterfield, and became the opposition's chief symbol of the administration's threat to liberty—must be viewed as the government's response to the whole complex of events in the spring of 1737, the most important element of which was the decision of the prince to move openly into opposition to Walpole. The press, as the *Gazetteer* itself admitted, could not be touched, but the stage could, and easily enough, given the history of efforts to regulate it on moral grounds and the previously successful efforts to suppress *Polly, The Fall of Mortimer,* and the like. Despite what Cibber and others were to claim, Fielding was not responsible for an act of Parliament which represented a simple countermove in a serious political game. Until 1737 Fielding was not primarily interested in political satire nor committed deeply to any political group; he was simply, in Sheridan Baker's words, "a talented young writer catching a popular advantage, willing to please the town, pleased to please his eminent and literate friends among the lords of the Opposition, really believing that most men have their prices, that Walpole has no monopoly on sin."[54] In his entire dramatic career he wrote only one play and one afterpiece that can be described accurately as thoroughly anti-Walpole or as comparable in any way to the level of satire familiar to readers of *Fog's,* the *Craftsman,* and the *Grub-street Journal.* These pieces appeared as part of a concerted literary-political campaign during three months of intensive opposition activity initiated by the Prince of Wales, and both Fielding and the stage suffered the consequences of events which had their origin in a family quarrel remote from the Little Theatre at the Haymarket.

Common Sense, the new weekly paper which did service in this campaign of wit, ran from 5 February 1737 until well after Walpole's fall; from November 1737 until June 1739 it was split, presumably because of a quarrel between printer and author, into *Old Common Sense* (issued from Bartholomew Close) and *Common Sense* (issued from White-Friars).[55] The paper which consistently retained the title *Common Sense* is of more than

ordinary significance in the relations between politics and literature in this period. Taking its name from Queen Common-
sense in Fielding's *Pasquin,* it was patronized by Chesterfield and
Lyttelton, both of whom were occasional contributors, and
conducted primarily by Charles Molloy, a minor dramatist who
had also written for *Fog's.* That the powers really behind the
paper may be more obscure is suggested by evidence which
George H. Jones discovered among the Stuart Papers at Windsor, evidence which provides a fascinating glimpse into the
literary-political intrigues of 1737. In the fall of 1736, these
documents indicate, the Pretender wrote his agent in Paris
urging that a new weekly paper be inaugurated, suggesting that
support would be given by English Jacobites, and recommending Charles Molloy as a good man who had offered his services.
The agent's response in February of 1737 cited a report by
George Kelly, a fellow conspirator with Atterbury, to the effect
that (1) Molloy was ready to start his paper; that (2) Pope, "qui
jusqua present, a evité dentrer dans aucune affaire de party,"
had offered *his* services to Molloy on the condition that his role
remain secret; and (3) that Chesterfield and Lord Grange had
offered their support as well. With such talent at their disposal,
the agent concluded, the venture could hardly fail. According to
Jones, the upshot of all this remains uncertain, since it is difficult
to determine whether Molloy actually received funds from
Jacobites or only from opposition Whigs.[56] Yet the correspondence clearly suggests Pope's willingness at this time to write for
a paper conducted by a man whom he may or may not have
known to be a Jacobite; this evidence is thus in some contrast to
Pope's high-sounding refusal in 1739 to allow Bolingbroke's
secretary to insert the *Essay on Man* into *Common Sense* "or any
avowed Party-Paper, on either side."[57]

Whether Pope did in fact contribute to *Common Sense* cannot
be known, but the paper was certainly a medium worthy of his
genius. Like *Fog's,* it has not been accorded the praise it is due by
literary historians, though even a hostile pamphlet at the time
was forced to admit that the "Wit, Humour, and Vivacity" of the
early issues promised a revival of a sort of writing that had been
absent from England for many years.[58] The "Printer to the
Reader" of the first collected edition (1738) indicates that its

style was intended to be one uncommon in political writings, "contrived as much to divert as to instruct the Publick, at the Expence of those who have long been diverting themselves at the Expence of the Publick."[59]

Chesterfield, in the opening issue, adopts the ironic, whimsical manner of the best of eighteenth-century periodical writers as he promises to judge all by the standard of common sense, whether authors, politicians, fine gentlemen, or the fair sex. Like Mr. Spectator, he sets for himself the general moral purpose of reforming abuses and shaming folly. There is no mention made directly of partisan politics, though his real intentions would have been clear to readers accustomed to the artful dodges of opposition journalism. In surveying the difficulty offered by his many rival papers, for instance, Chesterfield immediately places his paper in the proper camp: the *London Journal,* he says, "cannot possibly interfere with me, as appears from the very title of my paper"; *Fog's* is "now condensed into a cloud, and only used by way of wet brown paper, in case of falls and contusions"; the *Craftsman* is the only rival that troubles him—but there is world enough for them both and he never "observed Mr. D'Anvers to be an enemy to Common Sense."[60] The next issue, by another writer, then launches into the familiar Bolingbrokean attack on party divisions. The following week, Chesterfield returned to wax witty on an Indian mogul who was weighed on each birthday, an event turned by *Common Sense* into a connection between corpulence and stupidity with obvious allusion to Robert Walpole. The next issue, however, was a completely nonpolitical essay on foreign foppery and ladies' dress, only to be followed on 5 March by a pointed essay on avarice and on 19 and 26 March by the "Vision of the Golden Rump." The mixture of wit, morality, political discussion, and personal satire made the new organ a difficult one for Walpole's hacks to answer in kind, though Lady Mary Wortley Montagu tried her hand in the short-lived periodical *The Nonsense of Common Sense.*[61]

The superiority of opposition wit shines through many pages of *Common Sense,* then, but that familiar theme is manifested by precept as well as by example. The "Printer to the Reader" congratulates the nation on the fact that "all the Wit and Good

Sense should have appeared on the Side of Liberty," though the government writers have tried their best "to be arch and merry on the Side of Corruption."[62] But it is not merely a matter of the relative merits of the political writers on each side. In a brilliantly malicious essay on 8 October 1737, Chesterfield, as I have noted in the opening chapter, points to the astounding fact that all the poets and wits of distinction, all "the brightest Genius's of this Age," are agreed in their opposition to the administration, which appears "destitute of all Literary Support." The reasons for this are to be found, says Chesterfield, in the glaring corruptions of the government; and the consequences to Walpole himself are pointed up in the issue of *Common Sense* for 8 November 1740: "Posterity will not receive one Scrap of Paper in his Favour; whereas, on the other Hand, many of those Writings in which he is not very advantageously delineated will be preserved and read while Wit and Learning are tolerated or tasted in this Kingdom. In what a Light then must he inevitably, though unjustly, appear to Posterity?" This is merely a restatement, of course, of one of the great political myths of the opposition, but it must have seemed to have special relevancy in the years in which *Common Sense* appeared, after the open allegiance to the opposition shown by such writers as Thomson, Fielding, and Pope.

Pope's own contribution to the campaign of 1737 was one of his boldest. In the few years immediately preceding 1737, he had had little to say on politics, having remained relatively quiet since the flurry over his early Horatian Poems. The *Epistle to Dr. Arbuthnot* in 1735 had, it is true, made references to "Queens, Ministers, or Kings," had depicted the toad Hervey at the ear of Queen Caroline, and had made approving references to Swift, Gay, and Atterbury while pilloring Cibber, Henley, Lady Mary, Dodington, and Yonge; and perhaps, too, Pope's poem may have been responsible for the fact that nine days after its appearance the *Daily Courant* took the trouble to ridicule Dr. Arbuthnot as "Mr. *Florentine,*" the "*pastry Cook*" of the *Craftsman.*[63] But the bulk of the satire in that poem is personal and literary, not political, and it attracted no attention in political circles. Over the next two years Pope cemented his friendship with Lyttelton and with the Prince of Wales, who surprised him with a visit in October of 1735. By 1735, too, Pope was willing to publish letters containing malicious sneers at Walpole,[64] and it was in that same year that Lyttelton in the *Letters from a Persian* praised him for praising men out of power (Letter XXVIII). After the prince in the spring of 1737 finally accepted his role as titular head of the opposition, Pope—like Fielding—became more daring. In May appeared his *First Epistle of the Second Book of Horace*, usually called the *Epistle to Augustus*.

The central technique of Pope's poem, of course, is to apply to George Augustus, king of England, language appropriate to the Augustus whom Horace had addressed. The irony implied in the duplication of names and the contrast of characters had not gone unnoticed before Pope. Something of the sort, I think, had been hinted in the *Grub-street Journal* in 1732; in No. 106 (13 January 1731/2) an unnamed correspondent quoted lines on Augustus from another Epistle of Horace and added, "I wish I could translate them into two English ones as good; I would give 50 pounds. Let POPE himself do it, if he can, and apply them to our AUGUSTUS." His remark prompted not Mr. Pope but Mr. Maevius (one of the editors) to essay the translation in lines described by the *Journal* as "a short specimen of unpensioned Panegyric; intirely different from some *New-years Odes,* which, if the Author was not well known, might justly be looked upon as grave burlesques upon the Court." The slur at Cibber would ensure that Maevius's lines "To The King" would be taken ironically.

Pope's ironies in this remarkable Epistle have been often annotated. He works into the fabric of his praise sneers at the king's English, at his contempt for learning, his "repose" in the arms of his Hanoverian mistress, his (or Walpole's) pacific foreign policy in the face of threats to Britain's trade. Pope also contrasts George II to strong kings like Edward III or Henry V; praises Alfred, a king of central importance in the opposition view of history; and works in daring allusions to the feud within the royal family.[65] Even the literary sections of the poem would have seemed politically relevant to an audience conditioned to the reiterated laments in the opposition press that England had an Augustus but no Maecenas. In Pope's hands Horace's defense of modern poets somehow becomes another indictment of the decline of English culture, and a lecture on English literary history delivered to a monarch whose lack of interest in the arts was notorious seems beautifully inappropriate. Pope's completely utilitarian defense of poetry has special sarcasm: a poet is useful "to teach a Foreigner the tongue," and Pope

> scarce can think him such a worthless thing,
> Unless he praise some monster of a King,
> Or Virtue, or Religion turn to sport,
> To please a lewd, or un-believing Court.[66]

According to Swift's friend Alderman Barber, the lines in praise of Swift's *Drapier's Letters* almost brought government reprisals on Pope, but to my knowledge there is no reference to the *Epistle to Augustus* in the pro-Walpole press. Indeed the poem's irony made it difficult for the *Gazetteer* to maul Pope in the way that it was to do when faced with the openly partisan *Epilogue to the Satires* a year later; as I have noted earlier, the government preferred to ignore innuendoes in the works of writers of distinction like Pope and Thomson as long as it was possible to do so. But the lack of noticeable reaction in political journals does not mean that the poem was misread. Pope's sympathies had been made so obvious and his irony here is so pointed that it is doubtful that anyone familiar with the political world could have failed to see the real import of his lines. John Butt claims that the irony was "unnoticed" by the "vulgar," and he cites as evidence the following passage from *Common Sense* (8 October 1737): "Excepting a late Imitation of *Horace*, by Mr. *Pope*, who but seldom meddles with publick Matters, I challenge the Ministerial Advocates to produce one Line of *Sense*, or *English*, written on their Side of the Question for these last Seven Years."[67] In actuality, however, the passage (quoted earlier) is that by the earl of Chesterfield, a writer hardly unacquainted with irony or with Pope, and the essay in which it appears is devoted to sneering at the administration for its failure to win literary support.[68] The comment, appearing in a paper for which Pope himself had offered to write, is thus not a vulgar misreading but a nice irony itself, designed to amuse that literary-political "in-group" which constituted a part of its readership. The same paper, in fact, employed Pope's technique a few years later to draw an ironic parallel between George's reign and "the *Augustan* Age . . . famous for Learning, Arts, and

Sciences, for Politeness of Manners, and for the Wealth, Grandeur and Prosperity of the whole *Roman* Empire." The resemblance is so striking, he adds, that it is surprising "that our present Set of Bards have not made more Use of it than we find they have."[69] One such bard had indeed made use of it, and—if we may judge by the reaction in *Common Sense*—to good effect.

Though the *Epistle to Augustus* amused the knowledgeable and pleased the "patriotic" by its daring innuendoes, another year was to pass before Pope wrote a series of poems so openly political that they can be called a real contribution to opposition propaganda. In the interval the plans of his political friends took on an even more optimistic air than they had in the spring of 1737. The parliamentary moves in February to increase the prince's allowance had signaled the opening of a new antigovernment campaign, headed by the prince and supported in the writings of Fielding and Pope; and Frederick's final break with the royal family in July completed the formation of a more vigorous and determined opposition. When, in November, Queen Caroline died, the hopes of the opposition leaders soared. Chesterfield wrote Lyttelton, "It is most certain that Sir Robert must be in the utmost distress, and can never hope to govern the King as the Queen governed him. This truth is so obvious to everybody, that many people in place will act very differently with respect to Sir Robert from what they used to do, while they knew that he governed her, who absolutely governed the King."[70] And he advises how the prince should comport himself on this occasion and how Pulteney and Carteret, both of whom he distrusted, should be managed. Walpole did not succumb, however, to the difficulties posed by the death of the queen. It was not that event but the clouds of war with Spain which spelled disaster for the prime minister, a war encouraged by a tirade of propaganda in which both Patriot poetry and satiric ridicule played a significant role.

6 PRELUDE TO WAR: SATIRE AND PATRIOTISM, 1738–1739

WITH THE PRINCE of Wales now in their camp, the leaders of the opposition in the early months of 1738 had bright hopes for the accomplishment of their goal, the dismissal of Walpole. On 1 January Stair wrote to Marchmont in glowing terms of the possibilities of a party united behind the prince, and opposition newspapers all that year kept up a barrage of criticism of Walpole's peace policies. But the opposition was still too fragmented to succeed in a united effort. Marchmont's niece, Lady Murray, predicted in February that all her uncle's consultations would come to nothing, that Sir Robert would "outwit you every one." She blamed Pulteney for the collapse of such plans, and indeed Pulteney and Carteret, the nominal heads of the opposition in the Commons and the Lords, were viewed with hostility and suspicion by Cobham, Chesterfield, and other Patriot leaders. By May Marchmont had to admit that the opportunity offered by the prince's rupture with the king had been lost; he concluded, "In short, I look, as several others do, upon the opposition as at an end."[1]

There remained the issue of England's grievances over Spain's interference with her commercial interests, and here, of course, popular outcry drove Walpole eventually into war, declared against Spain in October 1739. But, again, in political terms the opposition gained little. When the signing of an Anglo-Spanish Convention worked out by Walpole's negotiators was debated in March 1739, a large group of his opponents abandoned the House for the rest of the session as a sign of protest. Again, Walpole adroitly converted their weapon into a boomerang, for the "secession," as it was called, afforded no advantage to the opposition.[2] One member complained that "leaving the House, and doing nothing on it but running up and down a-sporting, like a parcel of the silliest schoolboys when playing truant" was simply ridiculous; the popularity of the Patriots, he felt, had declined badly since the secession. Chesterfield gave directions that the secession should be "writ up" in *Common Sense* as much as possible, since it was generally misunderstood.[3] Even when the approach of "The War of Jenkins' Ear" became obvious, the opposition saw little to gain: "If Sir Robert carries on the approaching war with vigour, and like a man, who can hurt him? and if there is . . . some tergiversation, who can save him?"[4] So spoke the earl of Winchelsea and Nottingham in August 1739, but there seemed at the time little reason to expect tergiversation. Chesterfield put the same point wittily in a letter to Stair:

> What do you say to the vigour of our Administration? The sleeping lion is roused; and a hundred and twenty men of war now in commission, and forty thousand land-forces in England, will show our enemies abroad that they have presumed too much and too long upon Sir Robert's pacific temper. I say this on the supposition and hopes that these land-forces are only raised against our common enemies abroad, and not against Sir Robert's enemies at home; though I know which I believe.[5]

Sir Robert's enemies at home could see no immediate political advantage in the administration's sudden vigor, though the lion had been roused by the propaganda of their adherents.

Everyone recognized that the powerlessness of the opposition was the result of its very nature: an inharmonious, disorganized, fragmented coalition unable to mount a concerted attack. As Stair remarked astutely after the declaration of war, "Sir Robert's confidence is not in the strength of his own party, but in the disunion of his opposers; you know the skill he has to profit of the weaknesses of mankind."[6] Stair, Bolingbroke, Chesterfield, and others continued to call for unity and joint action, but the divisions within this amorphous and contentious group of malcontents continued to defeat them.

But if the parliamentary opposition failed in its maneuvers because of its own disunity, the literary figures toiling in the same vineyard found more fruitful soil. In contrast to the waverings which the correspondence of the politicians reveals, poets, playwrights, and satirists seemed to smell blood, and the two years just before the war with Spain were marked by a concerted outpouring of anti-Walpole literature which was to continue uninterrupted until his resignation four years later. In this period progovernment newspapers concentrated attacks upon literary figures and literary questions to a greater degree than they had deigned to do earlier. Though Fielding was silent until the end of 1739, writers as diverse in background as Pope, Glover, Thomson, Brooke, Whitehead, Akenside, and Samuel Johnson contributed their talents to protest ministerial corruption, the Licensing Act, and the Spanish depredations.

Even Gay must be included in such a list, for his *Fables Second Series* was published posthumously in 1738; written in 1731–32, these poems are, as the prefatory Advertisement admits, "mostly on subjects of a graver and more political Turn" than the First Series (1727), written before Gay's disappointment at court. Indeed, they are heavily political and rather heavy-handed as well. The usual themes of ministerial corruption, bribery, greed, and reliance on spies and informers permeate the stories of vultures, sparrows, baboons, poultry, and the like.[7] And Gay's ironic defense of his satire as general was also conventional:

> E'er I begin, I must premise
> Our ministers are good and wise;
> So, though malicious tongues apply,
> Pray, what care they, or what care I?
>   If I am free with courts; be't known,
> I ne'er presume to mean our own.
> If general morals seem to joke
> On ministers and such like folk,
> A captious fool may take offence;
> What then? He knows his own pretence.
> I meddle with no state-affairs,
> But spare my jest to save my ears.[8]

This declaration, its irony made obvious by the fears expressed in the last couplet, is followed at once by an explicit assault on wicked ministers surrounded by servile knaves who rise by "screening fraud," and finally by the fable of the greedy vulture who seizes ministerial power and is spurned by an honest sparrow (John Gay) scornful of preferment from rogues and liars. If a collection of such fables had been published in 1727, it would have aroused a storm; that Gay's *Second Series* went virtually unnoticed by the political press in 1738 is excellent testimony to both the intensity and the extensiveness of anti-Walpole literature in the waning years of his administration. Walpole's propagandists had more important literary targets to aim at than the generalized satire of a poet dead for six years.

The Politicizing of Pope

Above all the progovernment writers had Alexander Pope to contend with, for 1738 was the year when that poet became fully committed to politics. Before the year was over he had published poems in which, for the first time, he abandoned Horatian innuendo for overt castigation of the ministerial forces and in which he fused the two strains of patriotic and satiric literature of the opposition. And in the same year he was attacked by Walpole's propagandists with a fury which suggests they were venting anger and resentment long stored up against the wasp of Twickenham and only held in check previously for lack of sufficient provocation. At any rate, Pope's advance into open battle with the adherents of the administration put him at the center of the literary-political stage; he was vilified, defended, and imitated. Because of his entry into the fray, verse satires decrying the state of the nation under Walpole abounded, and the argument in the political press about the value of satire became intensified. During much of the period in question Bolingbroke was over from France, advising and consorting with opposition leaders as usual, and both his correspondence and Pope's show that by the end of 1739 the poet whose claims to political neutrality had so long been a byword was himself actively engaged in partisan plotting that went well beyond the writing of poems.

All this began with the publication in March 1738 of *The First Epistle of The First Book of Horace Imitated*. Not only does this poem address Bolingbroke the arch-conspirator in terms approaching deification ("That Man divine whom Wisdom calls her own"), it also presents in unmistakable terms the symbolic contrast between pursuit of virtue in the country and pursuit of wealth or place at court, a contrast which Maynard Mack has fully explored in *The Garden and the City*. The language spoken at Cressy and Poitiers—the language of militant patriotism—is contrasted to "the modern language of corrupted peers," as is the "good old song" to the "new Court jargon," virtue to avarice, and the armor of innocence to a "Screen" or "Wall of Brass," epithets conventionally applied, of course, to Walpole.

The poem was simply too provocative for the *Daily Gazetteer*, which had refrained from calling attention to the irony of *Epistle to Augustus* a year earlier; now it launched an attack on Pope at once (27 March 1738), concentrating its fire on the compliment which this "very great Writer" had paid to Bolingbroke and also deriding the earlier praise of Bolingbroke in the *Essay on Man*. In view of Bolingbroke's life, the *Gazetteer* asks, could not such praise of his virtue be taken as satire rather than panegyric? "Would not the Lord *B*—— himself consider such Verses from any other Hand, as meant rather to affront him than to do him Honour?" The same newspaper, after pausing on 5 April to sneer at *Gulliver's Travels* as an opposition treasure trove, repeated its attacks on Pope in its issues of 6, 11, and 12 April, while Pope was defended by wretched verses in *Old Common Sense* on 15 April. The first of the *Gazetteer* attacks (6 April) included a poem of some literary interest. Note these lines of advice to Bolingbroke, which put both Pope's praise and the ideal of virtuous retirement in a rather different light:

> Far, far from *Courts,* hence, wisely trust for Fame
> To *Twick'nam*'s Bowers, and the Banks of *Thame,*
> By gentle Bard be sung in gentle Strain,
> And the calm *Hero* of a *Couplet* reign;
> So may thy Virtues tinkle in our Ear,
> Thy *Honour spotless,* and thy *Soul sincere*;
> Safe from thy Arts, so may thy harml[e]ss Praise
> In harmless Song our *Doubt* and *Pleasure* raise;
> Our *Doubt,* so *true* a *Briton* e'er cou'd be;
> Our *Mirth,* to find that *B*——*ling*——*ke* is *He.*

The *Gazetteer* of 12 April more directly accused Pope of being a party writer, but the lines quoted above, which ridicule the essential irrelevance of imaginative writing and the harmlessness of tinkling verses, are more typical of the ambivalent attitude of Walpole's writers toward the literary opposition, an attitude which mingled respect with contempt.

Thus by May, when *One Thousand Seven Hundred and Thirty Eight* (Dialogue I of *Epilogue to the Satires*) appeared, the attention of the town was already focused on Pope's new posture as an openly political poet. Readers would have expected a new boldness in his new poem after such a torrent of criticism, and they were not disappointed. Pope begins, interestingly enough, with an echo of the dispute over the proper role of satire, a literary question with considerable political overtones. Horatian delicacy, the Friend objects, is missing in Pope's works:

> *Horace* would say, *Sir* Billy *serv'd the Crown,*
> Blunt *could do Bus'ness,* H——ggins *knew the Town.* . . .
> And own, the *Spaniard* did a *waggish thing,*
> Who cropt our Ears, and sent them to the King.
> (Lines 14–15, 18–19)[9]

Horace could make Augustus smile, and was

> An artful Manager, that crept between
> His Friend and Shame, and was a kind of *Screen.*
> (Lines 21–22)

In this remarkable passage Pope appears to have the Friend voice arguments in favor of the kind of satire approved by the ministerial advocates, but simultaneously manages—by Horatian insinuation—to ridicule Walpole's henchman Sir William Yonge, linked here with a shady figure like Huggins; to attack Walpole's pacific policy toward Spain; and to transform Horace into Walpole himself, the "artful Manager" who "screens" his friends from shame. The use of the conventional epithet "Screen" makes Pope's "complimentary" portrait five lines later of Walpole in his social hours seem a bit disingenuous.

The remainder of the poem maintains the brilliance of the opening, as, mingling innuendo and exhortation, Pope lashes out at the government forces, from courtiers like Hervey and Yonge down to scribblers like Henley, "Mother Osborne," and the writers of the *Gazetteer.* The final sections on the "dignity of Vice" look forward to the apocalyptic mood of the last book of *The Dunciad* in their vision of a world of lost patriotism and inverted values:

> Lo! at the Wheels of her Triumphal Car,
> Old *England's* Genius, rough with many a Scar,
> Dragg'd in the Dust! his Arms hang idly round,
> His Flag inverted trails along the ground! . . .
> See thronging Millions to the Pagod run,
> And offer Country, Parent, Wife, or Son!
> Hear her black Trumpet thro' the Land proclaim,
> That "Not to be corrupted is the Shame."
>   (Lines 151–54, 157–60)

It is true that the "Patriot" is included with the "Man in Pow'r" in the list of those who succumb to avarice and that Pope has hinted earlier in the poem that some patriots (Pulteney and Carteret) do not deserve that name; but about the partisanship of this vision of the triumph of Vice there can be no question. Not only is the contrast of "Old England's" heroism with modern-day cowardice a familiar theme of the opponents of Walpole's foreign policy, but the generalized picture of universal corruption and even specific details like the Pagod (George II and/or Walpole) are commonplaces of opposition journalism.[10]

The *Gazetteer* struck back at once with a serious, bitter essay which impugned the value of Pope's poem without ever mentioning his name or the poem's title (though specific lines are alluded to). Its approach in answering Pope is to apply realistic criteria to the satiric fiction and hyperbole which "these great Masters of Satyr" have created: "If their Representation of Things is true, there never was a People so degenerated and sunk so low in Vileness and Infamy as we; for I think, according to their Account of the Matter, there are not above ten or a dozen wise and honest Men in the Nation, and those all within the Circle of their own Friends and Acquaintance." The writer marvels sarcastically at the extraordinary transformation the British have undergone, so that suddenly, among a people once famous for knowledge and virtue, *"the Soldier, the Churchman, the Patriot, and the Man in Power, should all think it a Shame not to be corrupted. . . .* But as much a Prodigy as all this may seem, the Satyrist has said it, and therefore there is no disputing the Truth of the Fact." After this literal-minded but unsurprising objection that Pope's satiric rhetoric does not match the obvious facts of the real world, the *Gazetteer* attacks the use of real names in satire and bitterly points to the partisan bias of this poem by a "Writer who professes himself to be of no Party, and to be guided by no other Spirit, but that of Truth and Justice."[11]

The second Dialogue of *One Thousand Seven Hundred and Thirty Eight* appeared in July. Once again Pope opens with a discussion over the role of satire, a discussion which, as I have said, echoes the controversy over that genre in the political press of both sides. As in Dialogue I he had contrasted Horatian with Juvenalian modes, so here he defends the use of personal rather than general satire—perhaps as a response to the *Gazetteer*'s criticism of his use of proper names. Sarcastically he sketches the folly of damning the dice but not the sharper. Then, after touching on the proper objects of satire as well as its mode, Pope puts his principles into practice. Intermixed with sections which "maul" Walpole's "Tools" like Nicholas Paxton is panegyric on the opposition figures Bolingbroke, Pulteney, Chesterfield, Wyndham, Cobham, Lyttelton, Polwarth, and even the exiled Atterbury. His special love, he says, goes out to worthy men removed from a court. Argyle and Pelham, both at that point being wooed by the opposition, share in the praise.[12] When the Friend offers the usual ministerial jibe at the opposition, "I think your Friends are out, and would be in," the poet responds, "If merely to come in, Sir, they go out,/ The way they take is strangely round about" (ll. 123–25).

As in the first Dialogue, Pope carefully includes a "compliment" to Walpole himself. In a passage in which he pretends he is lying like the *Gazetteer* about public figures, he says, "Sir ROBERT's mighty dull,/ Has never made a Friend in private life,/ And was, besides, a Tyrant to his Wife." Moreover, he claims he will use no odious names like "Wolsey" for the minister: "Why rail they then, if but a Wreath of mine/ Oh All-accomplish'd St. JOHN! deck thy Shrine?" (ll. 133–35, 138–39). (Railing, of course, had been the response of the government press to his eulogy of Bolingbroke in *Epistle* I.i in March.) Just after the poem was published Pope called Fortescue's attention to these references to Walpole: "You see I have made him a second compliment in print in my second Dialogue, and he ought to take it for no small one, since in it I couple him with Lord Bol——. As he shews a right sense of this, I may make him a third, in my third Dialogue."[13] Though critics have taken the compliments with some seriousness, Pope's condescending tone leaves no doubt, I think, of his intention, nor do the passages themselves bear close examination. The prime minister could not have been greatly flattered to learn that only before assuming power could he be happy or have friends, or to be reminded that now he can smile only with art and win only with bribes, or to be praised for his indifference to his wife's notorious infidelity. And though Pope may not have been politically sophisticated, he must have known that Walpole could not have been less than insulted to be linked with his arch-enemy Bolingbroke. The distinction between Walpole's public and private lives need not be taken very seriously; where the minister himself is concerned, Pope will deal in dubious compliments rather than odious names, but the poem in sum is an indictment of a moral infection the source of which can only be found in the person of Sir Robert.

The final seventy lines of the Dialogue, indeed, put the issues squarely in moral rather than political terms. Pope's provocation is "The strong antipathy of Good to Bad"; he is

> So impudent, I own myself no Knave:
> So odd, my Country's Ruin makes me grave.
> Yes, I am proud; I must be proud to see
> Men not afraid of God, afraid of me:
> Safe from the Bar, the Pulpit, and the Throne,
> Yet touch'd and sham'd by *Ridicule* alone.
> (Lines 206–11)

In the impassioned praise of Ridicule which closes the poem Pope merges his assault on corruption of the body politic with an apotheosis of poetic art as the ultimate weapon of truth:

> Ye tinsel Insects! whom a Court maintains,
> That counts your Beauties only by your Stains,
> Spin all your Cobwebs o'er the Eye of Day!
> The Muse's wing shall brush you all away. . . .
> Truth guards the Poet, sanctifies the line,
> And makes Immortal, Verse as mean as mine.
>   Yes, the last Pen for Freedom let me draw,
> When Truth stands trembling on the edge of Law.
> (Lines 220–24, 246–49)

The references elsewhere in the poem to Paxton, Walpole's discoverer of libels, give more than rhetorical force to the last lines quoted; Pope clearly expected Truth to suffer at the hands of Law in the form of some extension of the Licensing Act to cover books as well as plays. Swift thought the second Dialogue equal to anything else Pope had written. And despite Pope's partisan bias—or rather because of it—the two Dialogues together represent perhaps the finest poems to spring from the opposition to Walpole, not only because of their rhetorical power or technical virtuosity but also because of their fervent defense of the role of the man of letters in political society at a time when such a role was becoming increasingly trivialized or contemned.

But the very loftiness of Pope's manner made his poem easy to mock, and the *Gazetteer,* which launched a second full-scale attack on 24 August in response to the second Dialogue, ridiculed the pious overtones. In "A Dialogue in Prose" between *A* and *B,* the *Gazetteer* has *A* ask, "Are you not afraid of Ridicule? That *sacred Weapon,* that, brandish'd by *Heaven-directed Hands,* strikes a Terror into those who are not in Awe of any thing else?" *B* says the Minister "only laughs at those things," but *A* warns that Pope will make him tremble. The *Gazetteer* then launches into a personal attack on Pope, with further lampoons following in the issues of 26 August, 12 and 19 October, and 19 December. Some effort was also made to mock Pope by imitating his Dialogues; *A Dialogue on One Thousand Seven Hundred and Thirty-Eight: Together with A Prophetic Postscript as to One Thousand Seven Hundred and Thirty-Nine* appeared in 1738, as did *A Supplement to One Thousand Seven Hundred Thirty-eight; Not written by Mr. Pope.* Although both these dull poems concentrate on personal attacks (the *Supplement* even drags out the old charges of Pope's Jacobitism), they are interesting because of the tone they take about satire and wit. In the *Dialogue,* the "Patriot stile" is identified with the satiric "itch" in England, and a horrific vision is presented of a future state in which the wits have triumphed, the government is administered by Lyttelton, and the lawyers pay homage to Fielding. The *Supplement* first ridicules Pope's lack of verisimilitude in his hyperbolic assumption that men out of power are endowed with virtue:

> What? knaves at ten, and honest folks at five?
> Say, dearest poet, does the convert tribe,
> Brib'd in the morn, that evening hate a bribe?
> Does the old thirst so soon the soul forsake?
> Is it, they will not—or they cannot take?
> Does *St*[owe]'s pure air, or *Dawl*[e]y's, in an hour,
> Cleanse just like soap; like purgatory scour?
> (P. 10)

After this application of political realism to the fiction of Pope's poem, the writer indicts satire which paints the whole world black and suggests a mercenary motive for Pope's inability to write panegyric. Like the *Gazetteer,* then, these poems—for patently political reasons—question the morality of both Juvenalian and personal satire. Pope's two Dialogues clearly intensified the literary-political dispute over satire which I have examined in Chapter 1.[14]

Though I have encountered no direct references to it in the political press, Johnson's *London,* published the same day as Pope's first Dialogue, may also have figured in the minds of those who questioned the moral utility of satire. Indeed, it may well have been included in the *Gazetteer's* contemptuous phrase "these great Masters of Satyr" in its opening blast at Pope's first Dialogue. For it is well known that Johnson's imitation of Juvenal's third satire, written within a year of his arrival in London, is unmistakably intended as a contribution to opposition propaganda. Like Pope's Dialogues, it intermingles patriotic romanticizing of Britain's past with Juvenalian castigation of her present degeneracy:

> In pleasing dreams the blissful age renew,
> And call Britannia's glories back to view;
> Behold her cross triumphant on the main,
> The guard of commerce, and the dread of Spain,
> Ere masquerades debauch'd, excise oppress'd,
> Or English honour grew a standing jest.[15]

Sir John Hawkins, in his *Life of Johnson* (1787), suggested quite accurately that the topics of the satire were drawn from "weekly publications," the *Craftsman* in particular, designed to furnish the malcontents with matters of complaint which Hawkins itemized unsympathetically as follows:

That science was unrewarded, and the arts neglected; that the objects of our politics were peace and the extension of commerce; that the wealth of the nation was unequally divided, for that, while some were poor, others were able to raise palaces and purchase manors; that restraints were laid on the stage; that the land was plundered, and the nation cheated; our senators hirelings, and our nobility venal; and, lastly, that in his visits to his native country, the king drained this of its wealth.[16]

All these complaints, of course, are aired in Johnson's *London*. As Donald Greene has pointed out, the poem also contains a recitation of many nonpolitical aspects of London which Johnson happened to dislike,[17] but that does not make the satire less political; Pope, after all, had intermixed social with political satire even in his most obviously partisan poems. Unlike Pope, however, Johnson has little personal satire here; Hervey (or Henley, as Greene suggests) is attacked, the *Gazetteer* is sneered at, and perhaps the portrait of Orgilio is meant to caricature Walpole; but the poem is declamatory and somber rather than vicious and witty. Greene puzzles a bit over Johnson's sudden plunge into partisan politics; without quarreling with the psychological explanation he offers and without denying the influence of Savage over Johnson at this time, one might again suggest that in the late 1730s no aspiring writer could ignore support of the opposition as the most likely way to literary success. According to Hawkins (p. 34), Lyttelton carried Johnson's poem "in rapture" to Pope, who praised it and made efforts to discover its author; even if the anecdote is untrue, Johnson, like Savage, would certainly have known the value in 1738 of a poet's dependence on the statesmen out of power.

Johnson's poem sold well, but it was virtually ignored by the government press, which—in what little space it gave to literary matters at all—had its hands full coping with the much greater impact on the town of Pope's Dialogues. For those poems seem to have encouraged a host of minor poets to try their hands at verse satires on the corrupt state of Walpole's England. These poems all appeared in 1738 and 1739: *The Present Corruption of Britons, Being a Paraphrase on the Latter Part of Mr. P——e's first Dialogue,* by Bezaleel Morrice; *The World Unmask'd: A Satire;* Paul Whitehead's *Manners: A Satire; The Sixteenth Epode of Horace, Imitated, and addressed to the People of England;* and *The State of Rome, under Nero and Domitian,* possibly by Whitehead also. The last poem, like Johnson's *London,* is an imitation of Juvenal, and there is a Juvenalian cast to many of these anti-Walpole productions in the late 1730s. One scholar has recently pointed to a preference for Juvenal as characteristic of the second half of the century; but I would add that the declamatory rhetoric and zeal for liberty which Dryden admired in Juvenal also made him an apt model for Patriot satirists in the last years of Walpole's power. As Howard Weinbrot has demonstrated, the reputation of Horace, the court poet and flatterer, was suffering a decline in these years for reasons that were more political than literary; a satirist, Pope and others were saying, must oppose a corrupt court, not befriend it—laughing at folly rather than attacking vice must be reserved for times less vicious.[18]

Of these poems Whitehead's *Manners* (published by Dodsley in February 1739) evoked the most significant reaction, though it is fairly conventional in its satire on corrupt courtiers, its denigration of the policy toward Spain, and its patriotic prophecy of a triumphant Britain united under Frederick. All major opposition leaders are praised, Pulteney and Carteret as well as Chesterfield and Cobham, and there is the obligatory ridicule of Cibber, Henley, Hervey, Yonge, the Licensing Act, and the *Gazetteer*. More significant is the reason Whitehead gives for not attacking Walpole himself:

> I name not W——e; You the Reason guess:
> Mark yon fell Harpy hov'ring o'er the Press.
> Secure the Muse may sport with Names of Kings,
> But Ministers, my Friend, are dang'rous Things.
> Who would have *P*[axto]*n* answer what he writ?
> Or special Juries, Judges of his Wit?
> *Pope* writes unhurt—but know, 'tis different quite
> To beard the Lion, and to crush the Mite.
> Safe may he dash the Statesman in each Line,
> Those dread his Satire, who dare punish mine.
> (Pp. 13–14)

These lines proved more prophetic than the rhapsodic vision of Frederick's future reign which closes the poem; the reaction to *Manners* was severe, and crushing the mite Whitehead was interpreted as warning, if not bearding, the lion Pope. The two were attacked in tandem by the *Gazetteer* (15 February 1738/9) in a leader accusing both poets of mistaking the true nature of satire, and again on 20 February in a *Gazetteer* farce called "The Mock Patriots: Or the Knights of the Close Stool." They were also coupled in a libelous poem called *Characters: An Epistle to Alexander Pope, Esq; and Mr. Whitehead.* But the real warning to Pope, if such was intended, was the fact that *Manners* was declared scandalous by the House of Lords, and Dodsley and

Whitehead were ordered into custody. Whitehead absconded, but the point had been made. One pamphlet two years later claimed that the government's action "struck Mr. *Pope* with such a Pannic and trembling in his Nerves, that he has not since been able to hold a Pen."[19] Pope's later note to the second Dialogue put his silence in a more favorable light: "Could he have hoped to have amended any, he had continued those attacks; but bad men were grown so shameless and so powerful, that Ridicule was become as unsafe as it was ineffectual."[20]

Whether Pope was indeed frightened into silence or merely gave up in despair, we cannot say; but the Dialogue published in July 1738 was his last poem during Walpole's administration. Yet the attacks on him by government writers continued through 1739 and beyond. The *Gazetteer* in January 1739 made much of the criticism of the *Essay on Man* by Crousaz, and hit at Pope more directly in its issues of 16 June and 6 July. In May it reprinted a vicious indictment of Pope from a political pamphlet called *Modern Characters,* of which a few lines will suffice as an example:

The Character I am now to delineate is not that of a Man, but rather the *Shadow* of one, who, puffed up to the highest Pitch of *Vanity,* imprudently steps out of the Road pointed out to him by Nature, to thrust himself into the Rank of *mock Patriots* and *Statesmen.* Would the Pride of his wasted Heart permit him to see how despicable a Figure he makes in the Company that admits him, I cannot but think he would quit it to return to his . . . Vocation of simple *Sonnateer.*[21]

The remarkable thing is not the abuse but the fact that a political pamphlet has thought the "simple Sonnateer" worth so much attention; Pope is, in fact, treated here as one of the "six chief incendiaries," a list including also Chesterfield, Bolingbroke, Pulteney, and Wyndham. That is tribute indeed to the political effect of his satire.

Pope was, at the least, nettled by these attacks, but he refused to answer. Writing to the countess of Burlington in September 1738, he mocked the quality of the diatribes against him in the *Gazetteer* but resolved not to reply even if Hervey "owned" them, "nay if Sir Robert, & his Brother, & Mr Paxton, & Ch. Churchill, & Mr Ripley, & Tom Walker, all begged me on their knees to take notice of them so far." Again in May 1739, just at the time

Modern Characters was being reprinted in the *Gazetteer*, he affected the same nonchalance in reporting these assaults to Swift: "The Ministerial Writers rail at me, yet I have no quarrel with their Masters, nor think it of weight enough to complain of them." Nonetheless, as Sherburn points out, in the same letter Pope quotes for Swift a passage of ten lines he has written for the next edition of *The Dunciad,* a passage attacking "Mother Osborne," Nicholas Paxton, and the *Gazetteer.*[22]

Pope was perhaps more stung by the railing of the ministerial writers than he cared to admit, and he certainly had more of a quarrel with their masters than he indicated to Swift. For in 1738 the poet who was now the chief literary voice of the opposition also began serving as a minor political go-between and serious expositor of a political credo. In October he apparently received some instructions of a political nature from the duke of Argyle, and that same month Lyttelton called upon him to keep company as much as possible with the prince, to "Animate him to Virtue," and—by implication—to immortalize him in some writings. Somewhat more menial is the task for Pope which Bolingbroke suggested to Polwarth at the time of the "Secession"; if Polwarth wishes to make use of Bolingbroke's memorandum on the affair, he should first call in Pope to disguise the style.[23] Again, writing to Lyttelton in November 1738, Pope gave a full report of a conference with Wyndham on the state of the opposition, which—Wyndham warns Lyttelton through Pope—will "become nothing more than a Bubble-Scheme" if its nominal leaders Carteret and Pulteney are not somehow separated from those who wish to follow its original principle. Pope ends this letter with his own Bolingbrokean praise of the Patriot prince: "I wish him at the Head of the Only Good Party in the Kingdome, that of Honest Men; I wish him Head of no other Party. And I think it a Nobler Situation, to be at the head of the Best Men of a Kingdom than at the Head of any Kingdom upon earth."[24] Moreover, he would do his part to disseminate his friend's ideas. In 1738–39 he was commissioned by Bolingbroke to arrange a private printing of the *Letters on History* and was also entrusted with the manuscript of *The Idea of a Patriot King,* which—in an act that infuriated Bolingbroke—he later had published in an unauthorized edition of 1500 copies.[25] The poet who for so long boasted that he was of no party had

now become thoroughly politicized; both in private and in
public voice he spoke of his complete commitment.

In retrospect, the whole process of Pope's transformation into
an openly political poet seems most remarkable for the violence
of the reaction it provoked. The government forces were
aroused by his entry into the fray with the *Dialogues* of 1738 as
they had been aroused by no other literary event in the decade.
Mack has argued (pp. 190–200) that Pope became a symbol, a
"spiritual patron," of the poetic opposition with the publication
of his first Horatian Imitation in 1733; for the literati, who could
read his verse with understanding, he may well have served as
such a symbol, but there is no evidence that the political
world—as that world is reflected in the political writings of both
sides—took real notice of Pope until 1738, when the greatest
poet of the age took a stand against the government, unmistakably and in full view. Despite a decade of ridicule of men of
letters as unfit for business, the ministerial writers found Pope's
outspoken pledge of allegiance and the brouhaha which accompanied it too much to stomach. The bitterness of their
reaction says much, I think, about the esteem in which "wit" was
still held and about the political impact still possible for literary
figures to make.

Patriot Poets and the War with Spain

From a political point of view Pope's onslaught in the spring
and summer of 1738 was easily the major literary event of the
year, but as agitation over the Spanish depredations increased,
the Patriot poets also claimed the attention of the town. The
allegations then current of crimes against humanity and of
threats to British trade made attacks on Spain and appeals to
patriotism a natural subject for poets writing in the tradition of
Whig panegyric; and the adulation of Elizabeth which was so
important a part of the Patriot view of history made inevitable a
contrast between the defeat of the Armada and Walpole's efforts
at conciliation.[26] Akenside's *The Voice of Liberty; or a British
Philippic* is typical of the strain in its call for patriotic fervor to
answer the Spaniards' insults and its lament for the lost spirit of
Britain, once so generous but now dissipated by vice:

> Each kindling Thought
> That warm'd our Sires, is lost, ignobly lost
> In Luxury and Av'rice. —Baneful Vice!
> How it unmans a Nation! Yet I'll try,
> I'll aim to shake this vile degen'rate Sloth.[27]

And try he does, very rhapsodically. Nothing in the poem is specifically political, but the context of controversy over Spain made this poem, like so many in the period, a party document. Literary indictment of Walpole's peace policy was not, of course, confined to such lofty exhortations but covered the range from serious poetry to ballads and lampoons. Thus Swift's little poem on the character of Walpole was picked up and used by *Common Sense* on 14 April 1739, when the lines "Cur-Dog of Britain and Spaniel of *Spain*" made it especially timely; and supporters of the administration resorted to similar lowly modes in their effort to defend the Convention with Spain and a pacific foreign policy.[28] Joseph Trapp even preached and printed a hilariously ironic sermon ridiculing Walpole's posture toward Spain; called *The Ministerial Virtue: Or, Long-Suffering Extolled in a Great Man,* the sermon "praises" the peaceable disposition of the king and chief minister: "Come hither then ye . . . turbulent Spirits. . . . *Consider and behold!* Was ever *Patience* like to this *Patience?*"[29] As with the excise affair, popular feeling over the Spanish depredations found expression in a variety of forms, subliterary as well as literary.

Another popular issue exploited to good advantage by the opposition in 1738–39 was that of censorship. Objections to the Licensing Act of 1737 and fears that its provisions would be extended to cover printed books were increasingly aired in 1738 and became a *cause célèbre* in 1739. A series of raids by government agents on the *Craftsman* and *Old Common Sense* gave substance to such suspicions.[30] Even Thomas Cooke, one of the figures of *The Dunciad* and no wit by any stretch of the term, objected in print to restrictions on the stage, and Lord Bristol, the father of Lord Hervey, regarded the Act as but one more sign of the "total disregard paid to the interests and affections of the people."[31] In this atmosphere, not surprisingly, Milton's *Areopagitica* was reprinted with a foreboding preface by "Another Hand"—James Thomson. As usual with such propaganda,

Thomson cautiously pretends he is warning about a dubious future rather than protesting present measures: "I hope it will never be this Nation's Misfortune to fall into the Hands of an Administration, that do not from their Souls abhor any thing that has but the remotest Tendency towards the Erection of a new and arbitrary Jurisdiction over the Press."[32] Though there are no direct references to the Licensing Act in the semireligious language of Thomson's preface, it is in the background of his assumption that complete censorship is just around the corner. Two months later Thomson published a translation of another tract by Milton, *A Manifesto of the Lord Protector of the Commonwealth*, designed to help inflame sentiment against Spain; to make his intention (and his hand) unmistakable, Thomson appended his poem *Britannia* to the translation.

But agitation over these two prime issues, Spain and censorship, reached its peak in the literary world in 1739, when the Patriot poets attempted a concerted campaign on the stage. Here, for once, there seems to have been a planned, organized literary attack from the circle surrounding Prince Frederick, with the prince himself taking a hand in the complicated negotiations over the order in which plays would be performed. The main parties were the playwrights Thomson, Mallet, Hill, and Brooke, with advice given by Bolingbroke, Lyttelton, and Pope. Pope may also have been considering a more active role, since his epic on Brutus was perhaps being planned at this time as a contribution to the opposition's effort to create an ethos of "Bolingbrokean" patriotism. But his correspondence reveals that he was kept busy enough soothing the easily wounded feelings of Aaron Hill, whose play *Caesar* was never accepted for performance.[33]

These negotiations occurred in the fall and winter of 1738–39; earlier, however, in April 1738, Thomson had demonstrated that little was to be feared from the lord chamberlain by producing his flagrantly political play, *Agamemnon*, in which the title character takes a role secondary to the evil Aegisthus-Walpole and a somewhat softened Clytemnestra-Caroline.[34] The play was reasonably successful and correctly interpreted (Pope was doubtless alluding to it when he cited "Aegisthus" as a name for Walpole in his first Dialogue the following month), but the licensers were somehow offended only by the last four lines of the epilogue. Encouraged by its successful run—Thomson himself seems to have expected it to be banned—the opposition dramatists went forward with their plans for the next season. First, by the prince's direction, Mallet's play *Mustapha* appeared in February 1739, complete with its evil minister plotting against a noble heir to the throne. Because of its success, the lord chamberlain soon took a more severe line.[35] While in rehearsal in March, Henry Brooke's contribution to this campaign, *Gustavus Vasa,* was prohibited, and about a week later Thomson's *Edward and Eleonora* was also denied a license for performance. Both writers promptly prepared subscription editions of their plays, which were printed in May. In each case the playwright profited by the subscription, since, as Douglas Grant points out, to subscribe became a gesture of allegiance to those in opposition to the government.[36]

Both playwrights declared themselves free of any political intentions, and the old duchess of Marlborough, having read *Gustavus Vasa* in manuscript, professed the same opinion: "The story is not at all applicable to our present times, but of a King of Sweden, and has nothing in it but characters of virtuous people and speaking on the side of liberty, which is now a great offence."[37] Yet the duchess need not have been surprised at these first two applications of the Licensing Act in its two-year history. In the highly charged atmosphere of 1739, with its crisis over the Spanish depredations, speaking on the side of liberty had indeed become a great offense, especially in plays coming from the circle around the prince and boasting the usual trappings of Patriot drama (corrupt ministers, heroic saviors, and the like). The fact that these plays were banned whereas more provocative plays, like *Mustapha* or Thomson's own *Agamemnon,* had earlier managed to reach the stage intact indicates that the government was becoming increasingly cautious and alarmed at the success of Patriot drama.[38] One can thus take quite literally a quip intended as irony in *Old Common Sense* (24 March 1739): "Considering the Title Mr. Brook has given his Play, *The* DELIVERER *of his* COUNTRY, how can we wonder that the LICENSER would think proper to reject it?"

Naturally enough, however, the opposition press was quick to capitalize on this new *cause célèbre* which the lord chamberlain had so obligingly handed them by banning Brooke's play. The

Craftsman and other antiministerial papers rang the usual changes on the themes of freedom from arbitrary suppression of ideas, and Samuel Johnson wrote a scathingly ironic *Vindication of the Licensers of the Stage, from the Malicious and Scandalous Aspersions of Mr. Brooke.*[39] Johnson's "Whiggish" defense of individual liberty here has given some pause to commentators concerned to reconcile the tract with his later political ideas, but perhaps it is unnecessary to regard the piece as an expression of political principles at all; Johnson is writing a partisan tract about a current issue, and the political language he uses is both appropriate to the moment and consistent with the propaganda emanating from other Patriot sources on this occasion. Indeed, despite its excellence, the *Vindication,* as far as I can determine, was neither answered, imitated, nor even mentioned in the uproar in the press that spring over the Licensing Act.

Much of that uproar, of course, consisted of personal attacks on Brooke and Thomson by ministerial writers. One poem called *The Satirists* included Thomson in its ridicule along with genuine satirists like Pope and Swift; and the *Gazetteer* attacked both poets on four separate occasions in April and May.[40] What is most interesting about the *Gazetteer* essays is that, although the writer began the series by accusing Brooke and Mallet of having become mercenary party-writers, he quickly shifted the attack into purely literary channels. In the issue for 21 May, for example, the *Gazetteer* went into some detail to show the deficiencies of *Gustavus Vasa* as a drama, concluding with this remark directed to Brooke: "Without one Qualification of a *Dramatick Poet* . . . you have not only ventured to *write a play,* but *loudly* and *publickly* to complain of all who dare to disapprove of it." That sentence—indeed, the whole essay—seems obviously designed to leave readers with a vague impression that the play had been suppressed on grounds of taste rather than politics. The play's literary faults may, in fact, have seemed more evident to the public than its political offenses; one Thomas Edwards, for example, spoke of the political harmlessness of both plays but continued as follows:

But should my L⁴ Chamberlain say he prohibited them because they were but indifferent performances, I do not know what could be said in answer to that, since many of the Subscribers themselves give up that question, and are ashamed of their patronage. I cannot tell how far party prejudice may carry an audience, but I think nothing else could have saved these pieces.[41]

It is both unusual and amusing to find the furor over censorship forcing the government's political writers to treat literature with some seriousness. The *Gazetteer*'s customary attitude toward the poets re-emerged, however, in the issue of 15 May, which chided Brooke for presuming to describe his play as a compliment to the present establishment. The *Gazetteer* suavely inquired "whether you have not very much *mistaken your Province,* in speaking of a Piece of *Entertainment,* as of such Importance to the *Government.*" There, at least, is the true voice of the Walpole administration making its usual "realistic" assessment of the relative importance of men of letters and men of affairs.

The government, indeed, had much to contend with, as satires, poems, and pamphlets continued to attack the Convention and to push for war with Spain. Johnson contributed to the flood of propaganda on this theme also, with *Marmor Norfolciense; or, An Essay on an Ancient Prophetical Inscription in Monkish Rhyme Lately Discovered near Lynn* (May 1739). As the references in the title to Norfolk and King's Lynn suggest, the pamphlet is a standard anti-Walpole satire. It tells of a stone unearthed in Norfolk bearing a prophetic inscription which is explained by a pedantic commentator. Through the irony Johnson parades the usual subjects of opposition writing, from standing armies to Jenkins and his ear.[42] The device of political prophecy was also conventional; in fact, as a response to its use in the opposition press, the *Gazetteer* had recently (27 December 1738) run a prophecy of its own, with lines like these:

> From *Boling's* Spring when *Brooks* shall go,
> And a wrong Course for ever flow; . . .
> A Traitor's Fame *Rome's* Poet sings,
> And pleads for Guilt—and libels Kings . . .

Nonetheless, Johnson's own use of the hackneyed device fit the mood of the moment, and his piece was praised by *Old Common Sense* (19 May 1739) and reprinted in part in the *London Magazine.* The *Craftsman,* incidentally, also praised Johnson for his account in the *Gentleman's Magazine* of the debates in Parliament, though in general the opposition papers favored the *London Magazine*. In the prefatory material to that series of debates, called the *State of Affairs in Lilliput* (1738), Johnson had also treated the Spanish depredations in terms of his view of colonial policies.[43]

Pamphlet warfare, meanwhile, was raging on the subject of Spain and the Convention. Lyttelton published *Considerations upon the present State of our Affairs* (1739), a polemic on the policy towards Spain which touched also on the prince and the civil list and denounced the government's efforts to suppress the *Craftsman*. He was answered by *Popular Prejudices Against the Convention and Treaty with Spain, Examined and Answered* (1739). Other pamphlets on both sides abounded, with their titles offering sure clues to their politics; *Spanish Insolence corrected by English Bravery* (1739) and *The Grand Question, Whether War or No War, with Spain . . . In Defence of the Present Measures Against those that delight in War* may serve as examples. Whether such tracts were actually read cannot be determined, but Walpole apparently thought they were; at his direction 10,306 copies of the latter pamphlet were dispersed in the period of one month.[44] Agitation for war was especially strong among the merchants in the City, where in September the aldermen set aside the choice of Sir George Champion as lord mayor because he had voted for the Convention. One of the discontented merchants was the poet Glover, who in October once more aroused the ire of the *Gazetteer* by sponsoring a "Representation" thanking the four Members of Parliament from the City for working against the Convention.[45] Glover's contribution to the pro-war forces had been poetic as well as political, for at this time he published *London: or, The Progress of Commerce*, a virtually unreadable poem which concludes with the usual belligerent strains of opposition agitation in 1739:

> To other shores
> Our angry fleets, when insolence and wrongs
> To arms awaken our vindictive power,
> Shall bear the hideous waste of ruthless war;
> But liberty, security, and fame
> Shall dwell for ever on our chosen plains.[46]

On 19 October 1739 the "grand question" was decided; war

was declared, and popular indignation at Spain's failure to carry through the terms of the Convention was momentarily appeased. The ear of Captain Jenkins would, presumably, be avenged. Walpole is supposed to have remarked gloomily on the celebrations which greeted the proclamation of war, "They now ring the bells, before long they will be wringing their hands."[47] Burke, much later, saw the decision which Walpole took so reluctantly as the result of a popular clamor in which literary men played a leading role:

Sir Robert Walpole was forced into the war by the people, who were inflamed to this measure by the most leading politicians, by the first orators, and the greatest poets of the time. For that war, Pope sang his dying notes. For that war, Johnson, in more energetic strains, employed the voice of his early genius. For that war, Glover distinguished himself in the way in which his muse was the most natural and happy.[48]

Burke has overstated the case; certainly the greatest poets of the age cannot really be said to have played a significant role in "forcing" Walpole into war, not even if we assume that the government merely acceded to popular demand in its declaration of war. Yet a later analysis tends to support Burke's appraisal of the effect of popular opinion in causing Newcastle, in particular, to act in a way which made war inevitable.[49] And it is at least true that in 1737–39 literary men, both great and small, seemed united as never before in their hostility to all aspects of the administration—its supposed corruption, its alleged threat to freedom of expression, and its presumed willingness to betray the traditions of British valor by seeking an accommodation with Spain. Both Patriotic poetry and Juvenalian satire had poured out with a frequency which forced the government's agents on occasion to prohibit and its apologists repeatedly to denounce the incursion of literary figures into political territories. In all this, the diminutive figure of Pope towered above the rest. Perhaps it was only his superior reputation which provoked the clamor against him; but perhaps, too, Walpole's writers were shrewd enough to recognize that the poet of Twickenham, unlike the Patriot dramatists, had succeeded in embodying political themes without the sacrifice of artistic power.

7 THE FALL OF WALPOLE, 1739–1742

IN THE VIEW of one historian, J. B. Owen, the last two years in which Walpole held power were a kind of epilogue; his fall had been made certain by events in 1739, when he was forced to support a war in which he did not believe. From that time on, says Owen, he was hampered in his efforts to function as a link between the king and the Commons, both in favor of war with Spain. And so, in 1742, an unprecedented climax occurred: a minister who retained the full support of the king was forced to resign because he could not control a hostile House of Commons.[1] Of course, as Owen points out, what seems clear now in retrospect was doubtful and confused to those caught up in political struggle; the opposition, strengthened by the addition of Bubb Dodington and the duke of Argyle, and nearly defeating the administration on a place bill in February of 1740, nonetheless was torn by the old discords and lacked anything remotely resembling "party discipline." It placed much of its hopes on a continuing attack upon the government's conduct of the war; and much was made of Admiral Vernon's triumph at Portobello and Walpole's supposed delay in reinforcing him. Yet even on this popular theme the opposition had little hope of ultimate political success; on 3 June 1740 Pulteney wrote gloomily to Swift:

Sr Robt will have an Army, will not have a War, & cannot have a Peace; that is the people are so averse to it, that he dares not make one. but in one year more, when by the Influence of this Army, & our money, he has got a new Parliament to his liking, then he will make a Peace, and get it approved too be it as it will; after which I am afraid we shall all grow tired of struggling any longer, & give up the Game.[2]

Pulteney's despair must have come, in part, from consciousness of the strife within the opposition coalition, not only
between Whigs and Tories, but between the Pulteney-Carteret
bloc and the "boy" Patriots as well. That the court party was
similarly torn by internal feuds offered little comfort.[3] On 13
February 1741 opposition factionalism reached its climax; Sandys moved an address to the king to remove Sir Robert Walpole
from his presence and councils forever, only to find that the
desertion of over sixty Tories gave Walpole one of the largest
majorities of his career as the motion went down to defeat.
Bolingbroke called the conduct of the Tories on this occasion
"silly, infamous, and void of any colour of excuse," yet found the
"behavior and language" of those who complained the loudest
(i.e., Pulteney and Carteret) also to blame.[4] Wherever the blame
lay, the damage was done; the notorious "Motion" was ridiculed
in caricatures and the press as a despondent opposition prepared for the general election of 1741.

Yet, despite this blow to their morale and the spreading
distrust of Pulteney and Carteret, the opposition found events
turning in their favor. Thanks to opposition victories in Scotland
and Cornwall, the election gave Walpole a majority of only
nineteen, the smallest he had ever had; and, thanks perhaps to a
visit to France by Chesterfield, the Pretender ordered his
adherents in Parliament to support the coalition against Walpole.[5] As the members waited for the new session to begin on 1
December, a political lull set in which was obviously a prelude to
a fateful struggle. Chesterfield entreated Marchmont not to
remain buried in Scotland during this "extraordinary crisis,"
and young Horace Walpole foresaw the unnatural quiet as
giving way to great violence the moment Parliament met.[6] In the
first weeks of the new session, Walpole's opponents—however
strong their continuing suspicion of each other—managed for
once to act as a cohesive unit. Their success in electing one of
their number as chairman of the Committee on Elections and
Privileges was taken as symbolic of the final victory yet to come:
"You have no idea of their huzza!" wrote Horace Walpole,
"unless you can conceive how people must triumph after defeats
for twenty years together."[7] As a result of careful opposition
strategy on the issues of election petitions and the conduct of the

war, on 2 February 1742 the great minister finally resigned his
offices.

For some in the opposition, however, the long-awaited moment seemed bereft of meaning as their fellows scrambled for
places in the new administration. Walpole, created earl of
Orford, not only escaped the Tower but continued to wield a
powerful influence. As Foord puts it, the contest had been
between men, not measures. Least of all could the change of
men in power satisfy Bolingbroke's restless spirit; government
by party and the subordination of British interests abroad to
those of Hanover, the two points which he had felt were ruinous
to the nation, were unaffected by Walpole's fall. After the event,
he reflected cynically: "Long before I left Britain, it was plain,
that some persons meant, that the opposition should serve as
their scaffolding, nothing else."[8]

The events which led to the resignation of Walpole were thus
marked by two very different political features: a new-found
unanimity in an opposition determined to oust the minister and
a growing disillusionment with the self-interested motivation of
some of its leaders. Both had their parallel in the literary world.
As had been true since the prince's break with the king and
queen in 1737, the literary forces aligned against Walpole had a
cohesiveness and semblance of organization in some contrast to
the occasional nature of their efforts earlier in the decade; at the
same time one of its principal warriors, Pope, remained for a
time in disillusioned retirement, and another, Fielding, appears
to have defected from the opposition ranks just as victory was
approaching. Needless to say, the literary figures with whom we
are concerned played no direct role in pressing measures in
Parliament; one cannot imagine that their writings had any
influence on the politicians themselves in this crucial period. But
insofar as Walpole's personal unpopularity was a primary factor
in his fall, the poets and wits played an active part indeed in
keeping the public inflamed against the government. The
Patriot poets seized on the conduct of the war as a popular
theme, with Glover, now active in opposition circles in the City,
triumphing with his ballad on Portobello called "Admiral Ho-
sier's Ghost." And another patriotic dramatic work, the masque
Alfred by Thomson and Mallet, was performed privately for the
prince, a circumstance which forced the *Gazetteer* (13 September

1740) grudgingly to defend it as innocent of political reflections. But the writers of greatest political-literary significance in the last two years of Walpole's administration were not those in the circle directly around the prince but Fielding, Pope, and their old enemy Colley Cibber.

Fielding, the Champion, and Cibber

On 15 November 1739 appeared the first issue of the *Champion*, a new journal of the opposition managed by Henry Fielding and James Ralph, in partnership with five others. We know from his signature code that between that date and 19 June 1740 (the terminal date for the collected edition published a year later, June 1741) Fielding contributed at least sixty-four leaders. We know, too, that Fielding had stopped writing for the *Champion* by at least June of 1741, for he says so in the Preface to his *Miscellanies* (1743). Beyond those facts, however, little can be said with certainty about Fielding's responsibility for specific essays or his exact role in the editorial management of the paper. The Bodleian Library contains a unique run of the paper for the period not represented in the collected edition, including all the numbers to 15 November 1740 and two numbers from early 1741; unquestionably Fielding wrote many of the leaders in that period. But the incomplete state of such original files, as well as occasional differences between the collected edition and the original issues, makes conclusions about the text difficult to reach; and assignment of authorship on stylistic grounds is as hazardous here as it usually is. Happily, these are not matters with which this study need be particularly concerned.[9] Suffice it to say that Fielding was popularly assumed to be the leading figure in this new venture, even after he had ceased his contributions to it, and that the finest irony and wit in the paper can safely be laid at his door rather than Ralph's.

As was true with *Common Sense*, the first numbers of the *Champion* were carefully nonpolitical. Readers were introduced to the family of Vinegars, headed by Captain Hercules, and the tone was self-consciously imitative of Addison and Steele. Though by the second week a puff of Glover's *London* gave its bias away, essays on moral topics continued to abound in the first few months; only gradually did the *Champion* take on a thoroughly political cast. By 14 February Fielding was ironically refusing to discuss politics, despite the supposed demands of his readers; the *Champion,* he said, must be regarded as a miscellaneous rather than merely political paper, and correspondents must ask him "Questions concerning Virtue, Wit, Gallantry, Love, Poetry, and such like." Others, he added sarcastically, must be consulted in politics, "since I declare for my Part, I am so far from knowing, I cannot even guess what we are about, what we intend to do, or what we shall be able to do."[10]

Such a disclaimer would not, of course, be taken seriously, for by the spring of 1740 the *Champion* had become indistinguishable from any other opposition organ in its relentless pursuit of Robert Walpole. The devices used were markedly similar to those of the *Craftsman* in its early days: mock advertisements, dream allegories, scatalogical visions, and straightforward discourses on the evils of prime ministers. All the usual themes were paraded out once more, from the old parallel between Walpole and Cardinal Wolsey to the need for a place bill. Sir Robert himself appeared under such names as Robin Brass, the Brazen Trunk, R. Booty, Forage, His Honour, and Hum Clum, the last in Fielding's satiric voyages of Job Vinegar. To well-established modes of decrying bribery and corruption, the *Champion* could really add little new. It doubtless seemed more innovative in its sneering accounts of the conduct of the war, such as its occasional "Journal" counting up British losses and Spanish victories, or the dream vision in which an autopsy on a Walpole minion revealed the bitter words engraved in his brain, *"Porto Bello demolish'd, by Admiral Vernon, with six Ships Only."*[11] And, of course, the *Champion* propagandized directly for the opposition in election matters, both with regard to politics in the City of London and the approaching general election of 1741. A series of papers appearing in November 1740 was issued as a separate pamphlet, called *An Address to the Electors of Great Britain.*[12] In June 1741 the collected edition of the *Champion* was dedicated to the new members just elected, warning them in the usual way to stay clear of the worshippers of Mammon and exhorting them—accurately enough, as it turned out—that the time was ripe to remove that "grand Anti-Constitutional First-Mover, a Prime M——r." The Dedication closed on a note of self-deprecatory despair about what literary efforts can accomplish in the political world despite their power to warn and inform: "WRITINGS, Gentlemen, may serve to discover Leaks in the Common-wealth, but want Power to stop them; and, among a Variety of other Pieces, these two Volumes are put into your Hands, to shew how much has been hitherto *said* in vain."[13]

Such a realistic assessment of the political efficacy of the written word did not prevent the *Champion* from harping on the decay of letters under Walpole, for this traditional and highly significant opposition motif had lost none of its force in the waning years of Sir Robert's administration. A dream allegory in the issue for 13 December 1739 depicted the corruption of Parnassus by Walpole, with some incidental praise of Glover, Lyttelton, and (ambiguously) Pope. Again, twelve days later, Fielding ironically proclaimed the modern discovery that poetry needs no assistance from learning, instancing Cibber and the "Poet of our Age, most cherished at Court" (Duck). Sometimes, too, the topic was approached more seriously; future generations, we are told, will scarcely credit the contempt of the muses evidenced by the laureateship of Cibber or the debauching of public taste evidenced by the kind of dramatic entertainment approved by a licenser.[14] Nor will Walpole himself fail to suffer in the eyes of posterity, since envy has caused the real men of letters to overlook his merits:

When future Writers shall render him that Justice which his Cotemporaries deny him, when he shall be hang'd up, as it were, in History for our Children to stare at, how will they wonder that his Glories never warmed a *Pope*, a *Swift*, a *Young*, a *Gay*, or a *Thompson,* to celebrate his Name, to see no Memorial of him, unless Peradventure in an ancient Trunk or rotten Bandbox, which some prudent House Wife hath savingly lined with an eleemosynary Bundle of *Gazetteers*![15]

Readers would have recognized immediately the innuendoes in "hang'd up" or "stare at," and perhaps they would also have read "his Glories never warmed a *Pope*, a *Swift*" and so on as referring not only to lack of inspiration but also to lack of that support and patronage which such writers deserve.

Curiously, the *Gazetteer,* whose "eleemosynary" distribution is hit at in the passage above, studiously ignored the *Champion* for the first eight months of its life. There is hardly a mention of

Fielding or his paper until 4 July 1740, when the government writer bemoaned his misfortune in coming under the displeasure of some of "the *greatest Wits,* the *choicest Spirits,* and most illustrious *Patriots* of the Age," namely the writers of the *Craftsman, Common Sense,* and the *Champion.* The delay in attacking the new opposition paper is puzzling, although Fielding's paper was much more heavily political in May and June than it had been earlier. At any rate, once Ralph Courteville ("Court-Evil," the *Champion* called him) and the other *Gazetteer* writers began their attack, they came down hard upon the new journal, asserting that though it was the most recent opposition paper it easily outstripped all the other vehicles of sedition. Because of the *Champion* they declared 1740 to be the worst year for sedition since the "Diminutive, Rhyming Crew" (the literary opposition) first began these scandalous assaults on the government.

Naturally enough, the *Gazetteer* directed a series of personal attacks on Fielding himself. In one allegory (30 July 1740) Fielding is the abusive bully of the town, who sang ballads about Tom Thumb to the mob until the justices intervened; though he talked then of turning solicitor, this champion instead took it upon himself to slander Mr. Friendly (Walpole) despite the fact that Friendly "has been very kind to some of his Relations." The notion of Fielding's "ingratitude" to Walpole and his "obligations" to the minister forms an occasional motif in these attacks, a motif that may allude either to patronage perhaps received by Fielding in the early thirties or, as I shall indicate, to some more recent "obligations" from Walpole.[16] Oddly enough, nowhere does the *Gazetteer* remind its readers of Fielding's dedication of *The Modern Husband* to Walpole in 1732, though such a reminder would seem an obvious move in any effort to depict the playwright as a turncoat. Moreover, Fielding's plays are attacked here as immoral and scandalous but *not* as political satires serving the opposition. Again this seems curious, since it was the *Gazetteer* itself that had denounced Fielding as a political "*Cat's Paw*" because of *The Historical Register.* One may only conjecture that the ministerial forces were now reluctant to indict those plays on political grounds, for to do so would be to admit that the Licensing Act was a weapon of political censorship and not the moral and aesthetic necessity the government claimed.

In 1740 the *Champion* devoted a fair amount of its leader space to ridiculing Colley Cibber, whose *Apology* for his life appeared in April. Cibber's modern biographers have missed the political significance of this episode; yet no figure illustrates better than the preposterous poet laureate the intertwining of literary and political worlds. Both his elevation to the laureateship and his ceremonial odes, as we have noted earlier, were commonly described as symptomatic of the debasement of belles-lettres under Walpole. In the reaction to the *Apology* the same theme appeared, as Fielding and others mocked the literary deficiencies of Cibber's effusive prose. At the same time, however, the *Apology* was indicted on more directly political grounds, for Cibber had not hesitated to include a few political reflections in his account of his stage career.

The *Champion* began its attack on Cibber even before the *Apology* appeared. In its issues for 13 December and 25 December 1739 Cibber's role in the decline of learning and the degradation of culture was given the usual witty turns, the former essay depicting him as vainly seeking access to Parnassus just before Walpole enters the scene to bribe his way in. Again, on 3 January 1739/40 the *Champion* ridiculed Cibber's "Ode-Royal," pretending uncertainty as to whether it began "*Sing* GEORGE *and War*" or "*Sing* GEORGE *and Peace.*" After the *Apology* appeared much of the criticism was on a more serious level; since both Cibber and his son Theophilus were suspected to be contributors to the *Gazetteer*—in the case of the son the suspicion amounted to certainty—the occasional political reflections he permitted himself in his autobiography seemed doubly offensive. What the opposition writers found particularly outrageous was Cibber's brief discourse on the Revolution, before which, he claimed, British liberty hardly existed: "I will boldly say then, it is, to the Revolution only, we owe the full Possession of what, 'til then, we never had more than a perpetually contested Right to." That argument, it will be recalled, had become commonplace earlier in the decade among Walpole's propagandists in their effort to counter the opposition's use of Whig history in the *Craftsman*, Thomson's *Liberty*, and the like.

But there was more. Since the Revolution, Cibber explains, the number of qualified statesmen has been greater than the number of available places; therefore all ministers since 1688 have been railed at, "Tho' I can hardly forbear thinking, that they who have been *longest* rail'd at, must, from that Circumstance, shew, in some sort, a Proof of Capacity." This remarkable conclusion, that fifteen years of railing at Robert Walpole only demonstrated his superior capacities, could hardly be ignored by those whom Cibber called "weekly Retailers of Politicks" who pick up a living "merely by making bold with a Government that had unfortunately neglected to find their Genius a better Employment."[17] The *Champion* (6 May 1740) asserted that even more audacious than Cibber's curious method of evaluating statesmen or his defense of the Licensing Act was the "one Stroke beyond all the *Osbornes, Walsinghams, Sidneys, Freemans*, all the BOB-tail Writers of the Age, viz. That *we had but a contested Right to any Liberty before the Revolution.*"[18] Cibber himself was regarded as one of those "Bob-tail" writers; the *Champion* for 6 September 1740 made the accusation at length, again alluding to his comments on the Revolution, and when Fielding put Cibber on trial for the murder of English (in the issue for 17 May 1740), a "certain fat Gentleman" attested to the laureate's character. Finally, a pamphlet called *The Laureat*, designed to ridicule the *Apology* but antiministerial in its bias, warned Cibber against further remarks about neglected wits who retail antigovernment politics each week: they may reply "that there is a certain Band of low pensionary Caterpillars who do really gain a comfortable Subsistence by retailing of daily Nonsense in Defence of a certain A—— in which Band it is thought you have been long inrolled, a private Centinel at least."[19]

Some direct response, then, was given to direct political commentary in the *Apology*. But the opposition writers more frequently alluded to the time-worn parallel of the stage and the state, a parallel Cibber himself had frequently used in the pages of his autobiography. Given the political orientation of "Keyber," the book could easily be read as an Apology for the Life of Sir Robert Walpole, Prime Minister, especially since opposition journals had made a habit even before its appearance of drawing parallels between Cibber, Rich, and Walpole.[20] Fielding, in the *Champion* for 22 April, pointed the way to such a reading; though one would have thought such a book would be confined to matters theatrical, he says, "yet certain it is that this valuable Work hath much greater Matters in View, and may as properly be stiled an Apology for the Life of ONE who hath played a very comical Part, which, tho' Theatrical, hath been Acted on a much larger Stage than *Drury Lane*."[21] On one level this is true quite literally; as a book indiscriminately mingling "Ministers and Actors, Parliaments and Play-houses, . . . C. C. R. W.," in Fielding's words, the *Apology*'s open political bias defends the administration quite directly. On another level Fielding is alluding to the equation popularly drawn between the theatrical and political stages, between "C.C." and "R.W." *Common Sense* makes the same point in its issues for 13 December 1740 and 17 January 1741, but oddly enough it allegorizes not the *Apology* itself but *The Laureat; that* pamphlet, says *Common Sense*, is not really about Cibber or his book but is an attack on Walpole, a worse actor by far. The *Craftsman* (19 July 1740) provides yet another twist; Cibber's *Apology* is intended as a *"most refined Piece of Politicks"* making use of the strong resemblance between the conduct of public affairs and the transactions of the stage, and the parallel is artfully contrived by Cibber to attack the person of Sir Robert Walpole! It is Walpole, says the *Craftsman*, whom Cibber intended by the "Manager" who "by his *Blunders*, his *Cowardice*, and his *tricking Arts*, had reduced his *Theatrical Empire* to the very Brink of Destruction." This was an amusing turn to Cibber's progovernment book, which seemed to invite such responses by its abundant use of political metaphor.

Though Fielding could not have appreciated the reference to him as a "broken Wit" in the *Apology*, the context I have sketched makes it clear that his ridicule of Cibber in the *Champion* and elsewhere is as much politically as personally motivated. Even more obvious is the political bias in the *Champion*'s attacks on Theophilus, Cibber's son, a figure who seemed to cry out for ridicule regardless of politics. He was generally coupled with his father in the opposition papers, though the *Champion* made a distinction between them: "The Father lulls you to sleep, the Son awakens you out of it; The Father sets your Teeth on Edge: The Son makes your Head ach."[22] In 1739–40 there seemed special reason for the antigovernment press to attack him, for it was assumed by both the *Craftsman* and *Common Sense* that "Antient Pistol"—his usual sobriquet—had "newly listed into the ministe-

rial Regiment of Pen-men" as a contributor to the *Gazetteer*.[23]
Common Sense, in fact, ran a blustering letter from "Pistol"
proclaiming himself a ministerial politician.

Earlier, in 1733, young Cibber had gained notoriety by
leading an actors' revolt against the patentees of Drury Lane.
Apparently, at that time the government propagandists themselves considered using the stage-state parallel so as to turn the
war at Drury Lane into a device for ridiculing the opposition;
among Walpole's papers there is a manuscript called "An Epistle
from Thiophalous Keyber Comedian to Caleb Danvers Esq."
asking conspirators against the state to support those opposing
authority in affairs of the stage: "Why should you then who are
attempting to bring about a Revolution in the one, be an Enemy
to us who attempt a Revolution in the other?"[24] Now, however,
Theophilus's ventures into antiministerial journalism made him
fair game for the wits. In 1740, having issued proposals for an
autobiography modeled on his father's, he was startled to find
published in July *An Apology for the Life of Mr. T—— C——,
Comedian*, and was forced to return his subscriptions. The bogus
autobiography, which Cross with no evidence to support him
thought Fielding might have written, is a close parody of
Cibber's *Apology* which manages to satirize father and son simultaneously.[25] Though the satire, naturally enough, is centered on
Cibber's career and on stage history, political satire is a minor
motif throughout. Cibber had dedicated his *Apology* "To a
Certain Gentleman"; the "Certain Gentleman" in the parody is
Walpole himself, to whose service of "Gazetteering and Pam-
phleting" Theophilus has been recruited by Paxton, the "Super-
visor-General" of such endeavors. Colley's curious method of
determining the virtue of a minister (in direct ratio to the length
of time he has been railed at) is applied to Walpole with the
obvious sarcasms; Theophilus is given credit for the banning of
Gustavus Vasa; Walpole is said to have directed the writing of *The
Golden Rump* (the play) so as to ensure passage of a Licensing
Bill; and so on. The satire is not, clearly, very adroit, and it is
difficult to believe Fielding had a hand in it; but both this parody
and the other reactions to Cibber's *Apology* show well enough
that for the witty world both Cibbers were held guilty of political
as well as literary-theatrical crimes.

Fielding's Defection

Though Cibber continued to be the butt of Fielding's wit in 1741 and 1742, there has been some mystery about Fielding's own political attitudes in the last twelve months of the Walpole administration. One scholar has argued cogently that he defected to Walpole's camp for pay late in 1741; another has read the most "damaging" political tract as only a "good-natured rebuke" of the leaders of his own party; and still another has seen Fielding's apparent shift of personal political allegiance as only a symptom of a general movement within the opposition.[26] Although no absolutely certain solution to the mystery is possible on present information, I think a review of the old evidence and consideration of a few pieces of new evidence will make the picture of Fielding's political behavior in this period reasonably clear.

My account of his changing attitudes must begin, in fact, with an important piece of evidence which has only recently come to light: Fielding's leader in the *Champion* for 4 October 1740. In that essay (signed with his signature code "L") Fielding pretends to have received a letter from a quack doctor named "Roberto" (Walpole) offering bribes of "Pills," 100 pills to keep quiet, 200 to say a single favorable word, and 300 plus semiannual doses for life if Fielding "will declaim handsomely upon my Nostrums." Fielding then rejects the offer with these words:

> Whoever the Quack is, from whom this Epistle is arriv'd, I believe the Public will sufficiently conclude that he is a very impudent Fellow. If I mistake not the Hand, it is one whose Pills I formerly refused on the like Conditions now offer'd, tho' I own, being in an ill State of Health, I accepted a few to stop the Publication of a Book, which I had written against his Practice, and which he threaten'd to take the Law of me, if I publish'd: These Pills, tho' a mere Matter of Bargain, he was pleas'd to Consider as a great Obligation: But I can tell him, his Nostrums have now done so much Mischief, that whoever takes any Reward of him to secure his Practice any longer, deserves to be hang'd. . . .[27]

Fielding's attitude toward Walpole's "nostrums" is clearly as harsh as ever, but he here admits that he has taken Walpole's money to suppress the publication of a book. Since *The Grub-Street Opera* was in fact published after being suppressed as a performance, the book in question is probably *Jonathan Wild,* which many believe was composed in 1740 and which if published in these years would have been Fielding's most devastating assault on the prime minister. Fielding's defensive tone and his remarkable admission in this leader may have been in reaction to the charges in the ministerial press that he was ungrateful to Walpole for some unspecified favor. The obligation, he now says, amounts to very little, and his pen is not for sale. At any rate, this surprising essay in the *Champion* of 4 October sets the stage for innuendoes that would begin appearing five months later in the *Gazetteer* about Fielding's willingness to defect to the ministry; and it indicates unmistakably that on one occasion he had already succumbed to the temptation of a bribe accompanied by legal pressure.

Nevertheless, in January 1741 Fielding published two works as obviously hostile to Walpole as had been any of his essays in the *Champion* the preceding year. The first was "Of True Greatness," a poetic epistle addressed to George Bubb Dodington, who had recently aligned himself with the opposition. The poem is ostensibly on a topic of "moral" interest—the distinction between true and false greatness—but few readers would have failed to apply it to the Great Man himself or to note the allusion to "Sir *B*.," who "denies/ True Greatness to the Creature whom he buys." There is also the usual opposition bill of complaints against this *"Gothick* Leaden Age" in which wit is banished, fools are preferred, and "Men are largely for such Writings fee'd,/ As *W*——'s self can purchase none to read."[28] But Fielding's Preface, which was not reprinted when the poem appeared in the *Miscellanies* of 1743, is especially interesting, for here he defends not only Dodington but himself against the calumny of Walpole's hacks. In replying to the charge of "ingratitude" made by the ministerial press, Fielding hints that some affair between him and Walpole has been deliberately misrepresented. The reference, I think, may be to the story that Walpole once sent Fielding money for bail after he had been arrested in a country town, a story which had been spread the preceding October by a pamphlet called the *Historical View . . . of the Political Writers of Great Britain.* Or, even more likely, it may refer to the monetary

"Obligation" dismissed as a "mere Matter of Bargain" in the *Champion* of 4 October 1740. As well as firmly defending himself against such charges, Fielding again claims in this Preface that he has been offered to name his own terms to exert his "Talent of Ridicule" against the *foes* of the administration but has steadfastly refused to do so. And he insists that he has never personally reflected on any man, though in the light of some of the traditional innuendoes about Walpole in this very Preface ("Incense to *Baal*" is his phrase for ministerial writing) that claim might not have been taken very seriously.

Nor did Fielding's second publication in January, *The Vernoniad*, appear to be the work of a man anxious to avoid personal ridicule of his opponents. In fact, as has been recently demonstrated, Pope's figure of Walpole as Magus the Wizard (*Dunciad*, Book IV) was based on a detail in this mock epic by Fielding.[29] The satire consists of a "fragment" of an epic poem with lengthy notes by a Scriblerian commentator; both poem and notes carry the same burden, a vicious but amusing indictment of Walpole for having failed to supply reinforcements to Admiral Vernon after the victory at Portobello. Walpole appears as Mammon, whose palace (Houghton Hall) is crammed with art he cannot appreciate and whose obsession is the amassment of riches and the exercise of power. Instructed by the Devil, Mammon bribes Aeolus to hinder the British fleet, for as a friend to "Iberia" and foe to merchants he must obstruct the progress of the war. The notes which embellish this plot make the usual jokes at Walpole's expense while also parodying classical scholarship; thus a citation is made to the "Latin *Sturdi Begares*, &c. which we can't render in *English*" (p. 3), a reference to Walpole's contemptuous dismissal of the crowds opposed to the excise bill as "sturdy beggars." Beyond such incidental jokes, however, *The Vernoniad* is notable for its portrayal of Walpole as a moral cripple; he is the pragmatic materialist, the least erected spirit that fell into politics: "Virtue's a Name a Bubble or a Fart,/ And starves the Belly where it rules the Heart" (p. 26). The portrait was conventional enough in opposition literature, but Fielding gives it a wittier turn than it usually took in the pages of the *Craftsman*.

By the end of January 1741, then, Fielding had admitted to accepting Walpole's money to suppress a book; had nonetheless published two resolutely anti-Walpole pieces, one under his own

name; and had on two occasions indicated in print his disdain
for offers he claimed were being made to purchase his pen for
the administration. At this point his movement in the political
spectrum becomes increasingly murky, for at some time in the
late winter or spring of 1741 he became sufficiently disillusioned
with antiministerial journalism to withdraw from the *Champion*.
We know that his break with that journal occurred at least by
June, from his later statement that he had made no contributions to it since that month; moreover, he attended a meeting of
the partners on 29 June and cast the only vote against the
reprinting of the early essays in a collected edition. But minutes
of a later meeting, in March 1742, show that Fielding had
withdrawn his services over twelve months earlier—i.e., in
February or March 1741. From this evidence Martin Battestin
has suggested that Fielding withdrew not only his assistance
to the *Champion* but his allegiance to the opposition as early as
February 1741; he also cites an allegorical letter in the *Gazetteer*
for 11 March suggesting that Fielding might be thinking of
deserting his party.[30]

Even more to the point is another issue of the *Gazetteer* (30
March 1741) which makes a comment on Fielding that, as far as
I know, has hitherto escaped notice. The paper opens with a
letter from "Hercules Vinegar":

> Having irredeemably mortgag'd my share of the little Profit, arising
> from the Sale of the *Champion;* I have determin'd to bite the Mort-
> gagee, (I'm a Lawyer you know, and understand Trap) by withdrawing
> my propping Hand from that falling Paper; and intend for the future
> to dedicate the Strength of my surprizing Genius to you. Publish what I
> have sent you therefore, as a Specimen of my Taste for *collecting*
> curious Pieces of Wit and Humour.

There follows a piece ridiculing the *Craftsman* in low Grub Street
style. Of course, political journalists customarily charge their
opponents with mercenary motives, and neither item in the
Gazetteer can be taken at face value. But would the *Gazetteer* use
such a forthright statement as the one I have quoted unless at
least strong rumors on the topic were current? That two such
items should appear at just the time when other evidence
indicates Fielding's possible withdrawal from the *Champion* lends
strong support to Battestin's suggestion that the rupture oc-

curred four months earlier than has usually been thought. And if one wishes to speculate on what event at this time could have prompted Fielding's sudden distaste for opposition journalism, I think a likely candidate is Sandys's famous "Motion" of 13 February. That débacle for the opposition dismayed and disillusioned many more actively involved in antiministerial politics than Fielding, who may well have decided to quit the fray after such a defeat.[31]

Whether the break occurred in February or in June, it is clear that Fielding brought a firm end to his work for the opposition early in 1741. Between February and December no work of a political cast can be ascribed to him with any certainty except *Shamela*; though the preliminary apparatus of that parody contains hits at Hervey and Walpole, and though the "world" of the book is the debased culture over which Walpole was figuratively said to preside, it could hardly be called a partisan political satire of the same cast as *The Vernoniad*.[32] Moreover, since *Shamela* was published by early April, it may well have been written before the rumors of Fielding's supposed political unsteadiness began in mid-March; and the same argument may be made about *The Crisis,* an anti-Walpole mock sermon which has sometimes been attributed to Fielding and which also appeared in April. By this time, too, he had apparently abandoned the writing of *Jonathan Wild* and turned to the composition of *Joseph Andrews*—if indeed *Jonathan Wild* had not already been voluntarily suppressed well before these months, as is perhaps indicated by the *Champion* of 4 October 1740. In short, by the spring of 1741 Fielding had, the evidence clearly suggests, simply dropped out of Patriot politics. But desertion of a cause does not necessarily mean defection to the enemy, and as yet nothing had appeared to indicate Fielding's enlistment in the ministerial ranks. As a matter of fact, it must be noted—and it has not been—that in the summer and early fall of 1741 the *Daily Gazetteer* continued to treat Fielding as an opposition hack writer and to make broad hints that he would soon be changing sides. Thus the issue of 3 July calls him the "reputed Author" of the *Champion,* and that of 5 August concludes an attack on that paper with an epigram which opens, "Patience, dear Sir!—you should not write,—but laugh/ At mad Sir F——d——g, and at dull 'Squire R——." Two days later (7 August) a mock letter from a "Patriot" warned the *Gazetteer* that, despite his indolence at the moment, Fielding would punish them when Parliament assembled, "or perhaps he'll write another Epistle to a *quondam Great Man* in Praise of *Steadiness*" (i.e., the *Epistle* to Dodington).

By 30 September the *Gazetteer*'s characterization of Fielding as indolent had become transmuted into a depiction of his political indifference. In a paper of that date describing a fictional meeting between the opposition writers and the *Gazetteer* writer, "Vinegar" is simply an unscrupulous buffoon: "as to Party, tho' my Principles allow me to write for all—they oblige me to stick to none." (Since "Vinegar" claims he has been a playwright and is now a lawyer, the allusion is to Fielding and not to Ralph). But the most explicit of these comments comes in the *Gazetteer* of 30 October 1741, where another "meeting" between "R. Freeman" (the *Gazetteer* writer) and Hercules Vinegar is depicted. Here Fielding (and again references to the Haymarket, Temple, and Bath make his identity obvious) is shown confessing that he writes only to please the taste of the town and that he is concerned about the possible triumph of the administration over its enemies:

> *H. V.* . . . But after all, if I thought it would come to that,—I wou'd not be—found o' th' wrong Side.
> *R. F.* I dare say you wou'd not, Captain.—But what will the Publick think, when 'tis told them, that this *mighty Hector!* . . . the *renowned* Capt. HERCULES VINEGAR! has been whimpering to get over, without once desiring the least Favour to be shewn to his COADJUTOR *R.*

Freeman then promises Vinegar, "Perhaps when you shew a thorough Repentance, something may be done for you—on our Side."

Such accounts need not be taken too seriously; that the *Gazetteer* continued to identify Fielding with the *Champion* months after he had definitely withdrawn from it does not encourage us to look upon it as a credible authority on the movements of opposition writers. On the other hand, the sum total of such innuendoes in the ministerial journal is impressive. One may well wonder why it is only Fielding, among all the journalists and writers opposed to Walpole, who was so often accused of political tergiversation. Ralph *had* in fact shifted his loyalties when he joined the opposition, but though the *Gazetteer* sometimes joked about this fact it was Fielding who developed the reputation for political unsteadiness. Moreover, it is notable that such hints and accusations abounded in 1741; a year earlier, when Fielding was hard at work for the *Champion,* he had been accused only of "ingratitude." Then, late in 1740 and early in 1741, he claimed that offers had been extended to him by the administration, and rumors that he had accepted those offers were spread widely enough to force him to protest in the preface to his *Miscellanies* that he had never written a *Gazetteer.* Possibly some reputation for changeableness still clung to Fielding from his about-face in 1732, which I have described earlier; but the attacks upon him in 1740 and 1741 made no reference to his play dedicated to Walpole. The evidence, though circumstantial, makes us hesitate to dismiss out of hand the *Gazetteer's* claim on 30 October 1741 that Fielding was "whimpering to get over."

Six weeks after the *Gazetteer* made that remark Fielding published a pamphlet which has formed the crux in all accounts of his politics. In Martin Battestin's view this allegory, called *The Opposition: A Vision,* demonstrates that Fielding's "whimpering" was favorably received by Walpole, that the playwright—faced as he was with serious financial problems—not only deserted his party but defected to the enemy for pay.[33] At the very least the pamphlet represented a complete shift on the part of the author of the *Champion*; as has often been remarked, it would be difficult to believe Fielding had written it had he not acknowledged his authorship. For there is no question of irony here; the satire is distinguishable from countless similar attacks on the opposition by ministerial apologists only by its literary superiority. The central image in the dream vision is a "Waggon" called the Opposition; it bears passengers and drivers, is drawn by asses in miserable condition, and is loaded with two trunks labeled Grievances and Public Spirit. Fielding, incidentally, may have used this image because of a satire by Lyttelton called *The Court Secret,* which had appeared three months earlier and had depicted the rule of Walpole in this manner: "The Nations under his Rod found themselves divided into two Tribes, Asses and Drivers; And, not having been used to the Whip or the Load, not only complain'd of the Impositions they felt, but struggled hard to remove them."[34] But Fielding turns the image against the opposition. The passengers are members of the parliamentary opposition who have gained their "Seats" because of alleged grievances; the drivers are their leaders; and the asses represent journalists and others who do the dirty work of the party. The wagon is at a standstill, directionless; the grievances are revealed to be imaginary, and the public spirit to be only disappointed ambition.

Moreover, the narrative framework appears to give a rough chronology of the fortunes of the opposition in this crucial year. One passenger, for instance, protests that the wagon has traveled through enough dirt: "I was so bespattered with the *last Motion* the Waggon made, that I almost despaired of ever making myself appear clean again"[35] (a reference to Sandys's disastrous motion in February). Fielding dwells at length upon the "dirt" which opposition politicians must utilize merely to reach the "Top of the Hill." Other details of the allegory then remind us of the quarrels and recriminations following the débacle of February, and the opposition appears *"stuck for seven Years longer"* (p. 18), that is, until the next general election. But when a supply of Cornish and Scottish asses arrives, the wagon finally moves—an allusion to the opposition's success in those areas in the election in the spring of 1741. Success now appears possible, but the place-seeking politicians still on board find the way to St. James blocked by Walpole, symbolized as a fat gentleman in a coach and six—a detail matching his appearance in a number of satirical prints ridiculing "the Motion." After one of the asses upbraids the opposition members for deserting the "Country" path and for attacking Walpole merely because he stands in their way, the allegory closes with the prime minister, having set the asses to graze in a greener pasture, moving unobstructed along the *"very Road* whither the other had *pretended* it was going" (p. 24).

Thus the allegory has moved from the effects of Sandys's motion to the election of the new Parliament and the opposition's new hope for success in the coming session. But in this pamphlet which appeared just as the new session was beginning, Fielding seems to say that such hope is illusory; the opposition, torn by dissension and unfaithful to its original principles, will end in defeat. The inaccuracy of the prophecy hardly detracts from the satiric brilliance of the piece, which is surely one of the most effective political satires of the Walpole years. In contrast to the heavy-handedness one usually encounters in political allegories of the day, with their "Norfolk Stewards" and the like, Fielding grounds his simple parable on novelistic images and aspects of character that take on a life of their own:

Then the Drivers put a Question to their Company, whether they would not go in a *Body* and drag the Gentleman out of the Coach; but being asked by some of them *what he had done?* They answered, damn *him, he stood in their Way*, and that was enough (p. 22).

The conventional charge by Walpole's advocates that grubbing for places lay at the root of the Patriot opposition to Sir Robert's measures had seldom been put so forcefully.

But why should it now be Henry Fielding who put this charge? In Battestin's view both this pamphlet and certain passages in the first version of *Joseph Andrews* make unavoidable the conclusion that Fielding changed sides for money. Of the scene in which the asses are set grazing in a delicious meadow, Battestin writes: "Fielding seems to say that his days of starving in the service of a false cause are over; Walpole's generosity has set him free and fed him."[36] He might have cited also the astonishing passage in which Fielding seems to complain that he and Ralph had been inadequately paid for their work: " 'Surely, considering the wretched Work they are employed in, they deserve better Meat' " (p. 17). Though Fielding's admirers have been reluctant to accept such a conclusion, the evidence—albeit circumstantial—seems to me to support the contention that Fielding not only shifted his allegiances but was probably rewarded for doing so; and such an interpretation of his political behavior in this period is obviously strengthened by the *Champion* of 4 October 1740, where Fielding admits that he has taken money from Walpole to stop the publication of a book. The only counterargument that has been advanced holds that Fielding's evident disillusionment with opposition politics was shared by many others within the anti-Walpole movement. The distrust of Carteret and Pulteney, the fiasco of Sandys's motion, the squabbling between Tories and the various Whig blocs—all provided a context in which Fielding's "apostasy" becomes understandable enough, the argument goes, without recourse to the theory that he sold his pen to the higher bidder. "Fielding changed his politics, to be sure," writes W. B. Coley, "but he changed with his party, so to speak, or with a considerable segment of it."[37]

Though the context Coley describes helps to explain Fielding's disillusionment, it by no means will account for the turnabout represented by *The Opposition*. When that pamphlet appeared, the Patriots, having scored election victories, were beginning the new Parliament in a mood of hope, not of despair; Chesterfield, for example, wrote Marchmont entreating him to come down speedily for what was clearly to be a crisis, and in the Commons victories were won by an opposition united as never before. Moreover, no opposition politician, however agitated he might have felt privately about the dissension within the party or however much he might have suspected the motives of its leaders, would have aided the ministry by anatomizing those sensitive areas publicly. Publicly, indeed, the large segment of the party to which Coley refers did not change its politics; Chesterfield, Pulteney, Carteret, Lyttelton, Dodington, and the rest all participated in Walpole's final defeat. And whatever discomfort some within the opposition ranks might have felt about the personal abuse heaped on Walpole, few would have depicted him at this crucial moment as Fielding did, "with a Countenance full of Benignity" (p. 23).

There is, in short, no escaping the fact that Fielding withdrew from opposition journalism and wrote a pamphlet that could easily have been published in the *Gazetteer,* so similar is it to the usual mode of proministerial propaganda. After Walpole's fall, Fielding used episodes in *Joseph Andrews* to express his disillusionment with the Patriots, and in the Preface to his *Miscellanies* (1743) he took care to explain that the revised portrait of Jonathan Wild would fit "more than one," at least in the eyes of any reader who "knows much of the Great World."[38] It was also in this Preface that Fielding disclaimed authorship of any political articles in newspapers appearing since June of 1741 and expressed his abhorrence of libels and personal satire—the "dirt" of which so much was made in *The Opposition.* The *Miscellanies* contained the poem to Dodington and another to Lyttelton on Liberty, but also the two jocular poems begging preferment from Walpole; and the subscription list included not only the major Patriots, headed by the Prince of Wales, but Walpole himself, now the earl of Orford. All in all, the *Miscellanies,* despite the political cast of much of the material, manages to project the image of a man of letters who has had ties on both sides in a struggle that is now mercifully over. Though Fielding here expresses his annoyance at having been accused of writing for both sides in the winter of 1741–42, no hint remains in these volumes of the events which fixed upon him a reputation for political inconstancy.

What lessons can be drawn from this remarkable episode? Years later, it will be recalled, one of Fielding's enemies summarized his career as one of political venality, referring first to an early episode in which the "Press-*Renegade*" suppressed a dramatic satire when paid to do so and then to his work on the *Champion*; Fielding, this writer charges, having written three libels a week against Walpole, "at last took a small pecuniary Gratuity to betray his Paymasters and the Paper, out of which he had for sometime extracted a precarious Subsistence."[39] Even when allowance is made for the rhetoric of a political enemy and the uncertainty of his sources, such a portrait is disturbing. Yet, even if solid evidence should come to light about the "pecuniary Gratuity" Fielding may have received for changing politics, one still need not pass a harsh judgment upon him. About the later period of his political satire as about his early plays, one may conclude simply that Fielding was primarily a wit rather than an ideologue committed to a specific political program. Although he was always a Whig in the broadest sense and would not, we may assume, have sold his pen to Tories or Jacobites, the fortunes of particular Whig politicians in their struggle for power were necessarily of less concern to him than his own literary career in a time of personal difficulty. He was drawn into political satire by the need to meet a popular taste for antiministerial ridicule, and he persisted in such a career through the flattering ministrations of Lyttelton and other lords of the opposition. Some disillusionment about their political cause is expressed in *The Opposition*, but what comes through just as clearly is distaste for the personal satire he was required to produce and simple dismay at the poor pay for his efforts. Writers are not, after all, politicians: " 'As to Asses, it's of little Consequence where they are driven, provided they are not used to such Purposes, as the Honesty of even an Ass would start at' " (p. 21).

Years later, in the *Jacobite Journal* No. 17 (26 March 1748), Fielding reflected on the relation of writers to great politicians in terms that, as Battestin points out, seem to fit his own case at the end of the Walpole era. The passage is important enough to be quoted once more:

> To confess the Truth, the World is in general too severe on Writers. In a Country where there is no public Provision for Men of Genius, and in an Age when no Literary Productions are encouraged, or indeed read, but such as are season'd with Scandal against the Great; and when a Custom hath prevailed of publishing this, not only with Impunity but with great Emolument, the Temptation to Men in desperate Circumstances is too violent to be resisted. . . .
>
> In a Time therefore of profound Tranquillity, and when the Consequence, at the worst, can probably be no greater than the Change of a Ministry, I do not think a Writer, whose only Livelihood is his Pen, to deserve a very flagitious Character, if, when one Set of Men deny him Encouragement, he seeks it from another, at their Expence; nor will I rashly condemn such a Writer as the vilest of Men, (provided he keeps within the Rules of Decency) if he endeavours to make the best of his own Cause, and uses a little Art in blackening his Adversary. Why should a Liberty which is allowed to every other Advocate, be deny'd to this?[40]

His loyalty, in short, is not to a particular set of Whig politicians but to himself as a writer. In the usual view, England in the last years of Walpole was indeed a country with "no public Provision for Men of Genius"; and that allegation, which had been a common motif in antiministerial propaganda and which had driven some writers into the arms of the opposition, drove this particular man of genius to seek patronage wherever he could find it, perhaps from the prime minister himself.

The Englishman in His Grotto

That Pope, like Fielding, despaired of the progress of Patriotism is amply demonstrated both by his letters and by one fragmented poem. The death of Sir William Wyndham seems especially to have affected him.[41] In the fragment *One Thousand Seven Hundred and Forty*, never published in his lifetime, Pope gloomily reflects on the passing of leaders such as Wyndham: "The plague is on thee, Britain, and who tries/ To save thee in th' infectious office *dies*."[42] In the same poem, moreover, our eyes are turned away from "wicked men in place" as we are shown sarcastically how little "succour from the Patriot Race" Britain can expect. Carteret and Pulteney are, of course, satirized rather nastily, and perhaps Sandys and Shippen as well. Gower, Cobham, and Bathurst are merely ineffectual; they pay Britain "due regards,/ Unless the ladies bid them mind their cards." Even Chesterfield is interested only in his wit. The rest, the country gentlemen, run up to Parliament every winter, clear that something must be done, listen to Carteret and Pulteney as they are alternately inflamed and cooled, follow admiringly anyone that can read or write, and hurry back finally to their "paternal ground": "Yearly defeated, yearly hopes they give,/ And all agree, Sir Robert cannot live" (ll. 41–42).

Fielding's disillusionment is here, and even his image of the opposition as a carriage bogged down in mire is coincidentally used by Pope as a metaphor for Britain's broken state:

> Can the light packhorse, or the heavy steer,
> The sowzing Prelate, or the sweating Peer,
> Drag out with all its dirt and all its weight,
> The lumb'ring carriage of thy broken State?
> Alas! the people curse, the carman swears,
> The drivers quarrel, and the master stares.
> (Lines 69–74)

But unlike Fielding, Pope savagely attacks Walpole and the court party as well as the opposition, and closes with a Bolingbrokean address to the Prince of Wales, who "unministered" can restore public virtue and redeem the land from the curse of false patriots, corrupt ministers, and partisan strife. By this time Pope had studied the manuscript of *The Idea of a Patriot King,* and the final lines of this poem are replete with its themes: the prince's "public virtue" will make "his title good," and his moral, rather than his political, qualities must constitute his "true glory" and enable him to restore "Europe's just balance and our own." Unlike Fielding, too, Pope continued active participation in opposition circles and closed his career with a poem epitomizing the opposition's vision of Walpolean culture.

That poem—*The New Dunciad* of 1742—was a long time
coming, and Pope's silence after 1738 seems to have annoyed
some among the opposition, especially since it was rumored that
he had been frightened off further political satire by the
prosecution of Paul Whitehead. Fielding, in an allegorical satire
in the *Champion* (13 December 1739), depicted Pope atop
Parnassus but too timid to defend the muses from their corruption by the mercenary hand of Walpole; and in the same journal
for 17 May 1740 he lightheartedly brought Pope to trial for his
failure to denounce the roguery of "Forage" (Walpole).[43] The
Craftsman, too, printed a poem (24 October 1741) complaining
about Pope's silence: "Not one Poetick Cobweb spun,/ From
Thirty-eight to *Forty-one.*" The italicizing of "Thirty-eight" suggests, of course, Pope's famous dialogues of that year, and the
couplet implies that the year "Forty-one" cries out for the same
satiric treatment. Although Pope was in no mood to respond to
these demands for further political satires, he had not, despite
his disillusionment with the Patriots, withdrawn from politics or
cried a plague on both houses. In September 1740 he expressed
to Bolingbroke his approval of the measures of Chesterfield and
Lyttelton, and, perhaps at Lyttelton's bidding, he wrote a month
later to Marchmont urging him to come down from Scotland to
"dash the Forehead and shake the soul of Guilty Wretches" in
Parliament. With Lyttelton he seems to have been on particularly close terms in 1740 and 1741; Lyttelton, significantly, was
not among the Patriots chided in *One Thousand Seven Hundred
and Forty,* and in November of 1741 he wrote Pope urging him
to continue his campaign against corruption. Even the minutiae
of party-writing continued to interest Pope, at least when a
Dunce like Ralph was involved.[44] In short Pope's poetic silence
may have piqued his admirers in the opposition, but it clearly
did not indicate any withdrawal from the commitment to politics
he had exhibited since the late thirties.

Meanwhile his reputation as Walpole's foe continued undi-
minished in the public mind. James Miller, a clergyman and
playwright, created a storm with his poem *Are These Things So?
The Previous Question, from an Englishman in his Grotto, to a Great
Man at Court* (October 1740), a satire in a vigorous Popean style
which makes the usual indictment of Walpole as the source of

Britain's moral plague and the gravedigger of British liberty. As Maynard Mack points out, Pope is clearly the "Englishman" intended, Pope as a symbolic figure in incorruptible retirement.[45] In one edition Pope's name appeared on the title page, and Horace Mann a year later still assumed the poem to be his; more commonly, however, it was ascribed to Whitehead or even Dodington.[46] Miller's poem was followed shortly by an even more vicious Juvenalian excoriation of "sinking Britain" called *Yes, They Are,* by Robert Morris, an architect who himself lived at Twickenham; this poem, among other things, suggested methods by which Walpole might commit suicide for the public good. The efforts by the government's supporters to counter with panegyrics like *What of That?* (1740) were feeble enough, and Miller provided his own "rebuttal" from Walpole in *The Great Man's Answer to Are These Things So? In a Dialogue Between His Honour and the Englishman in his Grotto* (1740). While the Great Man rationalizes his conduct, the Poet repeats the bill of complaint from the earlier poem, attacking corruption, the conduct of the war, the mistreatment of merchants, the minister's personal wealth, and the Licensing Act. But the statesman remains unmoved: "In vain you Patriot Oafs pronounce my Fall,/ Like the great LAUREAT, *S'Blood I'll stand you all.*"[47]

The tradition of Patriot satire to which such poems belong had, of course, received its impetus from Pope's two *Dialogues* in 1738. Another such poem, even more interesting because of its connection with *The Dunciad,* appeared in November 1741, just four months before Pope's *New Dunciad.* Called *The Year Forty-One: Carmen Seculare* and dedicated to the duchess dowager of Marlborough, the poem is described by its author—again James Miller, apparently—as "an honest Satire on the Degeneracy of the Age."[48] In verse inferior but not despicable, the poet catalogues the customary evidence for such degencracy: the decay of learning, national cowardice abroad and public roguery at home, the corruption of justice and Parliament, and so on:

> O for a Muse of Fire! as *Shakespear* cries,
> But not to paint a *Henry's* Victories . . .
> No—to describe our *Eminence* in *Shame,*
> Our *Impotence* in all that *merits* Fame;
> Our Sinews quite unnerv'd, our Spirits broke,

> Our Necks bow'd down beneath the *Gallick* Yoke. . . .
> Such Treating, Voting, Swearing, Bribing, Biting,
> Such *Dearth* of Learning, yet such *Crops* of Writing.
> (Pp. 4–5)

So far the poem has been conventional enough; what makes it worth special notice is the stress which the remaining sections put on the decay of culture as the prime symptom of political infection. The Spirit of Liberty, it is assumed, will abandon England to begin anew among some untutored peoples; there she will restore those arts which have degenerated in Britain (Posey, Painting, Music, Sculpture, Architecture, Logic, Eloquence). After describing each art rhapsodically, Miller tells us that this societal reconstruction is to be capped by another phenomenon, public rule for public good. Then will arise new Miltons, Lockes, Newtons, Argyles, Pulteneys, Burleighs, Elizabeths—and new Georges! But Britain will be left in the gloomy regions of Dullness and Chaos:

> Whilst WE, deserted, and in Bondage bound,
> With Horrors, Clouds, and Darkness circled round,
> See *Dullness* lift her *consecrated* Head,
> And smile to view her dark Dominion spread;
> *Chaos* o'er all his leaden Sceptre rear,
> And not *one Beam* throughout the Gloom appear.
> (P. 10)

The anticipation of the mood and imagery soon to pervade *The New Dunciad* is remarkable, but for political reasons this poem ends with its pessimism somewhat mitigated. The poet dreams that Liberty will return to Britain if her sons will prepare the way by purging the waste land—if, in fact, they will "To publick *Justice* publick *Plund'rers* bring,/ And *take the Wicked from before the King*" (p. 15). As such a conclusion makes clear, *The Year Forty-One* combines the two dominant strains of opposition poetry, the satiric exposure of a corrupt world in the tradition of Pope and the hortatory-patriotic mode of Whig panegyricists like James Thomson.

Such satires remind us again of the connection between antiministerial politics and the satiric "itch." That profound dissatisfaction which some writers felt with the world about them, that obsessive conviction that the times were out of joint, fixed upon

Robert Walpole as the symbolic progenitor of a sick society. The impulse is one which satirists have always felt, but in the eighteenth century it typically found expression in political terms. Pope had written that a plague was upon Britain, and in all the darker political poems disease images abounded. Whitehead, Miller, and others whose names have not survived took upon themselves the satiric diagnosis of the infection, finding it invariably in a government which twenty years of political propaganda had consistently depicted as corrupt. But the talents of these minor satirists were unequal to the task; it remained for the greatest poet of the age to paint the familiar black picture in a fashion that would be unforgettable.

When Pope's *New Dunciad* (i.e., Book IV of *The Dunciad*) appeared in March 1742, Walpole had already fallen, but the poem nonetheless must be read as an unforgiving indictment of his years of power. The political overtones of the satire have been often analyzed; indeed, the motifs of opposition propaganda and verse satire I have already traced make it plain that a contemporary could hardly have made a nonpolitical reading of such a powerful stock-taking of contemporary culture.[49] Nor is the poem without particular political barbs, such as the references to the muses imprisoned by the Licensing Act, and wit (i.e., Atterbury) forced into exile. Walpole himself appears as Palinurus, who nods at the helm, and as Magus, the wizard whose gold and pensions work a magic familiar to any reader of the *Craftsman* or of *Common Sense*:

> With that, a WIZARD OLD his *Cup* extends;
> Which whoso tastes, forgets his former friends,
> Sire, Ancestors, Himself. One casts his eyes
> Up to a *Star*, and like Endymion dies:
> A *Feather* shooting from another's head,
> Extracts his brain, and Principle is fled,
> Lost is his God, his Country, ev'ry thing;
> And nothing left but Homage to a King!
> (IV.517–23)

These lines, it has been suggested, may refer to Pulteney, whose betrayal of the opposition and acceptance of a peerage were momentarily expected; but Pope's disillusionment with the Patriots finds no other expression in the poem, and it is perhaps

better to read this passage as a generalized reflection on the
supposed system of bribery and corruption which Walpole had
operated for two decades.

Perhaps, too, Walpole was not the only victim Pope intended.
In a note to the culminating lines of the original version of Book
IV ("While the Great Mother bids Britannia sleep,/ And pours
her Spirit o'er the Land and Deep") Pope quotes a couplet from
one of his earlier satires to explain why the poem was unfinished:

> Publish the present Age, but where the Text
> Is Vice too high, reserve it for the next.

Given the all-encompassing satire of the poem as it stands, what
vice was so high that it must be reserved for castigation till the
next age? Maynard Mack has suggested that many of Pope's
allusions may in reality refer not simply to Walpole but to the
royal family, the "golden Hanoverian era . . . which had in fact
turned out to be an age of 'gold' in a less attractive sense."[50] His
reading, if accepted, would explain why Pope would persist in a
satire of this sort even after Walpole's fall; in 1742 anti-Han-
overian sentiment was running high.

Certainly when the revised edition of the entire *Dunciad* was
published in October of 1743, its political import was extended
rather than lessened. The substitution of Cibber for Theobald as
"hero" would only have increased the political atmosphere, since
the "Keyber"-Walpole association was a well-entrenched tradition. Indeed, in his notorious *Letter* to Pope Cibber suggested
that Pope's bias against him was partly political: "Whenever the
Government censures a Man of Consequence for any extraordinary Disaffection to it; then is Mr. *Pope*'s time generously to
brighten and lift him up with Virtues, which never had been so
conspicuous in him before."[51] The quasi-political aspects of their
feud were also pointed up by Hervey's poem "The Difference
between Verbal and Practical Virtue," an attack on Pope published after *The New Dunciad* and headed by a letter signed "Cibber"; Hervey, in turn, was answered by *The Scribleriad*, a mock
epic connecting the Hervey-Cibber brand of dullness with
Britain's political ills.[52] In the light of all this, it is not surprising
that in the final version of *The Dunciad* Cibber should exclaim:

> Hold—to the Minister I more incline;
> To serve his cause, O Queen! is serving thine.
> And see! thy very Gazetteers give o'er,
> Ev'n Ralph repents, and Henly writes no more.
> (I.213–16)

Since the revised version of the poem is a demonstration, in the tradition of opposition satire, of organically related cultural and political decay, Cibber's reputation for inclining to the minister made him a far more appropriate hero than Theobald.

Pope's scorn for the literary and intellectual values of Walpole's administration is everywhere made clear. His note to a line (II.314) about the *Gazetteer* (whose record is borne by "Monumental Brass") cites the vast sums which, according to the Secret Committee, Walpole had spent on hack political writers between 1731 and 1741. Pope then makes this comment:

Which shews the Benevolence of One Minister to have expended, for the current dulness of ten years in Britain, double the sum which gained Louis XIV. so much honour, in annual Pensions to Learned men all over Europe. In which, and in a much longer time, not a Pension at Court, nor Preferment in the Church or Universities, of any Consideration, was bestowed on any man distinguished for his Learning separately from Party-merit, or Pamphlet-writing.

There is the root of the matter, the old cry of the opposition press about Walpole's hostility to men of letters or learning. His patronage of hack writers like William Arnall (satirized in the passage following Pope's note) and his failure somehow to regard writers like Gay or Swift as worthy of reward, to overlook their distaste for his policies and their friendship with his political enemies, were inseparably connected with his authorship of the spiritual and moral ills of "sinking Britain." Though it may be too much to say, with Maynard Mack, that he is the real hero of Pope's poem, his spirit as commonly characterized in the antiministerial press obviously pervades the whole. Needless to say, *The Dunciad* in its final form is not a partisan document; the prime minister was, at least nominally, already out of power, and in Bolingbrokean manner Pope castigates the spirit of party as handmaiden to Dullness. But the mythological creature fashioned by opposition propaganda did not die easily. Walpole-

Wolsey-Haman-Sejanus still functioned as the symbolic source of the cultural changes which twenty years had brought in England, not least of which was a widening rift between men of business and men of letters; and it is apt that the period's greatest poet should make his final work an imaginative embodiment of that literary-political myth.

CONCLUSION

"LAST NIGHT at Strawberry Hill," wrote Horace Walpole in 1780, "I took up, to divert my thoughts, a volume of letters to Swift from Bolinbroke, Bathurst and Gay—and what was there but lamentations on the ruin of England—in that era of its prosperity and peace, from wretches who thought their own want of power a proof that their country was undone! Oh, my father!"[1] His outburst is understandable. From 1726 to 1742 his father's administration, in retrospect appearing so just and effective not merely to Horace but to many historians, was derided and denounced by poets, playwrights, and satirists. Those writers did not, however, form an organized "literary opposition"—only the circle around Prince Frederick in the very late 1730s can be said to have constituted such a group—but for the most part wrote independently of political direction and with little similarity of literary method. Obviously, it makes little sense to talk of Gay's *Beggar's Opera* and Glover's *Leonidas* as somehow connected in purpose, inspiration, or technique. One must, in fact, distinguish rather sharply between the Scriblerians, who were the first to enter the lists, and the later Patriot writers, who were patronized by the prince and inspired by the later writings of Bolingbroke. In literary terms, too, one must recognize the shift in tone and manner of antiministerial literature, as the dominant mode moved from satiric wit to patriotic exhortation to satiric gloom.

What was the effect of the wits' support of the opposition? In one respect Horace Walpole's comment could be slightly misleading. His easy linking of Swift and Gay with Bathurst and

Bolingbroke, as though they all moved in the same circles of power and exerted the same influence on events, is at odds with the realities of the situation. Poets and playwrights no longer inhabited the same world as politicians, as to some extent they had been able to do in the years of the last Tory ministry; for the most part, they no longer even wrote for the political press. Literary historians have occasionally tended to exaggerate the political significance of Walpole's literary opponents, with their accounts sounding sometimes as though only through his exceptional wile was the prime minister able for so long to escape the clutches of the wits.[2] But Walpole, who, as Swift reminds us, paid his literary workmen on the nail, had little to lose by his utter indifference to those superior talents who seemed somehow to expect his patronage without breaking their ties to his political enemies. As he well knew, it was in Parliament and not in the theater or in volumes of verse that the struggle for power was joined. The details of the political struggle itself, even of so crucial an issue as the excise bill, did not touch the imaginations of the literary intelligentsia, and they cannot be regarded as a political force of the same consequence as the pamphlets or newspapers of both sides. Of course works like *Gulliver's Travels* and *The Historical Register* were useful to the opposition and fully exploited; but what emerges most clearly from the foregoing study is that the *notion* of all the wit on one side was much more politically significant and had much more political utility than any of the works of wit themselves. Men of letters apparently still had sufficient standing in the public eye for the administration's disregard of belles-lettres to be effective, alongside "bribery and corruption," as a stock motif of opposition propaganda.

If we ask again, with Chesterfield, by what "uncommon fatality" the Walpole administration was destitute of literary support, it should be clear that no simple answer, indeed no single answer, will suffice. It is not quite enough to say, as H. T. Dickinson has argued, that Walpole failed to gain the support of the best writers of the age "because their talents were better suited to criticizing an administration and expressing dissatisfaction with contemporary life."[3] It is true that the later satirists, obsessed with their vision of a sick society, naturally seized upon the image projected by opposition propaganda of a corrupt prime minister and transformed such political commonplaces into moral symbols. But Dryden in *Absalom and Achitophel* and Swift in the *Examiner* had found satiric talents well suited to the castigation of the *opponents* of a regime, as did Fielding in *The Opposition*. Nor can one find a satisfactory explanation simply by positing a set of political ideas to which all these writers were committed. One may, of course, speak in very broad terms of their political principles—of Fielding's adherence to the Revolution settlement and the general ideals of Whiggism, for example, or of the Scriblerian wits' humanistic reaction against the "corrupting" effects of new financial institutions. But even Bolingbroke's ideas, as important as they were in furnishing the themes of the Patriot poets, do not constitute an ideological umbrella large enough to cover writers as diverse as Swift and Thomson. Problems arise when one attempts to use some broadly conceived political orientation—such as the "Country ideology"[4] —to account for individual responses to the immediate pressures of partisan politics; and the problems are compounded when the individuals in question are writers pursuing literary careers rather than politicians or political philosophers. At one time or another, most of these men of letters sought some accommodation with the administration: Gay hoped for advancement at court; Pope accepted a Treasury grant and maintained a dubious neutrality for much of the period; Thomson dedicated a poem to Walpole in a bid for patronage; Swift met with him to discuss Ireland; and Fielding's relations with the Great Man provide a convoluted record of a writer cautiously seeking his advantage wherever it lay. Their chance friendships with figures in public life—with Bolingbroke, Bathurst, Cobham, Lyttelton, and the like—were perhaps as significant in determining their attitude toward Walpole's policies as any abstract ideology.

I have argued that an equally significant element in that attitude was Walpole's failure to provide patronage to writers who expected both favor from the government and some voice in the world of affairs. To put it more precisely, the exploitation of that failure by the opposition press created an atmosphere that made the wits' antagonism to Walpole almost inevitable. The charge that the administration was hostile to men of letters found a place in opposition propaganda very early; the encouragement of men like Duck and Cibber seemed to give it substance; and the typical response in the ministerial press—that men whose skill lay in making "words clink" were unfit for "business"—served only to irritate the wound. Walpole, as one poem in his behalf put it, had no need for "Fancy's feeble Aid"; over and over his journalistic minions called for straightforward, plainspoken political discourse instead of the flashy, suspect, unanswerable wit which everyone recognized as the opposition's stock in trade. In such an atmosphere, when the administration seemed to set men of letters apart from the world of affairs and when its spokesmen appeared to impugn the values of literature itself, serious writers naturally gravitated toward the opposition. Though Edward Young, alone of the major figures, managed to retain both his literary reputation and his loyalty to Walpole, alignment with the opposition had become by the mid-1730s simply a matter of fashion in literary circles. For a contemporary parallel one need only look to the predictable political responses of many American intellectuals.

Serious writers could not escape making political choices, for politics touched and colored virtually every aspect of life in the world of letters, even the reception of plays or poems not overtly political. Those who used their talents openly to attack the government sometimes did so with a moral intensity which perplexed a later generation. Warton complained that Pope's *Dialogues* painted an absurdly dark picture of a nation overwhelmed with corruption: "Yet this very country, so emasculated and debased by every species of folly and wickedness, in about twenty years afterwards, carried its triumph over all its enemies, through all the quarters of the world, and astonished the most distant nations with a display of uncommon efforts, abilities, and virtues."[5] In such poems, indeed, political reality was made subservient to the demands of partisan propaganda; but it should not be forgotten that in the better writers those demands themselves were subservient to a literary imagination which created works at once politically useful and of lasting significance. The ends of politics could be harmonized with the ends of art. Maynard Mack has spoken of the inevitable division between the poet's conception of the good life and the existing world of power; Walpole, he says, was "better off without the dewy-eyed idealists who talked in high terms of culture and corruption and the decay of national virtue."[6] But Swift and

Pope were not Blake and Thoreau, and I think they might have been surprised at being relegated to an ivory tower by the nature of their craft; within their memory, after all, the relation between men of letters and men of power had been on a different footing. The best writers of the age saw the widening rift between the poet and the city, but they would not have agreed with Auden that the poetic imagination is an undesirable quality in a statesman or that poets are by definition ill-equipped to understand politics. They were not alienated artists. Their way was not to abjure the rough world of partisan politics but to enter that world and make it the subject of their art.

NOTES

Notes to the Introduction

1. Hume, *The Philosophical Works,* ed. T. H. Green and T. H. Grose (London: Longmans, Green, 1875), 4: 395; Pulteney, *An Humble Address to the Knights, Citizens, and Burgesses Elected to Represent the Commons of Great Britain* (London, 1734), p. 10.

2. Foord, *His Majesty's Opposition, 1714–1830* (Oxford: Clarendon Press, 1964), p. 134; for an analysis of the groups within the opposition, see J. B. Owen, *The Rise of the Pelhams* (London: Methuen, 1957), pp. 62–86.

Notes to Chapter 1: Literature as a Political Issue

1. *The Dyer's Hand and Other Essays* (New York: Random House, 1962) p. 84.

2. See Irving Howe, *Politics and the Novel* (Cleveland: Meridian Books, 1964), pp. 20–21.

3. See Jeffrey Hart, *Viscount Bolingbroke: Tory Humanist* (London: Routledge and Kegan Paul, 1965), pp. 4–8.

4. *Common Sense,* 8 Oct. 1737, as reprinted in the collected edition (London, 1738), 1: 248–49.

5. *Memoirs of the Life and Administration of Sir Robert Walpole,* rev. ed. (London: T. Cadell and W. Davies, 1800), 3: 354–55.

6. Greene, "Sir Robert Walpole and Literary Patronage," (Ph.D. diss., Columbia University, 1964). For the argument favorable to patronage under the Hanoverians, see Paul J. Korshin, review of *The Age of Patronage* by Michael Foss, *ECS* 7 (1973): 101–5, and Korshin's essay, "Types of Eighteenth-Century Literary Patronage," *ECS* 7 (1974): 453–73.

7. Swift, *Correspondence,* 3: 418; 4: 100.

8. See *Fog's Journal,* 20 March 1731; and Eustace Budgell, *A Letter to Cleomenes* (London, 1731), pp. 195–97.

9. For a similar exchange of epigrams on the same topic, see *Craftsman,* 3 Jan. 1735/6, and *Daily Gazetteer,* 12 Jan. 1735/6.

10. *Daily Courant,* 31 Aug. 1734; *Craftsman,* 9 May 1730, 28 April 1739; on the attacks on Augustus, see Howard D. Weinbrot, "History, Horace, and Augustus Caesar," *ECS* 7 (1974): 391–414.

11. See also Aaron Hill's Epistle Dedicatory to *Advice to the Poets: A Poem* (London, 1731); *Common Sense,* 8 Nov. 1740, 12 Dec. 1741.

12. *A Critical History of the Administration of Sir Robert Walpole* (London, 1743), pp. 375–76; cf. *Craftsman,* 12 June 1742.

13. 20 Feb. 1727/8; cf. *Daily Courant,* 27 July 1731.

14. *Free Briton,* 6 Aug. 1730; *London Journal,* 1 July 1732; *Daily Gazetteer,* 24 Oct. 1740.

15. *Free Briton,* 25 Dec. 1729; *Fog's Journal,* 17 Oct. 1730.

16. Ed. G. A. Aitken (London: Duckworth, 1899), 4: 4.

17. *A Letter from a Gentleman in Worcestershire to a Member of Parliament in London* (London, 1727), p. 26.

18. (London, 1738), p. 6.

19. Hervey, *Observations on the Writings of the Craftsman* (London, 1730), pp. 6–7; *The Counterpart to the State-Dunces* (London, 1733), p. 5; see also *Daily Gazetteer,* 27 March 1741, and *London Journal,* 10 Jan. 1729/30.

20. *British Journal,* 23 Nov. 1728; *Daily Courant,* 22 June 1734; *Daily Gazetteer,* 4 April 1740.

21. *An Historical View of the Principles, Characters, Persons, etc., of the Political Writers in Great Britain* (London, 1740), p. 24.

22. *London Journal,* 23 Nov. 1728; Hervey, p. 6; *Daily Courant,* 31 Aug. 1732.

23. (London, 1735), pp. 6–7.

24. *Daily Gazetteer,* 27 Oct. 1738, 15 Feb. 1738/9; *London Journal,* 5 Oct. 1728. On the legal treatment of libel, see Laurence Hanson, *Government and the Press, 1695–1763* (London: Oxford University Press, 1936).

25. *British Journal,* 27 July 1728, 5 Oct. 1728; see Weinbrot, pp. 406–13, and below, pp. 174–75.

26. Pope, *Correspondence,* 3: 420; Cibber, *An Apology for the Life of Mr. Colley Cibber, Comedian* (London, 1740), p. 23.

27. *Common Sense,* 5 Feb. 1734/5; *Craftsman,* 28 Sept. 1728; *Daily Gazetteer,* 26 May 1738.

28. *Craftsman,* 2 Aug. 1729; *London Journal,* 15 March 1728/9, 30 May 1730, 13 March 1730/31; *Free Briton,* 1 Jan. 1729/30. Indictment of "general" satire on purely literary or philosophical grounds was common enough; see my essay, "Satires on Man and 'The Dignity of Human Nature,' " *PMLA* 80 (1965): 535–41.

Notes to Chapter 2: The Scriblerians and the New Opposition, 1723–1728

1. C. B. Realey, *The Early Opposition to Sir Robert Walpole,* University of Kansas Humanistic Studies, vol. 4, nos. 2, 3 (Lawrence, Kansas, 1931), p. 105.

2. As quoted by Henry Beeching, *Francis Atterbury* (London: Sir I. Pitman, 1909), p. 306.

3. *The Political State of Great Britain*, ed. Abel Boyer, 25 (1723): 648–50; Pope, *Correspondence*, 2: 165.

4. *The Replies of Thomas Reeve, Esq; and Clement Wearg, Esq; . . . in Behalf of the Bill to Inflict Pains and Penalties on the late Bishop of Rochester* (London, 1723), p. 14; *His Grace the Duke of Wharton's Speech in the House of Lords, on the Third Reading of the Bill to Inflict Pains and Penalties* (London, 1723), p. 24.

5. George Sherburn, *The Early Career of Alexander Pope* (Oxford: Clarendon Press, 1934), p. 229; Pope, *Correspondence*, 2: 165 n.

6. See Pat Rogers, "A Pope Family Scandal," *Times Literary Supplément*, 31 Aug. 1973, and the reply by E. P. Thompson, "Alexander Pope and the Windsor Blacks," *Times Literary Supplement*, 7 Sept. 1973, pp. 1031–33; Pope, *Correspondence*, 2: 160, 161.

7. Swift, *Correspondence*, 2: 436; for a detailed discussion of the entire affair and of Swift's satiric reaction, see Edward Rosenheim, Jr., "Swift and the Atterbury Case," in *The Augustan Milieu: Essays Presented to Louis A. Landa*, ed. H. K. Miller, E. Rothstein, and G. S. Rousseau (Oxford: Clarendon Press, 1970), pp. 174–204.

8. Pope, *Correspondence*, 2: 184.

9. *The State Dunces, Part II* (London, 1733), p. 8.

10. *Poems*, ed. M. G. Segar (Oxford: Clarendon Press, 1937), pp. 124–26.

11. Ibid., p. 81 n.; Pope, *Correspondence*, 2: 332.

12. Swift, *Correspondence*, 3: 117.

13. Ibid., 2: 449.

14. *The Letters of John Gay*, ed. C. F. Burgess (Oxford: Clarendon Press, 1966), pp. 45, 49, 51.

15. Pope, *Correspondence*, 2: 332; W. H. Irving, *John Gay: Favorite of the Wits* (Durham: Duke University Press, 1940), pp. 212–13.

16. Pope, *Correspondence*, 2: 160 n.; the figure is confirmed by Walpole's private records, C (H) MSS. 61/ Vol. 4, fol. 242.

17. Pope, *Correspondence*, 2: 160–61, 276, 294; 5: 2.

18. Thompson, "Alexander Pope and the Windsor Blacks," p. 1032.

19. Pope, *Correspondence*, 2: 413, 368.

20. Oliver Ferguson, *Jonathan Swift and Ireland* (Urbana: University of Illinois Press, 1962), p. 98; J. H. Plumb, *Sir Robert Walpole: The King's Minister* (London: Cresset, 1960), pp. 72, 103.

21. Realey, p. 135; Plumb, pp. 74–75; *Letters Written by . . . Hugh Boulter, Lord Primate of all Ireland* (Oxford, 1769), 1: 62.

22. Swift, *Correspondence*, 3: 82. On the alliance between Pulteney and Bolingbroke, see Realey, pp. 193–95.

23. *Poems*, ed. Harold Williams, 2nd ed. (Oxford: Clarendon Press, 1958), 2: 388–89. The allusion is probably to Sir William Yonge, not to Edward Young.

24. Plumb, pp. 101–2; *Mist's Weekly Journal*, 10 Sept. 1726.

25. *The Instalment: To the Right Honourable Sir Robert Walpole, Knight of the Most Noble Order of the Garter* (London, 1726), pp. 5–6.

26. Thomson, *Letters and Documents*, ed. A. D. McKillop (Lawrence, Kansas: University of Kansas Press, 1958), p. 41.

27. *Remarks Critical and Political, upon a Late Poem, Intitled the Instalment* (London, 1726), pp. 12–13.

28. *Craftsman*, 13 Feb. 1726/7; Swift, *Poems*, 2: 650.

29. Swift, *Correspondence*, 3: 128 n., 132; Ferguson, pp. 140–41.

30. Swift, *Correspondence*, 3: 144.

31. Realey, pp. 158–59.

32. Swift, *Correspondence*, 3: 162, 172, 182.

33. Foord, *His Majesty's Opposition, 1714–1830*, pp. 120–21, 135.

34. C (H) MSS 74/72; but see a ballad of 1729 connecting Arbuthnot with the *Craftsman*, printed in Percival, p. 30.

35. *The Occasional Writer Numb. I: With an Answer Paragraph by Paragraph* (London, 1727), pp. 5–6.

36. *A Discourse to the Right Honourable Sir Robert Walpole* (London, 1727), p. 13.

37. For another view, see Mabel Hessler, "The Literary Opposition to Sir Robert Walpole" (Ph.D. diss., University of Chicago, 1934), p. 48.

38. John Gay, *Poetical Works*, ed. G. C. Faber (London: Oxford University Press, 1926), p. 242.

39. Swift, *Prose Works*, ed. Herbert Davis (Oxford: Basil Blackwell, 1939–68), 12: 35.

40. *Poems*, 3: 78.

41. *The Oak and the Dunghill: A Fable* (London, 1728), printed also in *London Journal*, 2 Nov. 1728; see answers and sequels in *Craftsman*, 9 Nov.; *London Journal*, 23 Nov., and *Fog's*, 23 Nov.

42. Thomson, *Letters and Documents*, p. 50.

43. (London, 1727), sig. A1.

44. *James Thomson: Poet of "The Seasons"* (London: Cresset, 1951), p. 72.

45. Swift, *Correspondence*, 3: 207.

46. *Prose Works*, 5: 96.

47. *Prose Works*, 5: 97. On Voltaire, see Calhoun Winton, "Voltaire and Sir Robert Walpole: A New Document," *PQ* 46 (1967): 421–24.

48. Swift, *Correspondence*, 3: 215; 4: 99.

49. See Plumb, pp. 162–72; *Craftsman*, 5 Aug. 1727, italics reversed.

50. Firth, "The Political Significance of *Gulliver's Travels*," *Proceedings of the British Academy* 9 (1920): 210–41; Case, *Four Essays on "Gulliver's Travels"* (Princeton: Princeton University Press, 1945), pp. 69–97; Plumb, p. 104; John Loftis, *The Politics of Drama in Augustan England* (Oxford: Clarendon Press, 1963), p. 94. Phillip Harth challenges the interpretation of Book One as a consistent political allegory in "The Problem of Political Allegory in *Gulliver's Travels*," forthcoming in *Modern Philology* for May, 1976.

51. See W. A. Eddy, *"Gulliver's Travels": A Critical Study* (Princeton: Princeton University Press, 1923), pp. 193–94; Case, 105–6; Harold Williams, ed., *Gulliver's Travels: The Text of the First Edition* (London: First Edition Club, 1926), p. xxviii; Herbert Davis, ed., *Prose Works*, 5: xv–xvi.

52. Swift, *Correspondence*, 3: 102, 181, 182, 189, 208.

53. *Parker's Penny Post*, 28 Nov. 1726; see Eddy, pp. 193 ff.

54. HMC, *Portland*, 7: 445–46; Atterbury, *Epistolary Correspondence*, ed. John Nichols (London, 1783–90), 4: 75–76, 84.

55. *Political State of Great Britain* 32 (1726): 460, 477, 515; 33 (1727): 27.

56. *Lemuel Gulliver's Travels . . . Compendiously Methodized* (London, 1726), key to Part One, pp. 13, 26; key to Part Three, p. 23; key to Part Four, pp. 16–17.

57. See Ralph Straus, *The Unspeakable Curll* (London: Chapman and Hall, 1927), pp. 101–20.

58. (London, 1726), pp. 9, 15–18, 21. Italics mine.

59. (London, 1726), p. 10. On the authorship of this tract, see the comment by Harold Williams in Swift, *Prose Works*, 11: xxii n.; it is viewed as an ironic defense of Swift by Martin Kallich, ed., *Letter from a Clergyman*, Augustan Reprint Society, no. 143 (Los Angeles: Clark Memorial Library, 1970), pp. vi–viii. But Kallich ignores the fact that this piece was one of the attacks collected and annotated by Pope; see *The Rape of the Lock*, ed. Geoffrey Tillotson, Twickenham Ed., 2 (1940): 393.

60. Pp. xii, 30, 38.

61. Swift, *Correspondence*, 3: 199, 201.

62. *The Occasional Writer Numb. I*, p. 8; *An Answer to the Occasional Writer No. II* (London, 1727), p. 9; *British Journal*, 25 Feb. 1726/7.

63. *A Letter to the Occasional Writer, on the Receipt of his Third* (London, 1727), pp. 22–23.

64. *Political State* 33 (1727): 149; Swift, *Correspondence*, 3: 207; Swift, *Prose Works*, 5: xiv.

65. See *British Journal*, 26 Aug. 1727; *Flying Post*, 4 April and 11 May 1728; *Like Will to Like* (London, 1728), pp. 31–32; *Worse and Worse* (London, 1728), p. 10; and *An Essay upon the Taste and Writings of the Present Time* (London, 1728), p. 8.

66. *Remarks on the R——p——n of the H—— of C——ns to the K——g* (London, n.d.), pp. 28–29.

67. *"Gulliver's Travels": The Text of the First Edition*, ed. Williams, p. 279.

68. *Prose Works*, 11: 6.

69. *Travels . . . Compendiously Methodized*, key to Part Three, p. 23.

70. *The Universal Passion: Satire the Last* (London, 1726), p. 1; in later editions *Satire the Last* became Satire VII of *The Love of Fame*.

71. *Poems*, 2: 391–92.

72. *The Correspondence of Edward Young, 1683–1765*, ed. Henry Pettit (Oxford: Clarendon Press, 1971), p. 53.

73. Printed in Arbuckle's *Hibernicus's Letters* (London, 1729), 2: 397–405.

74. *Poems*, 2: 548.

75. *Prose Works*, 5: 97.

76. *Poems*, 2: 550.

77. (London, 1727), p. v.

78. In her edition for the Facsimile Text Society (New York, 1940), Marjorie Nicolson discusses primarily the satire on the South Sea Bubble and the place of this volume in the tradition of "voyages to the moon." See also the review by James Sutherland, *RES* 16 (1940): 476–78.

79. *Prose Works*, 11: 6–7.

80. See the comment by Herbert Davis, ed., *Prose Works*, 5: xiii.

Notes to Chapter 3: The Triumphs of Wit, 1728–1730

1. Atterbury, *Epistolary Correspondence*, ed. John Nichols (London, 1783–90), 5: 109, 113. On Walpole's position at this time, see J. H. Plumb, *Sir Robert Walpole: The King's Minister*, pp. 176–83.

2. *British Journal*, 31 May 1729.

3. The letter is included in Wharton's *Select . . . Pieces* (Boulogne, 1731).

4. *Political State of Great Britain*, ed. Boyer, 35 (1728): 462–63.

5. On the *Universal Spectator,* see *London Evening Post,* 15 Oct. 1728; on Steele, see *British Journal,* 13 Sept., 4 Oct. 1729; *Daily Journal,* 10 Oct. 1729; *Craftsman,* 15 Nov. 1729.

6. *Mist's Weekly Journal,* 24 Feb. 1727/8, original in italics.

7. Pope, *Correspondence,* 2: 453; Swift, *Correspondence,* 3: 260, 4: 97–98.

8. W. H. Irving, *John Gay: Favorite of the Wits,* p. 213.

9. Swift, *Correspondence,* 3: 365, 4: 100; Pope, *Correspondence,* 2: 456.

10. *Poems,* ed. Harold Williams, 2nd ed., 2: 481–83.

11. For political exploitation of Gay's disappointment, see *Mist's Weekly Journal,* 13 April 1728.

12. W. E. Schultz, *Gay's "Beggar's Opera"* (New Haven: Yale University Press, 1923), p. 186. W. A. McIntosh has recently argued for a more cautious view of the political satire, but his account ignores the play's reception in the political press; see "Handel, Walpole, and Gay: The Aims of *The Beggar's Opera*," *ECS* 7 (1974): 415–453.

13. Swift, *Correspondence,* 3: 267.

14. *John Gay,* p. 256.

15. *A Collection of Poems on Several Occasions, Publish'd in the Craftsman* (London, 1731), p. 15; *Craftsman,* 2 March 1727/8.

16. C (H) MSS 74.

17. *Mist's Weekly Journal,* 23 March 1728; Swift, *Prose Works,* 12: 32–37.

18. "Some Immediate Effects of the *Beggar's Opera,*" in *Manly Anniversary Studies in Language and Literature* (Chicago: University of Chicago Press, 1923), pp. 180–89; Stevens's view is followed by John Loftis in *The Politics of Drama in Augustan England,* p. 95.

19. C (H) MSS 75/19.

20. See Swift, *Correspondence,* 3: 288; *Prose Works,* 12: 36; Atterbury, *Epistolary Correspondence,* 5: 110.

21. *London Journal,* 23 March 1727/8; *Weekly Journal, or British Gazetteer,* 30 March 1728.

22. *Twickenham Hotch-Potch* (London, 1728), p. ii.

23. Ibid., p. vi; see also *Flying Post,* 6 April 1728, reprinted in Matthew Concanen's *A Compleat Collection of All the Verses, Essays, Letters . . . Occasioned by the . . . Miscellanies by Pope* (London, 1728), pp. 25–26.

24. Jonathan Smedley, *Gulliveriana* (London, 1728), pp. 277–79; Concanen, p. 51.

25. 11 May 1728; see also *Like Will to Like* (London, 1728), p. 32.

26. *An Essay upon the Taste and Writings of the Present Times . . . By a Gentleman of C——st C——h, Oxon* (London, 1728), p. 19.

27. P. 8.

28. *Pope's "Dunciad": A Study of Its Meaning* (London: Methuen, 1955), p. 11.

29. See Maynard Mack, *The Garden and the City: Retirement and Politics in the Later Poetry of Pope* (Toronto: University of Toronto Press, 1969), p. 122.

30. *The Dunciad*, ed. James Sutherland, Twickenham Ed., 5 (1963): 183–84 (III.283–86). Subsequent quotations will be from this edition.

31. Ibid., p. 126 n.

32. Mack, pp. 155–62, traces the changes before 1743 which made the poem even more obviously political.

33. See, e.g., *Pope Alexander's Supremacy* (London, 1729), p. 14; *Weekly Journal, or British Gazetteer*, 14 Sept. 1728.

34. *A Compleat Collection*, pp. v–vi.

35. *A Compleat Key to the Dunciad*, 3rd ed. (London, 1728), pp. 7, 9, 18; Ward, *Durgen, or A Plain Satyr upon a Pompous Satyrist* (London, 1729), pp. 20–22.

36. Pulteney, *An Answer to One Part of a Late Infamous Libel* (London, 1731), p. 8; *A Proper Reply to Mr. P——'s Answer* (London, 1731), p. 9.

37. Swift, *Correspondence*, 3: 326; on Pope's reaction to Gay's activities, see Sherburn's comments in Pope, *Correspondence*, 3: 52 n.

38. *Letters of the Late Thomas Rundle, L.L.D., Lord Bishop of Derry . . . to Mrs. Barbara Sandys* (Gloucester, 1789), 2: 56; Swift, *Correspondence*, 3: 325–26.

39. See John Fuller, "Cibber, *The Rehearsal at Goatham*, and the Suppression of *Polly*," *RES*, n.s. 13 (1962): 125–34; and Schultz, p. 220.

40. *Letters of . . . Rundle*, 2: 63–64.

41. *Lord Hervey's Memoirs*, ed. Romney Sedgwick (London: William Kimber, 1952), p. 52.

42. Gay, *Poetical Works*, ed. G. C. Faber (London: Oxford University Press, 1926), p. 551 (I.xi), italics reversed. Subsequent references are to this edition.

43. Swift, *Correspondence*, 3: 357.

44. *Letters of . . . Rundle*, 2: 59.

45. See also *Craftsman*, 14 Dec. 1728. On Gay's authorship of the "Hilarius" Letter, see Fuller, pp. 128–29.

46. 28 Dec. 1728; reprinted in Percival, pp. 20–21.

47. The phrase is Lady Irwin's, HMC, *Carlisle*, p. 57.

48. *One Epistle to Mr. A. Pope* (London, 1730), p. 22; Victor, *Original Letters* (London, 1776), 1: 267.

49. (London, 1729), p. 23.

50. See A. D. McKillop, ed., *The Castle of Indolence and Other Poems* (Lawrence, Kansas: University of Kansas Press, 1961), pp. 159–61.

51. Ibid., p. 163.

Notes to Chapter 4: The Wits and the Government
in the Years of Crisis,
1730–1734

1. Swift, *Correspondence,* 3: 372–73.
2. See J. H. Plumb, *Sir Robert Walpole: The King's Minister,* chaps. 6–7.
3. *Select Letters Taken from Fog's Weekly Journal* (London, 1732), 2: 81.
4. See A. H. Scouten, ed., *The London Stage, Part 3, 1729–1747* (Carbondale: Southern Illinois University Press, 1961), 1: xlviii–xlix.
5. Croxall, *A Sermon Preach'd before the Honourable House of Commons* (London, 1730), pp. 5, 22; *Journals of the House of Commons,* 21: 429; *Daily Journal,* 12 Feb. 1729/30; *Dr. Croxall to Sir Robert Walpole* (London, 1730), pp. 1–4.
6. *A Letter to Cleomenes* (London, 1731), p. 97; *A Letter to . . . Ulrick D'Ypres* (London, 1731), pp. 76–77.
7. *Daily Courant,* 23 March 1730/31, 7 July 1732; see also *Free Briton,* 11 March 1730/31.
8. Swift, *Correspondence,* 3: 421; on Swift's reaction to Budgell, see 3: 437.
9. 40 (1730): 420–38.
10. *Memoirs of Charlotte Clayton, Lady Sundon,* ed. Katherine Thomson (London, 1847), 1: 187, 191–92, 197.
11. Swift, *Correspondence,* 3: 418.
12. *A Hymn to the Laureat: By a Native of Grub-Street* (London, 1731), p. 8.
13. *Grub-street Journal,* 24 Dec. 1730, printed as possibly by Pope in *Minor Poems,* ed. Norman Ault and John Butt, Twickenham Ed., 6 (1954): 450.
14. Swift, *Correspondence,* 3: 459.
15. 24 Dec. 1730; for a less political version, ascribed to Pope, see Pope, *Minor Poems,* p. 302.
16. 9 Jan. 1730/1; see also *Fog's,* 6 Feb. 1730/1, 24 April 1731. "Paraphonalia" repeats, as a stock jibe at Cibber, his misspelling of the word in the Dedication to *The Provoked Husband* (1728).
17. Thomson, *Letters and Documents,* ed. A. D. McKillop, p. 76; Pope, *Correspondence,* 3: 142.
18. *Gentleman's Magazine* 1 (1731): 22, italics reversed.
19. James T. Hillhouse, *The Grub-street Journal* (Durham: Duke University Press, 1928), pp. 6–7 and note. Pope's connection with this

paper, which Hillhouse attempts to demonstrate, must be regarded as unlikely; see my essay forthcoming in *Modern Philology*.

20. "Ruth Collins," *The Friendly Writer and Register of Truth*, Oct. 1732, pp. iii–iv; Budgell, *Bee* 4 (1733–34): 72 ff.

21. 9 Dec. 1731; see also a news item ridiculing the *Free Briton* in No. 36, 10 Sept. 1730.

22. Martin C. Battestin, "Fielding's Changing Politics and *Joseph Andrews*," *PQ* 39 (1960): 39–55; W. B. Coley, "Henry Fielding and the Two Walpoles," *PQ* 45 (1966): 157–78; and see below, pp. 197–208.

23. "New Verse by Henry Fielding," *PMLA* 87 (1972): 214.

24. Ibid., pp. 230–31. Grundy glosses "G——" as *God*, "M——" as *Minister*, and "M——y" as *Majesty*.

25. *Miscellanies*, 2nd ed. (London, 1743), 1: 41.

26. H. K. Miller, *Essays on Fielding's "Miscellanies"* (Princeton: Princeton University Press, 1961), p. 128.

27. H. Amory, "Henry Fielding's *Epistles to Walpole:* A Reexamination," *PQ* 46 (1967): 236–47. His argument is based largely on the supposed inconsistency of the epistles with the "violently pro-Opposition" plays of 1730–31. The 1743 version of the first epistle, he claims, was written in response to a charge in the *Historical View . . . of the Political Writers in Great Britain* (1740) that Fielding had written a "satyr" on Walpole and been charged by Sir Robert with ingratitude. Amory identifies this "satyr" with the 1738 version of the first epistle. But Amory has somehow failed to notice that the anecdote in the *Historical View* speaks of the episode of the "satyr" as occurring *before* Fielding "set up as a Play-Writer" and could thus hardly refer to a poem which Amory claims was written in 1738. There is no convincing evidence here for changing the traditional dating of the poems. Miller takes the poems and their dates at face value but suggests (p. 127) that the 1738 version may have been sent to the *Gentleman's Magazine* by someone seeking to embarrass Fielding. But would such a poem have embarrassed him in late 1738, after he left the stage and before he began the *Champion*? In 1739 a poem called *The Satirists* attacked all the opposition poets but referred to Fielding as having abandoned political scurrility for the peaceful pursuits of a law student (*The Satirists* is not dated but is listed in the *Monthly Catalogue* for December 1739).

28. See, e.g., "The Promotion" in Mitchell's *Poems on Several Occasions* (London, 1729), p. 33. Poems by Mitchell are to be found among Walpole's papers.

29. (London, 1735), p. 6.

30. Theobald, *Orestes* (London, 1731), sig. A3; Woods, "Fielding's Epilogue for Theobald," *PQ* 28 (1949): 419–24.

31. See Charles B. Woods, "Captain B——'s Play," *Harvard Studies and Notes in Philology and Literature* 15 (1933): 243–57.

32. Ibid., p. 255; on *The Modish Couple*, see *Fog's Journal*, 15 Jan. 1731/2. See also *Grub-street Journal*, 27 Jan., 10 Feb., 24 Feb., and 16 March 1731/2.

33. "Political Allusion in Fielding's *Author's Farce, Mock Doctor*, and *Tumble-Down Dick*," *PMLA* 77 (1962): 221–26.

34. *The Author's Farce*, ed. Charles B. Woods (Lincoln: University of Nebraska Press, 1966), p. 31 (II.vi). Subsequent quotations are from this edition.

35. Ibid., p. xv n.

36. *Tom Thumb and The Tragedy of Tragedies*, ed. L. J. Morissey, Fountainwell Drama Texts, No. 14 (Berkeley: University of California Press, 1970), pp. 112, 115.

37. Wilbur L. Cross, *The History of Henry Fielding* (New Haven: Yale University Press, 1918), 1: 103.

38. HMC, *Egmont Diary*, 1:97. G. M. Godden, in *Henry Fielding: A Memoir* (London: Sampson Low, 1910), Appendix J, cites but does not quote an item in the *Daily Post* for 29 March 1742 taking the play as a political allegory; by that time, however, with Walpole's fall fresh in readers' minds and with Fielding's reputation as a political satirist well established, a political reading of one of the early plays might well be expected.

39. *Free Briton*, 8 Oct. 1730; it was not Sir Robert who subscribed to *Hurlothrumbo* but his son, Lord Walpole.

40. *Political State of Great Britain* 39 (1730): 431. See also *The Life of Colonel Don Francisco* (London, n.d.), pp. 53–54.

41. Swift, *Correspondence*, 3: 385.

42. 39 (1730): 322–33; *Grub-street Journal*, 12 March 1730.

43. *The Complete Works of Henry Fielding*, ed. W. E. Henley (London: William Heinemann, 1903), 9: 145–46, hereafter cited as *Works*.

44. See the Biographical Appendix to Pope's *Imitations of Horace*, ed. John Butt, Twickenham Ed., 4 (1953): 351.

45. Swift, *Correspondence*, 3: 405; *Poems*, ed. Williams, 2: 560.

46. *Craftsman*, 8 Aug. 1730; *An Answer to One Part of a Late Infamous Libel* (London, 1731), p. 43.

47. Percival, pp. 34–36; cf. the epigram from the *Grub-street Journal* cited above, p. 96.

48. *An Answer*, pp. 43–44; *Daily Courant*, 3 Sept. 1731; Pope, *Epistles to Several Persons*, ed. F. W. Bateson, Twickenham Ed., 3, part 2 (1951): 84.

49. (London, 1731), pp. 20–21.

50. Fielding, *Works*, 9: 75–76.

51. Ibid., p. 147.

52. In an earlier version of this section I argued for the presence of personal satire and genuine commitment in this play; I now regard that case as overstated. See my "The Politics of Fielding's *Coffee-House Politician*," *PQ* 49 (1970): 424–29.

53. See Cross, 1: 106–7; Edgar V. Roberts, ed., *The Grub-Street Opera* (Lincoln: University of Nebraska Press, 1968), pp. xvii–xviii. Subsequent references in the text will be to Roberts's edition.

54. Roberts, pp. xiv–xv.

55. Roberts, p. xvi; see *The London Stage, Part 3, 1729–1747*, 1: xlix.

56. See *Remarks on an Historical Play, called the Fall of Mortimer* (London, 1731); *The Norfolk Sting: Or, the History and Fall of Evil Ministers* (London, 1732), p. 19; *The History of Mortimer, Being a Vindication of the Fall of Mortimer* (London, 1731); and *Fog's Journal*, 19 June, 24 July 1731.

57. *Daily Courant*, 8 July 1731; John Loftis, *The Politics of Drama in Augustan England*, p. 106.

58. Amory, "Henry Fielding's *Epistles to Walpole*," p. 238.

59. Roberts, p. xx.

60. P. xvii.

61. Woods, "Fielding's Epilogue for Theobald," p. 424 n. For ironic readings see G. R. Levine, *Henry Fielding and the Dry Mock* (The Hague: Mouton, 1967), p. 146 n., and S. M. J. Z. Rizvi, "Political Satire in the Plays of Henry Fielding" (Ph.D. diss., University of Edinburgh, 1967).

62. *The Modern Husband* (London, 1732), sig. [A3].

63. *Daily Courant*, 9 May 1732; Loftis, p. 130.

64. 5 August 1749, first cited by Martin Battestin, ed., *Joseph Andrews*, Wesleyan Edition of the *Works* (Oxford: Clarendon Press, 1967), p. xxi n.

65. Cross, 1: 122; Loftis, p. 131 and note.

66. Loftis, p. 131.

67. Goldgar, "Fielding, Sir William Yonge, and the *Grub-street Journal*," *Notes and Queries*, n.s. 19 (1972): 226–27.

68. (London, 1732), p. 8.

69. See Woods, ed., *The Author's Farce*, p. 96 n. Sheridan Baker, "Political Allusion," also finds political satire in *The Mock Doctor*, acted at Drury Lane.

70. See Loftis, p. 132.

71. Swift, *Correspondence*, 3: 506.

236   NOTES TO PAGES 116–128

72. Williams, ed., *Poems*, 2: 474; *Daily Journal*, 2 May 1730.

73. Letter to Stephen Fox, 25 Nov. 1728, printed in *Lord Hervey and His Friends, 1726–1738*, ed. the Earl of Ilchester (London: John Murray, 1950), p. 40.

74. *Poems*, 2: 536, ll. 143–56. Subsequent quotations of Swift's poetry in this section will be from this edition (ed. Williams).

75. See Williams, ed., *Poems*, 2: 551–53.

76. See Hervey's letter to Fox, 21 Dec. 1731, in *Lord Hervey and His Friends*, p. 125.

77. Williams, ed., *Poems*, 2: 629, 640. On this entire affair, see George P. Mayhew, "Rage or Raillery: Swift's *Epistle to a Lady* and *On Poetry: A Rapsody*," *Huntington Library Quarterly* 23 (1960): 175–77.

78. See, e.g., the *Daily Gazetteer*, 30 July and 6 Oct. 1735; 29 Aug. 1739.

79. King, *Political and Literary Ancedotes of his Own Times* (London: John Murray, 1818), pp. 14–15.

80. Pope, *Correspondence*, 3: 318, 332.

81. *Daily Courant*, 16 Feb. 1732/3; see also "Ruth Collins," *The Friendly Writer*, Dec. 1732, p. 12; Atex. [Alexander?] Burnet, *Achilles Dissected* (London, 1733).

82. Pope, *Correspondence*, 3: 90 n., 91, 133, 135 n., 276.

83. See Maynard Mack, *The Garden and the City*, chap. 6, passim.

84. Ibid., p. 128.

85. Ed. J. V. Guerinot, Augustan Reprint Society, no. 114 (Los Angeles: Clark Memorial Library, 1965), pp. 16, 19; *Fog's*, 30 May, 6 June 1730.

86. See Pope, *Minor Poems*, pp. 452–55; *Gentleman's Magazine* 1 (1731): 306.

87. Kathleen Mahaffey, "Timon's Villa: Walpole's Houghton," *Texas Studies in Language and Literature* 9 (1967): 193–222; Mack, pp. 122–26, 172–73, 272–78.

88. Pope, *Epistles to Several Persons*, ed. F. W. Bateson, Twickenham Ed., 3, part 2 (1951): 179–80.

89. *A Letter to Mr. Pope* (London, 1753), pp. 433–34.

90. Wasserman, *Pope's Epistle to Bathurst* (Baltimore: Johns Hopkins Press, 1960), pp. 54–55; and see Mack, pp. 163, 174.

91. Swift, *Correspondence*, 4: 131–32.

92. See Mack, pp. 176–77.

93. P. 186; it should be noted that in early editions of the poem, Trebatius is not identified with Fortescue.

94. *The First Satire of the Second Book of Horace, Imitated, in a Dialogue between Alexander Pope . . . and the Ordinary of Newgate* (London, 1733), p. 28, printed with Burnet's *Achilles Dissected*.

95. *The State Dunces: Inscribed to Mr. Pope* (London, 1733), pp. 4–5; subsequent quotations are from this edition.

96. *Bee* 2 (1733): 758–61; *The Counterpart to the State-Dunces: By a Native of New-York* (London, 1733); *A Friendly Epistle* (London, 1733).

97. *The Works of Alexander Pope*, ed. W. Elwin and W. J. Courthope (London: John Murray, 1871–89), 5: 437.

98. Mack, p. 190.

99. See John Butt, ed., *Imitations of Horace*, Twickenham Ed., 4 (1953): xviii.

100. *Tit for Tat: To which is Annex'd, An Epistle from a Nobleman to a Doctor of Divinity* (London, 1734), p. 9.

101. Lines slandering the queen and attacking Walpole as "This M——r that can't indite" were suppressed; they are present as a MS addition in the B.M. copy and are printed by Ilchester, *Lord Hervey and His Friends*, p. 300. See also a mock obituary of "Fannius," whose estate included a satire on Pope and a defense of the excise scheme, *Grub-street Journal*, 14 Feb. 1733/4.

102. *Works*, ed. Elwin and Courthope, 5: 439.

103. *Imitations of Horace*, p. 39; see Introduction, p. xxxvii.

104. For Hervey's view of Pope's lines on Bolingbroke, see *Lord Hervey and His Friends*, p. 192; on Walpole's speech, see Plumb, pp. 306–7.

105. Plumb, p. 325.

106. *The Proper Reply of a Member of Parliament* (London, 1733), p. 9; on Walpole's indifference to public opinion, see Plumb, p. 245.

107. Swift, *Correspondence*, 4: 143.

Notes to Chapter 5: The Prince and the Poets, 1734–1737

1. *Letters to and from Henrietta, Countess of Suffolk*, ed. J. W. Croker (London: John Murray, 1824), 2: 146–48.

2. *Daily Gazetteer*, 13 Sept. 1736; on Pulteney's absences, see Romney Sedgwick, *The House of Commons, 1715–1754*, The History of Parliament (London: HM Stationery Office, 1970), vol. 1, p. 43.

3. See *Craftsman*, 21 Aug. 1736.

4. Sedgwick, 1: 43; Archibald Foord, *His Majesty's Opposition, 1714–1830*, p. 183.

5. Foord, pp. 128–29.

6. *An Humble Address to the Knights, Citizens, and Burgesses, Elected to Represent the Commons of Great Britain* (London, 1734), p. 10.

7. See, e.g., *Gentleman's Magazine* 4 (1734), 506; and epigrams in *Daily Courant*, 24 Sept. 1734; *Grub-street Journal*, 19 Sept. 1734; *Craftsman*, 3 Jan. 1735/6; and *Daily Gazetteer*, 12 Jan. 1735/6.

8. *Gentleman's Magazine* 6 (1736): 225.

9. *The Crafts of the Craftsman: Or a Detection of the Designs of the Coalition* (London, 1735), p. 6.

10. C. A. Moore, "Whig Panegyric Verse, 1700–1760: A Phase of Sentimentalism," *PMLA* 41 (1926): 362–401.

11. *A Review of the Controversy* (London, 1734), p. 6.

12. *The Rise of the Pelhams*, pp. 69–70.

13. *Letters of the Late Thomas Rundle, L.L.D., Lord Bishop of Derry . . . to Mrs. Barbara Sandys* (Gloucester, 1789), 2: 241–45.

14. Bolingbroke, *Letters on the Spirit of Patriotism: on the Idea of a Patriot King: and on the State of the Parties at the Accession of King George the First*, a new ed. (London, 1775), pp. 140, 172. On the literary use of the *Patriot King*, see Mabel Hessler Cable, *"The Idea of a Patriot King* in the Propaganda of the Opposition to Walpole, 1735–1739," *PQ* 18 (1939): 119–30. For analysis of its ideas see Harvey C. Mansfield, *Statesmanship and Party Government* (Chicago: University of Chicago Press, 1965), pp. 70–80; Jeffrey Hart, *Viscount Bolingbroke: Tory Humanist*, pp. 83–163; Isaac Kramnick, *Bolingbroke and His Circle* (Cambridge, Mass.: Harvard University Press, 1968), pp. 30–38, 163–69; and H. T. Dickinson, *Bolingbroke* (London: Constable, 1970), pp. 259–66.

15. Rose Mary Davis, *The Good Lord Lyttelton* (Bethlehem, Pa.: Times Publishing, 1939), pp. 72–73.

16. For a different view, see Cable, p. 123.

17. *The Works of George Lord Lyttelton*, ed. George Edward Ayscough, 3rd ed. (London, 1776), 1: 343, 371, letters lxv, lxxiv; on the relation of these ideas to Bolingbroke's, see Kramnick, pp. 230–33.

18. Davis, p. 36; *Daily Courant*, 23 April 1735; *Daily Gazetteer*, 28 May 1738.

19. (Dublin, 1735), p. 25; see also *Of Liberty and Stediness: A Poem* (London, 1735), Preface.

20. *The Crafts of the Craftsman*, p. 13.

21. *Letters and Documents*, ed. A. D. McKillop, pp. 83, 84 n.

22. Pope, *Correspondence*, 3: 395 n. See Douglas Grant, *James Thomson, Poet of "The Seasons,"* p. 170.

23. *Lives of the English Poets*, ed. George Birkbeck Hill (Oxford: Clarendon Press, 1905), 3: 289.

24. A. D. McKillop, *The Background of Thomson's "Liberty,"* Rice Institute Pamphlet: Monograph in English, vol. 38, no. 2 (Houston: Rice Institute, 1951), pp. 86–93; Kramnick, "Augustan Politics and English Historiography: The Debate on the English Past, 1730–35,"

History and Theory 6 (1967): 33–56.

25. *Complete Poetical Works*, ed. J. Logie Robertson, Oxford ed. (London: Oxford University Press, 1908), p. 379 (IV.775–90). Subsequent quotations are from this edition.

26. *Memoirs of Charlotte Clayton, Lady Sundon*, ed. Katherine Thomson (London, 1847), 2: 212–14; HMC, *Carlisle*, p. 146; *Bee* 8 (1735): 457–58.

27. *Lives*, ed. Hill, 3: 289.

28. See A. D. McKillop, "The Early History of Thomson's *Liberty*," *Modern Language Quarterly* 11 (1950): 307–16.

29. Foord, p. 127.

30. *Complete Poetical Works*, pp. 464–65.

31. *Letters and Documents*, pp. 114–15.

32. *Poetical Works*, in *A Complete Edition of the Poets of Great Britain*, ed. Robert Anderson (London, 1795), 11: 515.

33. See W. R. Irwin, "Prince Frederick's Mask of Patriotism," *PQ* 37 (1958): 380.

34. *Poetical Works*, p. 485.

35. *Works*, ed. Ayscough, 3: 193–96.

36. Pope, *Correspondence*, 4: 72.

37. Thomson, *Letters and Documents*, pp. 110–11, 112 n.

38. *Works*, ed. Ayscough, 1: 400.

39. As reprinted in *Gentleman's Magazine* 7 (1737): 290–91.

40. See D. Torchiana, "Brutus: Pope's Last Hero," *JEGP* 61 (1962): 853–67.

41. *The Complete Works of Henry Fielding*, ed. W. E. Henley (London: W. Heinemann, 1903), 11:7–8; hereafter cited as *Works*.

42. Wilbur L. Cross, *The History of Henry Fielding* (New Haven: Yale University Press, 1918), 1: 160.

43. Ibid., 1: 179.

44. *Works*, 11: 199. Both Cross and John Loftis, I believe, exaggerate the political bias of this plot; a more temperate view is taken by O. M. Brack, Jr., William Kupersmith, and Curt A. Zimansky, eds., *Pasquin* (Iowa City: University of Iowa, 1973), pp. xiv–xvii.

45. See Sheridan Baker, "Political Allusion in Fielding's *Author's Farce, Mock Doctor*, and *Tumble-Down Dick*," *PMLA* 77 (1962), passim.

46. *Works*, 11: 224.

47. *Grub-street Journal*, 22 April, 6 May 1736; see Cross, 1: 189.

48. *Bee* 8 (1735): 350; for remarks critical of the opposition, see *Prompter*, 29 Nov., 10 Dec., 17 Dec. 1734; 28 Jan. 1734/5.

49. Baker, pp. 228–31, finds veiled allusions to Walpole in *Tumble-Down Dick* (1736).

50. See Emmett L. Avery and A. H. Scouten, "The Opposition to Robert Walpole, 1737–1739," *English Historical Review* 83 (1968): 331–36.

51. *Daily Gazetteer*, 7 May, 4 June 1737.

52. Quoted by Charles B. Woods, "Notes on Three of Fielding's Plays," *PMLA* 52 (1937): 369.

53. For the attacks, see *Daily Gazetteer*, 14 April, 7 May, 4 June, 6 July 1737; for Fielding's reply see *Common Sense*, 21 May. Much of this material is reprinted in *Henry Fielding: The Critical Heritage*, ed. R. Paulson and T. Lockwood (London: Routledge and Kegan Paul, 1969). On the Licensing Act see John Loftis, *The Politics of Drama in Augustan England*, pp. 138–53.

54. Baker, p. 231.

55. See Davis, *The Good Lord Lyttelton*, pp. 82–83.

56. George H. Jones, "The Jacobites, Charles Molloy, and *Common Sense*," *RES*, n.s., 4 (1953): 144–47.

57. Pope, *Correspondence*, 4: 209.

58. *A Letter to the Author of Common-Sense . . . of April 16* (London, 1737), p. 3.

59. (London, 1738), 1: sig. [A3v].

60. *Miscellaneous Works of the Earl of Chesterfield*, ed. M. Maty (London, 1777), 1: 21.

61. Ed. Robert Halsband, Northwestern University Studies in the Humanities, no. 17 (Evanston, Ill., 1947).

62. Sig. A5.

63. *Daily Courant*, 11 Jan. 1734/5.

64. Pope, *Correspondence*, 3: 500, 125 n.

65. See Maynard Mack, *The Garden and the City*, pp. 131 and note, 139–40; Manuel Schonhorn, "The Audacious Contemporaneity of Pope's *Epistle to Augustus*," *Studies in English Literature* 8 (1968): 431–43; and the notes to *Imitations of Horace*, ed. John Butt, Twickenham Ed., 4: (1953): 195–231, passim.

66. *Imitations of Horace*, p. 213, ll. 209–12.

67. Ibid., p. xxxviii.

68. *Miscellaneous Works*, 1: 75; see above, p. 9. The B.M. copy of this volume has MS notes by Horace Walpole, who rejects the ascription of some of the essays from *Common Sense* to Chesterfield but accepts the essay in question.

69. *Common Sense*, 12 Dec. 1741; see also *Old Common Sense*, 8 April 1738.

70. *The Letters of . . . Chesterfield*, ed. Bonamy Dobrée (London: Eyre and Spottiswoode, 1932), 2: 311.

Notes to Chapter 6: Prelude to War: Satire and Patriotism,
1738–1739

1. *Marchmont Papers,* 2: 91–94, 96; 100–101.
2. See Archibald Foord, *His Majesty's Opposition, 1714–1830,* pp. 197–98.
3. *Marchmont Papers,* 2: 158–59, 165; *The Letters of . . . Chesterfield,* ed. Bonamy Dobrée, 2: 372.
4. *Marchmont Papers,* 2: 133.
5. *Letters,* 2: 372.
6. *Marchmont Papers,* 2: 169. On the makeup of the opposition at this time, see the analysis by John B. Owen, *The Rise of the Pelhams,* pp. 62–86.
7. See Edwin Graham, "John Gay's Second Series, the *Craftsman* in Fables," *Papers on Language and Literature* 5 (1969): 17–25.
8. *Poetical Works,* ed. G. C. Faber, p. 279.
9. *Imitations of Horace,* ed. John Butt, Twickenham Ed., 4 (1953): 298. Subsequent quotations will be from this edition.
10. On the Pagod, see Maynard Mack, *The Garden and the City,* pp. 141–49.
11. *Daily Gazetteer,* 26 May 1738; for other attacks on Pope, see the same paper for 30 May and 15 June.
12. See Butt, ed., *Imitations of Horace,* pp. 316 n., 318 n.
13. Pope, *Correspondence,* 4: 114.
14. See, e.g., *Craftsman,* 7 Oct. 1738, and *Daily Gazetteer,* 27 Oct. 1738.
15. *Poems,* ed. E. L. McAdam, Jr., Yale ed. of the *Works of Samuel Johnson,* 6 (New Haven: Yale University Press, 1964): 49.
16. Sir John Hawkins, *The Life of Samuel Johnson,* ed. and abridged Bertram H. Davis (New York: Macmillan, 1961), pp. 34–35.
17. *The Politics of Samuel Johnson* (New Haven: Yale University Press, 1960), p. 88.
18. W. B. Carnochan, "Satire, Sublimity, and Sentiment: Theory and Practice in Post-Augustan Satire," *PMLA* 85 (1970): 260–67; Weinbrot, "History, Horace, and Augustus Caesar," *ECS* 7 (1974): 391–414. Perhaps in reaction to Pope and this parade of Juvenalian imitations, the *Gazetteer* in the fall of 1738 printed an unusual number of poems praising Walpole—poems on his illness, his recovery, his departure for Houghton, etc.
19. *The Tryal of Colley Cibber, Comedian* (London, 1740), p. 30 n. The text of this pamphlet consists simply of extracts from the *Champion.*
20. *Imitations of Horace,* p. 327 n.

242   NOTES TO PAGES 176–182

21. *A Hue and Cry after Part of a Pack of Hounds . . . To Which is Added, Modern Characters, by Another Hand* (London, 1739), p. 27.

22. Pope. *Correspondence*, 4: 124, 178–79 and note.

23. Pope, *Correspondence*, 4: 138–39; *Marchmont Papers*, 2: 190.

24. Pope, *Correspondence*, 4: 142–44.

25. See George H. Nadel, "New Light on Bolingbroke's *Letters on History*," *Journal of the History of Ideas* 23 (1962): 550–57; Giles Barber, "Bolingbroke, Pope, and the *Patriot King*," *The Library*, 5th Series, 19 (1964): 67–89; and F. T. Smallwood, "Bolingbroke vs. Alexander Pope: The Publication of the *Patriot King*," *Papers of the Bibliographical Society of America* 65 (1971): 225–41.

26. C. A. Moore, "Whig Panegyric Verse, 1700–1760: A Phase of Sentimentalism," *PMLA* 41 (1926): 400; Isaac Kramnick, *Bolingbroke and His Circle*, p. 233.

27. (London, 1738), 6.

28. See the *Daily Gazetteer*, 15 March 1737/8; and the ballad *Lord B——ke's Speech upon the Convention* (1738), reprinted in Percival, pp. 117–19.

29. (London, 1738), pp. 8–9; on Trapp's authorship, see *Gazetteer*, 20 Feb. 1738/9.

30. See E. L. Avery and A. H. Scouten, "The Opposition to Robert Walpole, 1737–1739," *English Historical Review* 83 (1968): 331–36; the essay traces the career of James Lacy, a minor actor who tried to circumvent the Licensing Act and ended in jail.

31. Cooke, *The Mournful Nuptials* (London, 1739), p. viii; *The Letter Books of John Hervey, First Earl of Bristol*, ed. S.H.A. Hervey, Suffolk Green Books, no. 1 (Wells, 1894), 3: 222.

32. *Areopagitica: A Speech of Mr. John Milton . . . with a Preface by Another Hand* (London, 1738), p. vi, original in italics.

33. See D. Torchiana, "Brutus: Pope's Last Hero," *JEGP* 61 (1962): 853–67; Pope, *Correspondence*, 4: 145–68, passim.

34. See Douglas Grant, *James Thomson, Poet of "The Seasons,"* pp. 178 ff.; and Jean B. Kern, "James Thomson's Revisions of *Agamemnon*," *PQ* 45 (1966): 289–303.

35. See Grant, pp. 186–87; and Percival, pp. xxvi–xxvii.

36. Grant, pp. 187, 189.

37. *Memoirs of Sarah, Duchess of Marlborough . . . Together with Her Characters of Her Contemporaries and Her Opinions*, ed. William King (London: Routledge, 1930), p. 295; see also *Craftsman*, 14 April 1739.

38. See John Loftis, *The Politics of Drama in Augustan England*, pp. 150–151.

39. For full discussion of Johnson's piece, see Greene, pp. 99–108, and Loftis, pp. 145–47.

40. *The Satirists* (London, n.d.), p. 7, listed in *Monthly Catalogue* as published Dec. 1739; *Daily Gazetteer*, 12, 26 April, 21 May 1739.

41. James Thomson, *Letters and Documents*, ed. A. D. McKillop, p. 129.

42. See Greene, pp. 96–98.

43. *Craftsman*, 3 Feb., 10 Feb. 1738/9; for analysis of the *State of Affairs*, see Greene, pp. 92–95.

44. C (H) MSS 73/ 12, 13.

45. Alfred J. Henderson, *London and the National Government, 1721–1742* (Durham: Duke University Press, 1945), pp. 190–94; *Daily Gazetteer*, 15 Oct. 1739.

46. *Poetical Works*, in *A Complete Edition of the Poets of Great Britain*, ed. Robert Anderson (London, 1795), 11: 552.

47. Quoted by Henderson, pp. 194–95.

48. *Two Letters . . . on the Proposals for Peace with the Regicide Directory of France* (London, 1796), pp. 71–72.

49. H. W. V. Temperley, "The Causes of the War of Jenkins' Ear," *Transactions of the Royal Historical Society*, 3rd Ser., 3 (1909): 197–236.

Notes to Chapter 7: The Fall of Walpole, 1739–1742

1. Owen, *The Rise of the Pelhams*, pp. 34–40.

2. Swift, *Correspondence*, 5: 190.

3. On the groups within the opposition, see Owen, pp. 62–86.

4. *Marchmont Papers*, 2: 246; see also Owen, p. 74; and Archibald Foord, *His Majesty's Opposition, 1714–1830*, pp. 139–41.

5. Romney Sedgwick, *The House of Commons, 1715–1754*, 1: 46, 71.

6. *Marchmont Papers*, 2: 263; *Yale Edition of Horace Walpole's Correspondence*, ed. W. S. Lewis (New Haven: Yale University Press, 1937–), 17: 171.

7. *Yale Edition*, 17: 243.

8. Foord, p. 216; *Marchmont Papers*, 2: 273–74; R. J. Phillimore, *Memoirs and Correspondence of George, Lord Lyttelton* (London: J. Ridgway, 1845), 1: 196–97.

9. For discussion of such problems, see W. B. Coley, "The 'Remarkable Queries' in the *Champion*," *PQ* 41 (1962): 426–36. I am indebted to Martin Battestin for information about the numbers of the *Champion* in the Bodleian Library.

10. *The Champion*, collected ed. (London, 1741), 1: 273.

11. Ibid., 2: 206.

12. For arguments questioning and supporting the attribution of this pamphlet to Fielding, see W. B. Coley, "The Authorship of *An Address to the Electors of Great Britain*," *PQ* 36 (1957): 488–95, and Thomas R. Cleary, "The Case for Fielding's Authorship of *An Address to the Electors of Great Britain* (1740) Reopened," *Studies in Bibliography* 28 (1975): 308–18.

13. *Champion*, 1: viii.

14. *Champion*, 8 July 1740, as reprinted in *The Patriot* (Edinburgh, 1741), pp. 105–6.

15. 6 Sept. 1740, as reprinted in *The Patriot*, p. 290.

16. See *Daily Gazetteer*, 24 July 1740; 12 Nov. 1740. The issue for 10 Sept. 1740 seems to accuse Fielding of having written for the ministry, but the reference is probably to Ralph.

17. *An Apology for the Life of Mr. Colley Cibber, Comedian* (London, 1740), pp. 40, 23.

18. *Champion*, 2: 183.

19. *The Laureat: Or, the Right Side of Colley Cibber, Esq.* (London, 1740), p. 21.

20. See Sheridan Baker, "Political Allusion in Fielding's *Author's Farce, Mock Doctor*, and *Tumble-Down Dick*," *PMLA* 77 (1962): 221, 229 n.; and Maynard Mack, *The Garden and the City*, pp. 158–62.

21. *Champion*, 2: 129.

22. 6 Sept. 1740, as reprinted in *The Patriot*, p. 323.

23. *Common Sense*, 22 March 1740; see also *Craftsman*, 26 May 1739; *Common Sense*, 19 May 1739.

24. C(H) MSS 73/ 24.

25. Wilbur Cross, *The History of Henry Fielding*, 3: 337; R. H. Barker, *Mr. Cibber of Drury Lane* (New York: Columbia University Press, 1939), pp. 201–2.

26. Martin Battestin, "Fielding's Changing Politics and *Joseph Andrews*," *PQ* 39 (1960): 39–55; Cross, 1: 298; W. B. Coley, "Henry Fielding and the Two Walpoles," *PQ* 45 (1966): 157–58.

27. This number of the *Champion* is in the Bodleian Library; I am indebted to Martin Battestin for calling it to my attention, providing a transcription, and suggesting its relevance to *Jonathan Wild*.

28. *Miscellanies, Vol. One*, ed. Henry K. Miller, Wesleyan Edition of the *Works* (Oxford: Clarendon Press, 1972), pp. 25, 27; Fielding's Preface is printed in Appendix A.

29. Martin Battestin, "Pope's 'Magus' in Fielding's *Vernoniad:* The Satire of Walpole," *PQ* 46 (1967): 137–41. My quotations are from *The Vernoniad* (London, 1741).

30. G. M. Godden, *Henry Fielding: A Memoir*, pp. 115–16, 135–39; Battestin, "Fielding's Changing Politics," pp. 47–48 n.

31. W. B. Coley, in "Henry Fielding and the Two Walpoles," p. 161 n., argues that rumors in the summer of 1740 of Fielding's overtures to Walpole make "a little less certain the case for 1741," but his evidence is misleading; he cites the *Gazetteers* of 30 July, and 1 and 2 Aug., but the first speaks only of Fielding's "ingratitude," and the others refer to Ralph, not Fielding. See Pope, *Correspondence*, 4: 255, and note.

32. See Eric Rothstein, "The Framework of *Shamela*," *ELH* 35 (1968): 381–402. A far-fetched account of the politics of *Shamela* is offered by Hugh Amory, "Shamela as Aesopic Satire," *ELH* 38 (1971): 239–53.

33. "Fielding's Changing Politics," pp. 44–46.

34. *The Court-Secret: A Melancholy Truth* (London, 1741), pp. 4–5.

35. *The Opposition: A Vision* (London, 1742), p. 7; subsequent quotations are from this edition.

36. "Fielding's Changing Politics," p. 46.

37. "Henry Fielding and the Two Walpoles," p. 178.

38. *Miscellanies*, ed. Miller, p. 9 and note.

39. *Old England*, 5 Aug. 1749, cited by Battestin, ed., *Joseph Andrews*, Wesleyan Edition (1967), p. xxi n.

40. As quoted by Battestin, "Fielding's Changing Politics," p. 55.

41. Pope, *Correspondence*, 4: 249–50.

42. *Imitations of Horace*, ed. John Butt, Twickenham Ed., 4 (1953): 336, ll. 75–76. Subsequent quotations are from this edition.

43. The name "Forage" alluded to Walpole's supposed corruption as secretary at war in the matter of two forage contracts for Scotland, for which he was committed to the tower in 1712; see *DNB*.

44. Pope, *Correspondence*, 4: 261, 273, 369, 255.

45. *The Garden and the City*, pp. 194 ff.

46. *Yale Edition of Horace Walpole's Correspondence*, 17: 388; *Daily Gazetteer*, 11 Nov. 1740; *Letters of Sarah Byng Osborn*, 1721–1773, ed. John McClelland (Palo Alto: Stanford University Press, 1930), p. 49.

47. Miller's two poems are reprinted in Augustan Reprint Society, no. 153, ed. Ian Gordon (Los Angeles: Clark Memorial Library, 1972).

48. (London, 1741), sig. A2; subsequent quotations are from this edition. The poem was advertised in the *Champion* (14 Jan. 1741/2) as "by the author of *Are These Things So?*" For additional evidence of Miller's authorship and for information about Robert Morris, I am indebted to Mrs. Paula O'Brien, Westfield College, University of London.

49. See James Sutherland, ed., *The Dunciad*, Twickenham Ed., 5 (1963): xxx; quotations in the text will be from this edition. See also Mack, pp. 150–55.

50. P. 154.

51. *A Letter from Mr. Cibber to Mr. Pope* (London, 1742), pp. 23–24.

52. *The Scribleriad,* ed. A. J. Sambrook, Augustan Reprint Society, no. 125 (Los Angeles: Clark Memorial Library, 1967); not to be confused with a poem of the same title by Richard Owen Cambridge.

Notes to the Conclusion

1. *Yale Edition of Horace Walpole's Correspondence,* ed. W. S. Lewis, 25: 6.

2. See, e.g., Ian Gordon, ed. James Miller's *Are These Things So?,* Augustan Reprint Society, no. 153 (Los Angeles: Clark Memorial Library, 1972), p. ii.

3. "Walpole and His Critics," *History Today* 22 (1972): 416.

4. For an analysis of this ideology, see J.G.A. Pocock, "Machiavelli, Harrington and English Political Ideologies in the Eighteenth Century," in his *Politics, Language and Time* (New York: Atheneum, 1973), pp. 104–47; and Pocock's *The Machiavellian Moment* (Princeton: Princeton University Press, 1975), pp. 466–67, 478–79, 486.

5. *An Essay on the Genius and Writings of Pope,* 2 (London, 1782), p. 426.

6. *The Garden and the City,* p. 228.

INDEX